ADVANCE PRAISE FOR

TEACHING
BLACK GIRLS

"*Teaching Black Girls* is told by a voice so rich in character that it challenges us to deal effectively with the intersections of race, gender, and class. Through richly intertwined personal narratives we are reminded or introduced to what it is like growing up as an African American female. The voices of these resilient students stand out among the common discourse in which educational policies are too often based. This book should be a vital resource for teachers, educational administrators, university faculty, and policy makers who are change agents within urban schools."

Dawn G. Williams, Professor of Educational Administration,
Howard University

"*Teaching Black Girls* is a beautifully written ethnography that performs what it promises. Namely, Evans-Winters challenges the reader to redefine resiliency for African American girls as hybrid and participatory. Utilizing 'Black Womanist' thinking, Evans-Winters develops critiques that are as complex as the lives of the girls she portrays, and compellingly argues we are all responsible for and to the resiliency of youth."

Wanda Pillow, Professor of Educational Policy Studies,
University of Illinois at Urbana-Champaign

TEACHING
BLACK GIRLS

Studies in the Postmodern Theory of Education

Joe L. Kincheloe and Shirley R. Steinberg
General Editors

Vol. 279

PETER LANG
New York • Washington, D.C./Baltimore • Bern
Frankfurt am Main • Berlin • Brussels • Vienna • Oxford

Venus E. Evans-Winters

TEACHING
BLACK GIRLS

Resiliency in Urban Classrooms

PETER LANG
New York • Washington, D.C./Baltimore • Bern
Frankfurt am Main • Berlin • Brussels • Vienna • Oxford

Library of Congress Cataloging-in-Publication Data

Evans-Winters, Venus E.
Teaching Black girls: resiliency in urban classrooms / Venus E. Evans-Winters.
p. cm. — (Counterpoints; v. 279)
Includes bibliographical references and index.
1. African American girls—Education. 2. Urban youth—United States—
Social conditions. 3. Resilience (Personality trait)—United States.
4. Critical pedagogy—United States. I. Title.
II. Series: Counterpoints (New York, N.Y.); v. 279.
LC2731.E92   371.829'96073—dc22   2004001654
ISBN 0-8204-7103-8
ISSN 1058-1634

Bibliographic information published by **Die Deutsche Bibliothek**.
Die Deutsche Bibliothek lists this publication in the "Deutsche
Nationalbibliografie"; detailed bibliographic data is available
on the Internet at http://dnb.ddb.de/.

Cover design by Joni Holst

The paper in this book meets the guidelines for permanence and durability
of the Committee on Production Guidelines for Book Longevity
of the Council of Library Resources.

Printed in the United States of America

This book is dedicated to Grandma, Mama, and Tubuka (Tam). Grandma, thank you for teaching me to carry myself with self-respect and poise. It was your example that taught me that women had the right to fight for "us" and "ours." Mama, thank you, for giving me a tongue of fire. We have not forgotten that you were an artist and that your creative gift was passed to me through the womb. And, Tam, thanks for instilling in me a drive to be stronger, faster, and smarter (than you). Big brother, your death was not in vain. You died in this ongoing struggle for humanity. This work is dedicated to all of our ancestors, for their vision of our future.

Table of Contents

Acknowledgments

There are many individuals whom I would like to acknowledge for their guidance, moral support, and constructive criticism throughout the duration of the research and writing phase of this book. Only after coming out on the opposite end of elongated process, such as the writing of a six-chapter book, I am able to finally understand what steadfast dedication entails. Due to the commitment of those who have stood by my side, or at the least, sat in my cheering section, I can begin to share "our stories." Keeping with one of the major themes of this work, I would like to say thanks to all who have contributed to my quest to blur the boundaries between the personal and political. Especially, I would like to thank the young women and their families, who allowed me into their lives for three years.

Second, I want to thank my student research assistant, Khalilah Muhammad, for her untiring dedication to meeting deadlines and contributing her extra touches of creativity in the editing process. Also, I would like to thank Kelly Lawton for helping with editorial changes in the original manuscript. Furthermore, I would like to acknowledge my UIUC mentoring team—Wanda Pillow, Lawrence Parker, Arlene Torres, Luis Miron, and Rochelle Gutierrez. I am much grateful to Shirley Steinberg and Joe Kincheloe for believing in my potential for growth. Their thoughts are obviously present in this book. I am also grateful to the Peter Lang editing team and staff, including Phyllis Korper. Your work and optimism is appreciated. And, thanks to the Evans "clan"— Bryant (Taylor), Kenya (Keke), Tubuka (Tam), and Glen. Our struggles and triumphs are interwoven into these pages. Their stories are our stories. Last, but certainly not least, thanks to my "boys," Steve and Stevie, and my niece, Destini, for putting up with my mood swings, as I tried to meet deadlines and my own and others' expectations of me.

Chapter One

Introduction:
Where I'm Comin' From

All over the country, the Black world was thrusting its girls and boys into the White world to represent the race. Intellectual inquiry became both our weapon and a political act requiring great courage because there were absolutely no role models or books and nothing to sustain us except the training and encouragement we received from our families and communities. (Omolade, 1994, p. xi)

Ummm…(short pause) I'm just trying to graduate, make something out of my life, because a lot of people in my family, they just like nothing. Just drink beer every day and stuff. And, I don't want to end up like them. I want to end up a better person, so I can do something with my life. (Yssis, a first-year high school student discussing her goals)

In private conversations, my close friends and I often compete to prove that one's own family is more dysfunctional than another's. An unspoken rule is that these stories never go beyond the conversation that it came up in, and the divulged information is never shared with others, not even other friends or family members. The family-dysfunction competition of family dysfunction over the years has included a range of stories about our immediate and extended family members, from the more "lighthearted" stories of disorderly drunkenness and arrest to the more serious stories of sexual innuendos. These gendered exchanges serve as a form of therapy for a group of individuals who feel that traditional therapy may not accommodate our experiences as women reared in African American families and communities. Also, we are a group of professional Black women who do not readily believe in airing our dirty laundry, which most of us deem to be a bigger social taboo than anything that could ever occur within the confines of our familial boundaries.

My most recent competition of "My family is more dysfunctional than yours" took place with a younger mentee. Usually one opponent will never admit that her challenger's family has caused more stress or complications to the confidante's life, but having heard her story on multiple occasions, I know that my life circumstances may not have been as difficult as my mentee's life. Nevertheless, the purpose of these exchanges is to serve as a form of positive reinforcement and pseudo-counseling for both opponents. The underlining message of these sessions is that conditions and predicaments could have been much worse for you growing up and that there is always another woman who has experienced something similar or something more difficult. However, this time the conversation became more serious. After the dysfunctional-family competition, my mentee wanted to know why some Black girls were more resilient than other Black girls. She wanted to know *why* young women like ourselves overcame the various challenges we experienced growing up, while other young women became the stereotypical "baby mothers" and/or "crack heads." My mentee, who happened to be a young single parent herself, concluded that our positive outcomes had to be the work of something greater than we were, but she wanted my professional opinion in this matter, along with my wisdom as an "older" (I was only five years her senior) African American woman who had "made it."

The young single mother's inquisition forced me to take an even closer look at this idea of resilience and African American girls. It seems that Black women also wanted to know *why* some Black girls blossomed in the face of adversity, while others stayed in segregated downtrodden communities and withered in the storm. My counterpart chose to attribute success and failure to a higher being, for in her mind only divine intervention could explain why Black girls could overcome some of the hardships that we experience. In all honesty, I was not intellectually willing to give up on millions of Black urban girls, by attributing my resilience to some restricted private connection to a higher being. Her question is one I have been pondering for a few years, but it is easier to observe and examine *how* girls succeed versus *why* girls are resilient in the face of adversity. *How* questions attempt to analyze the processes that lead to resiliency; therefore, in addition to looking at supports we will also be required to "air dirty laundry." Sharing becomes difficult because many children are taught at home not to share family business and happenings with outsiders. However, I told my young counterpart about my research work on girls and resiliency and suggested that maybe we both should reexamine the supports and setbacks in our own lives that may have attributed to our "making it." I explained that if these things could be identified and operationalized for research and practice reasons, then just maybe we could help other young women become more resilient.

Personal Reflections: An Urban Girl's Story

As a young girl, I attended high school in a majority Black low-income and working-class neighborhood. Young people were taught early that education opened doors to social and economic opportunities. The motto over the entrance of my high school read: Education is the key to success. Although we all received the same message on the importance of education, all of us did not overcome many of the social barriers that affect school achievement. Many students struggled with issues of poverty, violence, and drug and alcohol abuse at home, in the neighborhood, or at school itself. Some girls got pregnant; some boys went to jail for selling drugs; some students even experimented with drugs; and other students did not make it out of the ghetto alive.

Yet, the majority of us made it through and realized that schooling, like our families and neighborhoods, could be both a barrier and a hurdle. Students who stayed in school survived those barriers that were related to our race, class, and gender with the support of the people and physical resources around us. When reflecting on my own schooling experience, I realize that my family, the African American community, and adults at school played a major role in my personal and educational development. My teachers, godparents, grandparents, the church, successful adults, and others encouraged me to be a strong-minded individual as well as the best student that I could be. Students learned that we did not need privilege on our side to succeed at schooling, simply courage and endurance. Girls were told that with a good education you "won't have to depend on no man," and that "White folks can't deny you anything with an education." In other words, education was promoted as an opportunity to open doors and to battle the inequalities present in our daily lives. Thus, most of us struggled through racism, sexism, and classism at home, school, and in our neighborhoods and against larger forces outside our communities and completed school successfully.

Far From Home

However, in my Master's of Social Work program, I found that most of the literature on African American female students focused on pathology and deficits, e.g., school dropout and teenage pregnancy. Besides the abundance of research that focused on social problems, African American girls were also absent from the school resiliency literature. School resiliency literature focused on adolescents and/or minorities overall, ignoring the influence of the interaction of race, class, and gender on students' vulnerabilities and/or strengths. African American girls' absence from the resiliency literature presented a challenge as well as an opportunity. The challenge related to my observation that not many research studies were available that focused on the positive outcomes of African American girls, nor were there many studies available that examined the process by which school success is accomplished in the face of adversity. My personal experiences obviously contradicted what I was learning in my graduate studies, for I knew that the majority of African American girls were not high school dropouts or teenage mothers. The problem was that there were not enough educational and social science research studies available to support my claims.

The absence of African American girls in the resiliency literature presented the opportunity to fill this gap, and to implement alternative theoretical approaches to the study of the interaction of race, class, and gender on educational experiences. For example, instead of looking at how students fail, *Teaching Black Girls* focuses on how students succeed and focuses on resiliency and resiliency-fostering factors in the lives of three Black girls, growing up and attending school in an urban neighborhood. I identify and discuss support systems available to the young women that increase their chances of achieving their educational goals. I also attempt to illustrate how these support systems are effective in promoting educational resiliency. Through dialogue and self-reflection, the girls and I reconstruct and retell our stories of resiliency to derive practice from theory that is gender and culturally relevant to the experiences of urban Black girls.

Most researchers ask the basic "Who, what, when, where, and why?" questions in educational research studies. These basic inquisitive research questions are usually deficit oriented. For example, researchers may be concerned with "Who drops out of school, when are students most at risk, or what communities are more likely to have a high student dropout rate?" I will also ask these questions, but from a strength-oriented perspective. I attempt to move beyond the five basic research questions, to assimilate more in-depth "process" questions. As best articulated by Gulbrium and Holstein (1997), "The commanding focus of much qualitative research is on questions such as what is happening, what are people doing, and what does it mean to them? The questions address the content of meaning as articulated through social interaction and as mediated by culture. The resulting research mandate is to describe reality in terms of what it naturally is" (p. 14). However, the authors further explain, those concerned with "how" questions emphasize the production of meaning and how the production of everyday life is accomplished (Gulbrium & Holstein, 1997). In this book, those of us involved in the education and advocacy on behalf of urban girls will examine how everyday life affects how and what Black girls learn.

As a participant in the ethnography, I did not take for granted that educational achievement simply existed or "just was." I looked at the processes that gave meaning to educational achievement for the students in the ethnography. Thus, I was led to reinterpret educational resilience, and frame the following questions in a way that was inclusive of and sensitive to the social experiences of African American female students: (a) What are the coping strategies of the most resilient students? (b) What factors contribute to students staying in school? (c) When are students at their most resilient? (d) What are the historical, economic, and political conditions in which the students are experiencing schooling? (e) How do African American female students cope, resist, or buffer adversity? and (f) How can educators apply these findings to the urban class-room?

For multiple reasons, researchers in the field of urban education have tended to focus on deficits and pathology among African American adolescents and African American females. However, other researchers are critiquing the problems and failures of urban education research itself (instead of those of the students). In the *Social Construction of Urban Schooling*, Miron (1996) questions how the proportionally small amount of social and economic problems in inner-city schools have come to be generalized as the failure of all urban schools. He points out that the problems in some inner-city schools have been interpreted by some groups as simply that "most urban schools have failed their students" (p. 17). Miron describes the generalized failure of urban schools as a socially constructed reality. He contends that political parties and their ideologies over the last thirty years have participated in the social construction of the failure urban schooling with the help of the media and researchers. It is not unusual to read or view derogatory stories of urban schools and students in the newspaper, on the news, in movies, and televisions shows.

The negative images of public urban schools have served individuals' and groups' economic and political needs. For example, Anyon's (1997) qualitative research and historical analysis of Newark's Marcy School support the argument that educational reform efforts have to be a part of a larger effort if they are to address the problems of poverty and racial isolation in central city schools. Anyon's analysis also supports Miron's (1997) argument that urban schools have been affected by political and economic decisions of the power elite throughout history. On the other hand, Anyon focuses strongly on the hopelessness of the residents of Newark, the students' and community's hostility toward the school staff, and indirectly suggests the deficiency of the teachers, students, and parents of Marcy School. I contend that Anyon's analysis simultaneously politicizes urban education reform by situating reform efforts within a larger sociopolitical economy while ghettoizing children of color and their families who live in urban areas. A focus on hostility and hopelessness only contributes to and perpetuates folk theories that are situated in societal relationships of power and dominance (Lee, 2003). *Teaching Black Girls* attempts to avoid frameworks that depend on lenses of deficiency and hopelessness, which are much too prevalent in urban education research. Instead the book focuses on advocating for, empowering, and teaching Black girls from a strength perspective. It also addresses the shortcomings of current research and practice that continue to marginalize the school experiences of urban Black girls.

Payne (1994) traces the shortcomings of traditional research paradigms and models in social science research and questions how these traditions have harmed or simply not contributed to educational reform. Payne explains that the deficit-oriented focus of traditional and current research findings can be traced back to the original research question itself and the motives of whoever asked the question in the first place. For example, placing African American female students at the center of this discussion, one would ask, "Why has educational research traditionally focused on the number of out-of-wedlock births, sexual practices (read: promiscuity), and dropout rates among low-income minority adolescent girls?" Also, whose interests are being served by looking at the aforementioned behaviors? Last, why does more research not focus on those girls who do not become pregnant, stay in school, and are resilient despite the odds stacked up against them?

Payne offers one explanation as to why pathology remains at the core of social science and education research and its negative effects on minority students such as African American female students. In Payne's opinion, how researchers see educational inequality is related to how they see race and class inequalities overall. He cites research that found that theories of racism have ordinarily taken approaches that were high on victim blaming and low on embeddedness. Degree of embeddedness refers to whether racism is seen as central or peripheral to U.S. society. In sum, traditional social science research normally points to the personal and cultural characteristics of racial minorities, while failing to acknowledge racism as something embedded in or central to U.S. society. Consequently, the research paradigms that educational researchers and reformers have had to depend on regularly target the victim and ignore the role of social structures in our society.

Payne also argues that denial thinking is directly linked to the thinking of social scientists themselves, asserting that "The underlying similarity between much of sociological thinking and the thinking of laypersons results from the fact that the two are molded by a common culture than from the accuracy of folk wisdom" (1994, p.15). Payne suggests that sociological thinking is informed by everyday beliefs and assumptions about low-income minority groups and women. The same folk wisdom or stereotypes that are held by laypersons become a part of sociological inquiry. Payne's accusation supports other claims that racism is deeply ingrained in Western society and is merely rationalized through various disciplines and social philosophies (Smith, 1999). As a result, low-income minority students are targeted as problems and low achievers who refuse to learn, and then the role of larger social systems in the continuation of education inequality is ignored or theoretically underdeveloped in research.

Obviously, the various racist theories, disciplines, and philosophies present a threat to Black girls' social and educational development. Urban girls' educational development is negatively affected by outsiders' perceptions of inherent pathology and deficiency. Coupled with the media, social science and educational research may lead the public and educators to become focused on Black girls as prostitutes, welfare queens, and crack addicts. There is little or no attention given to achievement, success, and resiliency. Therefore, the threat is that teachers unenergetically approach teaching Black girls from a disembodied standpoint, building from a fixation on immorality, contamination, and/or in a more liberal state, absolution. It is from the same standpoint that urban educational policy and school policy is derived, being developed and implemented from a fixation on containment and surveillance.

Is it possible or even necessary to know the origins of denial, pathology, and "victim"-blaming theories? If we come to understand the derivation and function of pathology frameworks, maybe they can be deconstructed and counteracted. Miron (1996) argues that the dominant group's agendas were reinforced and legitimated by an overreliance on and belief in positivism, which was affirmed by an acceptance of objectivity. For example, Foster (1999) maintains that science itself was controlled by White European males, who established distant and hierarchal relationships between the researcher and researched as well as unequal and dominant gender relationships, so this type of research engagement came to characterize much of educational research.

As a result, girls, children from working-class families, and children of color were measured against White middle-class boys. Current theories of development, intelligence, curriculum, and pedagogy have been devised from the experiences of what has been discovered to be best for White middle-class boys. It sets those who are different apart and makes those children appear to be abnormal and culturally deficient. Children of African American descent, in particular, have had to carry the burden of racism, sexism, and classism in educational inquiry (Smith, 1999). The burden is a systematic problem that is embedded in everyday cultural practices and beliefs.

As an example, by the 1950s and 1960s, concepts like cultural deprivation, cultural deficit, and disadvantaged emerged in the educational literature. The concepts were used in psychological research to claim, because of linguistic and cognitive deficits, groups of children, mostly children of color from working-class backgrounds, were incapable of high academic achievement. In the article "Race, Class, and Gender in Education Research," Foster declares that these theories and conceptualizations that were advanced by racism served to support and reinforce White racial superiority. Foster concludes that this "academic supremacy research paradigm" is still present in educational research today; however, it was rephrased by the language of "at_risk" in the 1980s and theories of genetic inferiority in the 1990s (Foster, 1999).

Today the words "urban" and "inner city" have come to be synonymous with inferiority. Those two words have also come to be associated with Black and poor, and people psychologically and physically respond to these words in the negative. People withdraw from, detest, avoid, and admonish inner cities and low-income Black people because the two are viewed as interconnected. Racism is evident in everyday discourse and effortlessly finds its way into educational theories and research methodologies. In language and research, racism has consequences that affect individuals' and communities' thinking and behavior. Everyday language and research combine and interfere with meaningful urban educational reform efforts.

Both the traditions of early ethnography and comparative approaches to the study of cultures and racial groups continue to have a negative influence on educational research. John Stanfield II, a leading theorist on racism in social science research, contends that reasoning based on racial categories is embedded in American society and the Western world. Stanfield (1998) defines racial categorization as the ways people learn to think about human beings in terms of races. He strongly asserts, "Race is a mythology rooted in the false notion that social and cultural characteristics and abilities, such as moral character and intellect, can be attributed to real or imagined phenotypical traits" (p. 420). The principles of race and racialism and racial categories, contends Stanfield, indirectly shape the definitions and functions of institutions and communities, including communities of social scientists. There still exists a line of logic that races are ordered vertically from most to least able intellectually and socially, and there have been frequent "high-profile pseudo-scientific claims" pertaining to the place and abilities of African Americans. Stanfield, like Foster, contends that it has become normative to use Eurocentric notions and experiences as the baseline and yardstick to compare and contrast the notions and experiences of racial and ethnic minorities in the United States and abroad. Positivism's methodological approach of comparing and ordering racial, cultural, and gender groups remains a major aspect of social science and educational research.

As raced, classed, and gendered subjects, African American female students are multiply affected by racist, sexist, and classist research paradigms and resulting policies. Needless to say, these racist and sexist frameworks have affected research on or about Black girls and women, whether they are researchers or researched. In the lives of African American girls and women, racism, sexism, and classism are three interdependent control systems (King, 1995). White racism has suppressed them within racialized identities and patriarchy has subordinated them and deemed them powerless, concurrently their lower-income and working-class status have forced them to the peripheral of society.

Because African American females experience the intersection of race, class, and gender simultaneously, they become easy targets in the subordination and legitimation process in Western society (Miron, 1996). As articulated by Patricia Hill Collins (2000), "Portraying African American women as stereotypical mammies, matriarchs, welfare recipients, and hot mommas helps justify U.S. Black women's oppression" (p. 69). Collins further states that these socially constructed images are designed to make racism, sexism, and poverty, and other injustices appear to be a normal part of life.

Politicians, the media, social service personnel, religious groups, and researchers tend to focus on teenage pregnancy and high school dropout rates among urban African American adolescent girls. Very rarely do we hear discussions about the majority of Black girls from urban and inner-city communities who graduate high school and college. There is a strategic focus on social problems, and most of these social problems are inflated. The generalized depressing statistics about poor minority girls erase the role of discriminatory practices in education and other social structures (Leadbeater & Way, 1996). African American female students, as raced, classed, and gendered individuals, are particularly vulnerable to the consequences of the social construction of the "urban crisis."

In social science and educational research, African American female adolescents experience, in particular, have been left out, whited out (subsumed under White girls' experiences), blacked out (generalized within the Black male experience), or simply pathologized. The history of the study of Black girls has a cyclical pattern of excluding her experiences or simply suppressing her story within (White) feminist or Afrocentric led studies. Moreover, I agree with Smith (1982, p. 261) that "The black female adolescent has been underrepresented in educational, psychological, and career literature. Consequently, much of what we know about young Black females consists of bits and pieces of fragmented knowledge."

There are several reasons why Black female adolescents are absent from the literature. Compared to Black males, Black females have fewer behavior problems. African American girls' behaviors are least likely to affect others; thus, research and the resulting reform efforts tend to focus on Black males. Another factor is that White women have dominated the women's movement, which means their research is conducted on themselves or White adolescents. Last, researchers tend to assume that White females and Black females have similar socialization processes. Although there are some similarities between the two groups, Smith notes that there are important cultural and historical differences (Smith, 1982). By ignoring or subsuming Black girls' experiences within White girls' and Black boys' experiences, we overlook the inimitable experience of the

Black girl. Her experiences as a racialized "other," girl, and of the lower caste in the United States, makes oppression nearly ineluctable.

Postmodernism and Black Feminism

As mentioned above, research in education has worked to serve and protect the needs of the dominant elite. Consequently, many of the shifts and trends in qualitative and ethnographic research are results of epistemological and methodological challenges to traditional ways of "knowing." Together, epistemologies and methodologies are guides for how researchers approach the study of the social world.

Epistemology answers questions about who can be a "knower," what tests beliefs must pass in order to be legitimated as knowledge and what kind of things can be known (Harding, 1987). Epistemologies provide the justification for particular methodologies. Methodology is defined as "a particular social scientific discourse (a way of acting, thinking, and speaking) that occupies a middle ground between discussions of method and discussions of issues in the philosophy of social science" (Schwandt, 2001, p. 161). Based on this definition, it can be concluded a relationship exists between issues in the philosophy of social science, methods, and methodologies. We need educational and social science philosophies, methods, and methodologies that give voice to and empower urban African American girls. Also, we need epistemologies and methodologies that invoke discourse centered on agency and resiliency while simultaneously enacting critical practice and urban education reform.

Even more relevant to critical education research, Gloria Ladson-Billings (2000) makes it clear that epistemology is more than a way of knowing. She clarifies epistemology to be a "system of knowing" that has both an "internal logic and external validity" (p. 257). Therefore, a researcher's epistemology is well thought out and later justified by outside entities. Ladson-Billings further explains that epistemology is linked to one's worldview. How one views the world is influenced by the knowledge she possesses, and the knowledge she is capable of obtaining is influenced by her worldview. As a result, the theorist asserts, the conditions under which people live and learn shape their knowledge and worldviews simultaneously; thus, it becomes difficult to escape the dominant worldview of knowledge production. However, as Ladson-Billings points out, many theorists have been able to challenge and rework traditional Eurocentric worldviews to develop systems of knowledge or epistemologies that stand in contrast to the dominant Euro-American epistemology (Ladson-Billings, 2000). It is at the nexus of the relationships among worldviews, epistemologies, and methodologies that researchers' alternative and critical approaches to the study of education and the interaction of race, class, and gender arise.

Many women of African descent have lived and learned about the harsh realities of patriarchy and its intimate allies, racism and sexism. Nearly every day we have to be on guard against racial profiling that occurs when shopping and driving while Black. We know the anger that arises in us when we are asked for identification to verify our credit cards, while the White person next to us is not extended the same "protection." Most of us also know how it feels when we grocery shop and are mistaken for the young female single mother on welfare. Unfortunately, most of us know how it feels to sit in a college classroom full of our White peers and have to defend our competence and right to be there while defending our brothers and sisters who could not be there sitting beside us. Nevertheless, these experiences and emotions do not simply yield feelings of anger or hopelessness, they also bring forth distinct ways of interacting with and viewing the social world.

Traditional research questions and interpretations have not led to effective educational reform efforts. Theorists and educational researchers have substantially noted the current limitations of traditional research paradigms and methodologies. Rigsby (1994) states that "resilience research, like many areas of social science, needs serious attention given to theory building that focuses on understanding the causal structures and processes that give meaning and direction to social life" (p. 91). For example, structural influences like institutional racism, sexism, and classism work simultaneously to influence the behaviors and experiences of African American female students. Structural inequality leads to stress, strain, and, eventually, conflict in urban adolescent lives.

Not only does structural inequality shape the specific stressors in urban girls' lives, but it also shapes the systems of support that Black girls depend on to cope. African American female students' educational experiences are impacted by their race, class, and gender status; therefore, we need a framework in order to understand how structural forces and context-specific social conditions negatively and positively influence schooling experiences. Thus, researchers in urban education and gender studies need to embrace alternative and innovative methodological and theoretical approaches to the schooling experiences of African American girls, in particular. As urgent, is the need for theory-building that has practical implications for curriculum, policy, and pedagogy. At this moment in history, research and theory devoid of meaningful educational reform efforts are simply rhetoric contributing to cyclical patterns of marginalization and domination.

Miron (1996) and other researchers point out the usefulness of postmodernism in urban and educational ethnography. There is no one definition available to define the concept, theory, or discourse of postmodernism. Lyotard described postmodernism as a social condition that recognizes the myth of metanarratives that have legitimated scientific knowledge for the past two hundred years (Marshall, 1998). In other words, postmodernism represents a moment in time when theorists begin to question universal "truths," and asks what is rationality or science. I have chosen to consider postmodernism as a philosophy that serves to question essentialism, challenge metanarratives, and speak against the notion of scientific method or one particular way of knowing.

Miron wants educational researchers to embrace the tenets of postmodernism. He suggests that postmodernism offers a way to reinterpret existing ethnographies, and postmodern tenets have the potential to inform critical urban ethnography. For those who do research on urban Black girls, the tenets of postmodernism allow the opportunity to critique and reinterpret existing research. In the postmodern moment, urban girls are extended the rare opportunity to refocus the lens, snap the shot, decide the image, paint the portrait, touch up the proof, and present the picture of their own lives. Miron further suggests, for urban ethnographies, the postmodern leaning toward difference actually fosters the multiple vocular narratives of marginal groups. Researchers and the researched can begin to be understood as individuals who share distinctive historical and cultural experiences. From these commonalities and differences, meaningful contributions to urban educational reform and pedagogy can take place.

In "Poststructural Feminism in Education: An Overview," St. Pierre (2000) agrees that postructuralism (and the tenets of postmodernism) allows those interested in education reform to understand how knowledge, truth, and subjects are produced in language and cultural practice. She further asserts that reason or a foundation of true knowledge has never been objective but instead has always been produced by accident, passion, and chance. Furthermore, St. Pierre argues that educational researchers who understand power, resistance, and freedom are more likely to produce more complex and subtle analysis of social life. Similarly, educators who understand the dynamics can also produce and actively participate in pedagogy that is complex and transformative for themselves and their pupils. The feminist poststructural critique of epistemology is also useful for women who work to produce different knowledge "in different ways and to trouble what counts as truth" (St. Pierre, 2000, p. 500). Thus, poststructural feminism in education is an ongoing political strategy.

In "The 'Question of Belief': Writing Postructural Ethnography," Britzman (2000), like St. Pierre, challenges the "clean-cut" responsibility of the author, participants, and reader. Britzman reminds educational researchers that educational ethnography is both a set of practices and a set of discourses in which readers, participants, and the author are textualized identities. In the end, educational researchers like me admit to being involved in a political endeavor and writing partial and complex truths. My goal is to inform theory and practice that speaks to agency and resiliency in urban classrooms.

In addition, McCarthy (1988) asserts that postmodernism brings new insight to the study of the interaction of race, class, and gender. The theorists suggest that another approach to studying this intersection in education is to end the practice of explaining social difference as structure versus culture, the macro versus micro, and the disconnection between practice and theory. More specifically, McCarthy points out that some educational theorists have tended to look at human agency or a student's internal values while undertheorizing the effects of social and economic structures on educational experiences. Meanwhile, many other theorists undertheorize the effects of human agency and subjectivities on educational experiences.

Furthermore, McCarthy contends that microperspective analysis that looks at students' "abnormal" attitudes and behaviors actually places the burden of racism, sexism, and classism on the individual. In contrast, macrostructural analysis focus on the deeply embedded racism, sexism, and classism in U.S. culture but does little to show how these dynamics operate in schools. In short, McCarthy is calling for a nonsynchronous parallel approach to educational research. Nonsynchronous research does not dichotomize race, class, and gender or the various relationships, like human agency versus structure. Each relationship is seen as contributing to the educational experience. Lastly, theory must be linked to political action. These suggestions are strongly linked to postmodern thought (but not to postmodern action).

The postmodern nonsynchronous approach to urban education research works for the ethnography presented in this book, because race, class, and gender are not dichotomized. African American girls' schooling is viewed as affected by their race(d), class(ed), and gender(ed) status in our society. Furthermore, this book takes into account the economic, political, and historical context in which the students live, play, work, and experience schooling. Too many researchers study schooling and the school as if they were isolated spheres separate from students' everyday experiences with living and society. Students' experiences in their school environment are strongly tied to their experiences at the micro-level and at the macro-level; therefore, their interactions with individuals, groups, and their social context must be considered in an analysis on school resiliency.

In addition to its exclusionary language, lack of practicality, and lack of politics, three central features of postmodernism pose a challenge to Black feminist thought: decentering, deconstruction, and difference. These core themes are in alignment with as well as incongruent with Black feminist politics. First, decentering consists of moving those in power and the knowledge claims that defends their power away from the center. The challenge this poses for Black feminist thought is that postmodernism is exploding the center at a time when Black feminists and other racial and ethnic minority scholars are beginning to claim the margins. As articulated by Collins, "Within power relations that constructed whiteness, maleness, and wealth as centers of power, African American women were relegated to positions as marginalized Others. One 'decentered' hierarchal power relations by claiming the marginalized and devalued space of Black womanhood not as one of tragedy but as one of creativity and power" (1998, p. 128). However, postmodernism contends that any individual or group can claim marginalization, for power is unstable and at different moments in time different entities hold power.

Second, the postmodernist practice of deconstruction is accomplished by rejecting any discourse or theory that claims to explain universals, for no absolute "truth" exists. The problem that deconstruction poses is that it deconstructs or does away with social identities and structures like notions of race and culture. However, most Black feminists would argue that social identities are real and have real-life consequences in our society. Furthermore, within postmodern paradigm, theorists are becoming more concerned with differences among individuals or within groups. In the past, identity politics has been a form of political resistance in which an oppressed group rejected its devalued status and claimed its difference as positive (Collins, 1998). Yet, in the era of postmodernism, "difference" has largely come to focus on differences between individuals and groups. Due to the limitations and challenges brought forth in regards to postmodernism and the problems that it poses to the study of race, class, and gender, it is necessary to merge it with a more critical lens. I propose a necessary union between Black feminism and postmodernism.

There is little doubt that Black feminism is the most exhaustive theory available to study the African American female students' experiences. The various principles of Black feminism and its methodological analysis of the interaction of race, class, and gender depict the very essence of many Black girls' experiences. Black feminist thought is an example of oppositional knowledge formed at the margins. As a multifaceted concept, Black feminism/womanism means different things to different people. The term "Black feminism" is usually used to denote an intellectual and political movement, referring specifically to the work of Black female intellectuals and activists "who are rethinking Black experiences from a feminist perspective and revising white feminist politics from an Afrocentric perspective" (Cashmore, 1996, p. 50).

In *Fighting Words: Black Women and the Search for Justice*, Patricia Hill Collins describes Black feminism as a critical social theory. She defines critical social theory as "bodies of knowledge and sets of institutional practices that actively grapple with the central questions facing groups of people differently placed in specific political, social, and historic contexts characterized by injustice" (1998, p. 276). A critical social theory is "critical" due to its commitment to justice, for one's own group and/or for other groups. As a critical social theory, Black feminism is concerned with fighting against economic, political, and social injustice for Black women and other oppressed groups. Because theory-building is inevitably connected to transformation and change, research in urban education must lead to new ways of thinking and behaving.

As an ideology and political movement, Black feminism/womanism examines issues affecting African American women in the United States as a part of the global struggle for women's emancipation (Collins, 1998). Even more, explains Collins, the term "Black feminism" disrupts the inherent racist assumption that feminism is a "Whites-only" ideology and political movement. The term "Black feminist" reminds White women that they are neither the only nor the normative feminists. Furthermore, Collins points out that no one Black woman's standpoint exists, instead Black women's standpoint exists. For me, Black feminism is an act of self-definition that describes one's state of mind, directs one's research questions and methodology, announces one's embracement of Afrocentrism and mainstream feminism, and proclaims one's awareness of the interlocking systems of race, class, and gender oppression. Also for me, to even use the terms "Black feminism" or "womanism" amounts to activism. Critical urban education ethnography from this lens inevitably is a part of vital social, intellectual, and political politics.

J.A. Ladner's research with African American girls in the 1970s is an example of alternative approaches to traditional methodologies for studying the interaction of race, class, and gender. Ladner reveals that traditional methodology and theory required that she study subjects from an objective stance and view them as deviants. Of course, she rejected that. Drawing from her own experiences instead and the knowledge that African American girls held valuable perspectives on their own lives, Ladner chose to study their beliefs in the girls' specific social environment. She interviewed the girls; thus, their voices were central to the study. She placed their experiences in the historical (she began with discussions of slavery) and current context (the housing projects which the girls lived) (Harding, 1987).

Even more, Ladner's interpretive framework drew from various social science and research traditions. Ladner was admittedly not objective and searched for stories of strength and adaptability in the Black community, and urging other researchers of color to do the same. Her method responds to studies that focus on pathology and make residents look responsible for their predicaments. Ladner's work is only one example of ethnography from a Black feminist standpoint. From this research, we can learn about the importance of the participants' voice, the researcher's experience, and contextuality.

As Ladner demonstrates, Black feminism/womanism is the most comprehensive theory for framing African American female students' experiences. As a critical social theory, it bolsters and encourages research on resilience and resiliency-fostering factors in the lives of Black girls, and considers how historical and current social factors impact their lives. The Black feminist/womanist practice of placing Black women at the center and viewing Black females as subjects is what I have attempted to adopt in *Teaching Black Girls*. Traditionally, social science has "othered" young African American girls by incorporating deficit models into the mode of analysis. *Teaching Black Girls* looks at how a group of African American female adolescents from a strength perspective and views them as active agents in the schooling process. Theoretically, Black feminism provides a foundational approach that subverts societal images of urban Black girls as societal parasites. Its premise of confronting the issues that affect Black women in our society makes it an ideal theoretical lens for capturing the school experiences and resilience of African American girls as does its history of fighting racism, sexism, and classism.

A merge between Black feminism and postmodernism is useful for at least two reasons: (1) it reveals the racist assumptions in White feminist discourse, and (2) it challenges the essentialist stance of Black feminist theory. Black feminists have always critiqued the feminist humanist project of emancipation. Feminism has traditionally universalized a "woman's" experience, subsuming issues of race and class differences within White women's experiences. But, postmodern talk has forced White feminists to deconstruct their ideal universal woman.

Postmodernism has also allowed critique of the essentialist stance of Black feminism. For example, Caraway (1991) writes that Black feminist Patricia Hill Collins' (in 1989 works) vision of Black culture ignores these contradictory tendencies, Collins risks romanticizing Black culture and creating another essentialized countermythology. Black feminist bell hooks argues that a narrow cultural nationalism prevents Black liberation struggles (1990). Simply put, there is no one Black experience and the construction of a monolithic African American culture prevents political solidarity. Specific to urban education, researchers will note that not all African American female students are poor or working class, live in the inner city or urban areas, nor all identify as Black or perform the

"Blackness" in the same way. Thus, most will benefit from a more all-embracing multivocular Black feminism.

Of course, it is important not to ignore or minimize the importance of social facts. African American girls are more likely to experience social barriers, in a society that values White over Black, men over women, and wealth over poverty. Also, African American female students are more likely to encounter race, class, and gender discrimination in classrooms, curriculum, and pedagogy, putting them at risk of school failure. However, for Black feminist theorists to successfully question how some students are able to remain in school while others are pushed out, we first have to shed our essentialist stance. Otherwise, Black feminism has the potential to limit the study of African American female adolescents, for essentialism and neglecting the process of self-identification cause researchers to overlook how African American girls are simultaneously affected by and perform their race as well as their gender and class.

Toward Post-Womanist Research

Postmodernism has the potential to aid Black womanism/feminism as a theoretical lens to explain how African American girls' school experiences are related to their experiences as racialized, classed, and gendered subjects in society. For instance, Michel Foucault's primary concern was the process by which human beings are made subjects (objectification). Foucault refers to one mode of objectification of the subject as "dividing practices." Dividing practices occur by using diverse procedures, in which ultimately the subject is objectified by a process of division, either within him-/herself or from others. Foucault asserts, "Essentially dividing practices are modes of manipulation that combine the mediation of a science (or pseudo-science) and the practice of exclusion—usually in a spatial sense, but always in a social one" (1984, p. 8). This point allows us to begin to understand how girls and women of African descent have been raced, classed, gendered, and excluded based on divisions that privilege White over Black, male over female, and wealth over poverty.

A Black feminism/postmodernism will ask: To what degree have urban African American female students been subjects of objectification? How have dividing practices affected the study of urban African American female students as subjects in the social (and biological) sciences? For example, do researchers study low-income and working-class urban African American girls' school experiences as girls or as race(d), class(ed), and gender(ed) subjects? How do "dividing practices" that use the categories Black/female/lower income affect the education of these girls? Even more important, how do students, parents, communities, educational, and social institutions participate in dividing practices? These questions are important, because Foucault claims that there is an interconnection between modes of classification, control, and containment. Furthermore, Foucault and others (hooks, 1990; West, 1999; Goldberg, 1993) claim that dividing practices have been associated with reform and progress but have mostly affected and impacted oppressed groups such as urban Black girls?

Foucault argued that during the nineteenth century the body was treated as a thing; thus, social institutions were designed to complement dividing practices as witnessed through spatial, temporal, and social compartmentalization of institutions. Foucault asserts that social institutions are politically driven and serve to control the conduct of individuals through real or perceived rewards. I would argue that educational institutions are such social institutions and that they are politically driven. Therefore, it is useful to add Foucault's idea of social institutions as politically driven entities and scientific classification of the body to educational analyses.

Next, subjectification is the process through which an individual turns himself or herself into a subject, based on his or her own thoughts and conducts as well as those of others. "These operations characteristically entail a process of self-understanding but one which is mediated by an external authority figure, be he confessor or psychoanalyst," explains Foucault (1984, p. 11).

The process of subjectification allows us to understand Black females as active agents and participants in their own lives. Furthermore, we are able to study the processes by which urban girls are socialized into their gender roles, identify with their "Blackness," and act in or react to these roles as students from lower-income groups. In relation to Black girls, ethnographers want to ask: What role does the student play in her subjectivity and self-formation, and what are the (negative or positive) consequences of her identity formation to her educational goals? Can we teach students that they have been subjects of objectification? How can researchers and writers avoid further categorization and objectification of urban girls?

Other important tenets of postmodernism that function well in urban educational ethnography are (adapted from Miron, 1996, p. 56):

Opposes metanarratives	Against generalizations and one big story to explain social life; therefore, emphasizes the need for careful analysis of "local practices."
Antirepresentationalism	Against the idea that "truths" are representative of reality and does not believe that scientific knowledge and the validation process are independent of one's cultural or political beliefs.

Orientation to the "other"   Emphasizes a concern for those who have been oppressed or exploited, such as women, children, people of color, prisoners, and the underprivileged.

Based on these three tenets, postmodernism appears to be an ideal paradigm for an ethnography on urban girls. The findings presented in this book examine the school experiences of individual girls in a small city and cannot be generalized beyond the individual women's stories, families, communities, or schools (opposes metanarratives). I acknowledge that their experiences cannot necessarily be measured or verified by the powers that be (antirepresentationalism), but their realities can be told and given self-validation. Also, I draw conclusions and make recommendations for urban educators and advocates based on my own raced, classed, and gendered perspective. Even more important, the ethnography gives voice to a historically oppressed group that has been traditionally absent in educational research on resiliency. Therefore, throughout the book, readers will hear the voices of students in their own words (orientation to the other).

This book attempts to combine the tenets of both postmodernism and Black feminism. We ask: How do the Black family (as a socially constructed entity), the Black community (comprised of subjects of objectification), and the school (as a politically driven entity) impact the schooling experiences of Black girls (active in subjectification), who experience the intersection of race, class, and gender (as marginalized subjects of objectification)? How do African American female students interact with and shape those entities?

As pointed out by Miron (1996, p. 55), "all around us in literature, architecture, film, and video the postmodern paradigm is evident; in public schooling, especially in the inner-city schools, a cultural/theoretical lag exists." Black female students are more likely to live in urban areas and attend public schooling; therefore, their education too is stuck in a "cultural/theoretical lag." I am suggesting that when the theoretical bases of Black feminism and postmodernism form a magnetic attraction, we can begin to move educational research away from outdated positivist paradigms. Lastly, Collins (2000) admits that postmodernism can challenge existing dominant discourse, and hooks (1990) proposes postmodernism, as an answer to the "yearning" for oppositional practices. The integration of the tenets of postmodernism and Black feminism is pioneering methodological and theoretical approaches to including African American girls in education research as resilient active participants in their own lives. This lens is more likely to discover resiliency and its development instead of failure. I believe that social and educational transformation may occur with these new discoveries.

African American female students are more likely to attend schools in urban neighborhoods with high poverty, unemployment, and crime rates than their White counterparts (Wilson, 1996; Fine, 1991; Anyon, 1997), and to live in a world that privileges White over Black, male over female, and wealth over poverty. In spite of social and institutional racism and sexism, the majority of African American females have been able to achieve academically. More resilient adolescents may obtain support from the family, community, and/or school that serve as protective factors against academic failure. Although adolescents have some needs in common, these needs are structured by where and how they live. Factors that influence negative educational development can be buffered by external assets in community systems as well as internal assets.

Historically, family and community have served as a support system to protect many Black girls' self-esteem in the larger society and the school system. In addition, teachers, coaches, friends, extended family members, other unrelated adults, or mentors have played a central role in promoting adolescents' positive life experiences. For African American girls, mentors enhance girls' ability to appreciate the positive aspects of their social support networks, cope with problems in family relationships, and pursue activities related to their career goals (Davis & Rhodes, 1996). Other women can also serve as inspirations for success. Aunts, adult sisters, sisters-in-law, older friends, and neighbors were among the women who, many urban girls said influenced their achievement (Sullivan, 1996).

Teaching Black Girls looks at how support from the family, community, and school promotes educational resiliency among a group of African American girls in a midsize urban milieu in the Midwest. The theme of resiliency dominates the theme of subjugation in the lives of the selected students. Resiliency is the ability to recover from or adjust to problems, adversities, and stress. For women and African Americans, academic achievement has been associated with social and economic mobility; however, very little research has focused on the factors that enhance positive educational development amongst African American females. Instead, the majority of research on African American female adolescents focuses on social problems such as school dropouts, drug and alcohol use, welfare dependency, and teenage pregnancy.

Although Barbara Omolade was referring to African American children and parents participation in early de jure desegregation in the quote at the beginning of this chapter, her words represent the multiple themes of this book—individual agency, family and community influence on education, and education as a vehicle for social change.

At first glance, it appears that Omolade and Yssis are telling different stories in the epigraphs. The first quote seems to see the Black family in a positive light, while the second young woman appears to contradict the first statement. However, the women's words share the common theme of how Black folks have traditionally viewed education as a tool to change one's (or the collective) life circumstance. For the young women discussed in this book, like many other young women of color, educational stories are interwoven with the motivational voices of our families and communities. It is important that we tell others how to respect the interweaving of these support systems. Also, as we hear in Omolade and Yssis' words, our educational experiences are complicated and at times contradictory. Alongside stories of success and contentment, there are stories of failure and disappointment. The purpose of this book is to examine how a group of African American female students approach failures and successes in their everyday lives that lead to processes of educational resiliency. As I struggle to reconstruct "truths" and (re)tell their experiences, Omolade's and Yssis' words will serve as a reminder of the multiple realities that exist in the lives of those who experience the interaction of race, class, and gender simultaneously.

Chapter Two

(En)gendering Resiliency
in Urban Education

It is essential to "set the record straight," but how to do so is not always evident. To focus only on the strengths, accomplishments, and victories does not give sufficient attention to the system of domination. Yet to emphasize too heavily the structure of oppression underplays the creative energy and history of a people. (Mullings, 1997, p. xii)

Although an abundance of literature has focused on defining, conceptualizing, and constructing resilience, little or no research in this area has focused on African American female students in particular. Current conceptualizations of resilience have the potential for placing all blame on or giving all credit to individuals for their successes and failures, which ignores many important structural influences on the behaviors we may otherwise call resilient (Rigsby, 1994). To understand educational resilience and African American female students, we have to look at how larger historical forces and social structures affect their families, communities and schools as well as their individual choices.

In this chapter, I look at the social and political actions that have contributed to the current educational problems that so many urban African American children are facing today. Smith (1999), a legal scholar, brilliantly traces the disenfranchisement of Black children to the creation of the U.S. Constitution. Segregation, hostility, and indifference have greatly impacted the way educational policy is implemented and development. These negative sentiments also affect how educators and policymakers view and treat urban adolescent girls. The chapter also examines the current themes in education that affect reform initiatives and ultimately policy development. I lay out the major findings that have supported themes of a "crisis," then cite research that focuses on resiliency. The resiliency literature shows that because of segregation and discrimination, educators, communities, and the Black family have been sources of support for many African Americans.

The U.S. Constitution

For Smith, the original Hydra of the disenfranchisement of African American children is the Constitution and its framers. De jure segregation and de facto segregation, the author argues, are simply the Hydratic heads that sprang forth when the original Hydra was attacked or threatened. Smith explains that because the U.S. Constitution was built on the belief that all men were created equal and were born with certain inalienable rights, it became necessary to rationalize slavery, and that religion, science, sociology, biology, culture, history, literature, and education were all employed to justify and ensure the inferior status of African Americans. Undoubtedly, Smith's accusations sound far-reaching, but other cultural theorists (Foucault, 1984; Giroux, 1997; Blakey, 1997; West, 1999) have made similar claims.

It is at the least deplorable and disheartening to learn that the disenfranchisement of Black children can be traced back to the beginnings of American democracy itself. Today, too many Black children and their families are still fighting for the right to be included in our democratic social structure. For centuries, individuals and groups have tried to justify the alienation of retribution of children of African descent; such justification has only continued the educational inequality that we are witnessing today in many urban schools. Fortunately, these justifications have not always been effective, but they continue to pose a threat to the social, psychological, and educational development of many children.

Smith also avows that two historical and present customs in the United States, White supremacy and the practice of sacrificing the rights and liberties of Blacks, can be traced back to the U.S. Constitution. Smith explains that White supremacy predated the Constitution, but the moral compromises made in the Constitution and the justifications of those moral compromises solidified White supremacy in the minds of White Americans. In the same fashion, the practice of bargaining the rights and liberty of Blacks was witnessed when the Framers failed to address the injustices of slavery and gave up slaves' rights in order to maintain slaveholders' support of the Constitution (Smith, 1999). Of course, the long-term consequences of White supremacy, then and now, could not and cannot be predicted. Forgoing the rights of African Americans as a political strategy was at the time clever, but it set a precedent for the overall treatment of Black people. We are in the midst of finding out what occurs when one group's liberties are negotiated on behalf of another group's economic gain.

As a result of the moral compromises made in the original Constitution, our society is entrenched with indifference and hostility towards African Americans. As Smith articulates, once slavery was forcibly ended in order to win the Civil War, "Blacks, in the mind of the nation, were still slaves: non-persons to be treated with great disrespect, little recognition, and great criminality" (Smith, 1999, p. 164). Smith comprehensively details the many heads that sprang from the original Hydra after emancipation.

Jim Crow Laws and Black Codes, de facto and de jure segregation, resegregation (or "white flight"), transracial teacher hostility and indifference, and intellectual segregation has contributed to the disenfranchisement of African American children. (Note: The different practices should be read as interrelated social trends.) It is interesting that Smith focuses on the moral compromises made at that moment in history, because countless urban children and their families have been deemed immoral and undeserving of one our nation's greatest resources, a free and appropriate education.

As a final point, Smith makes a convincing case that Black children carry the burden of most European Americans' indifference and hostility toward African Americans. Not only do indifference and hostility affect funding and educational opportunity, but they also affect how Black children are treated within the boundaries of the school system. Smith uses quantitative and qualitative data to show that African American children are victims of verbal and physical racial assaults by teachers, are more likely to be classified as mentally impaired, emotionally disturbed, or labeled as having a learning disability than any other group of students, and, more likely to be suspended or dismissed from school than other students. These statistics are consistent with transracial teaching, declares Smith. She names Black boys as those most affected by transracial/transgendered teaching. Transracial teaching is a predominance of White teachers teaching Black students, a trend that has taken place since desegregation, due to a direct result of government actions that replaced Black teachers in Black neighborhoods.

The simple fact that the legal historian can trace the disenfranchisement of African American students to the U.S. Constitution presents multiple problems for African American female students. The Constitution states that all men are created equal, but it infers that Blacks are not human but mere chattel. In other words, the Constitution never granted African American women the same liberties as White men, because of their gendered and racialized identities. Black and White feminists have voiced the struggles they endured, because of their absence in the minds of the framers of the Constitution (Wollenstonecraft, Anthony, and Truth, in Ruth, 1990). Angela Davis, for example, asserts that the end of slavery did not offer African American women freedom from racism or sexism or economic exploitation.

In agreement with Davis, I extend this conclusion to African American female students. Smith's conclusion does not recognize that even if racism were eradicated today, Black girls would still have to live with sexism. Their educational experiences are tied to African Americans' and women's overall mistreatment in U.S. history and their lack of significance to the framers of the Constitution. There is no doubt that racism, sexism, and economic exploitation negatively affect all Americans. However, some benefit more than others from our nation's practice of excluding some from valuable resources, while others are placed on an unattainable pedestal. African American girls are one of the groups most at risk of experiencing the backlash of an indifferent and hostile populace.

Black Girls, White Teachers

In addition to larger structural factors, many African American female students also face barriers from their classroom teachers. Clark and Scott-Jones (1986) found that teachers' expectations of students vary with race and gender. Teachers look for and reinforce achievement-oriented behaviors in White students more often than they do in Black students. Teachers are also more likely to give White students praise and attention, and they have higher performance standards for White students than Black students. Furthermore, it was found that male students receive more attention, praise, encouragement, and criticism from teachers than female students did.

Additionally, teachers are more likely to perceive their Black female students as socially mature and White female students as intellectually competent. On the other hand, teachers praise academic performance more often than they praise social behavior amongst students. Black females received more praise for behavior than any subgroup of students. The intersection of race, class, and gender has a direct impact on African American female students' experiences inside and outside of the school environment. These findings show that African American female students' multiple identities affect their schooling and have separate and distinct consequences from those of their White peers and male counterparts. The interaction of race, class, and gender leaves African American young women vulnerable to multiple oppressions, causing them to rely on alternative support systems.

Three main themes are currently at the focal point of urban education reform initiatives and research. The themes generally center on (a) the idea that urban education is in a state of crisis, (b) low-income minority children are not thriving or fail to achieve, and (c) some African American students are a part of a new culture that opposes achievement. All of these points are separate themes, yet they operate interdependently. Support for one depends on support from another. For example, the idea that Afican American students have formed a culture that opposes achievement is reliant on the theory that low-income students fail to achieve, and the latter also depends on the former. Similarly, the urban education crisis theory can only be supported if research shows that low-income minority children are not achieving and that students in urban areas oppose education.

To begin with, probably some of the most-cited research in educational anthropology and urban education literature is John Ogbu's work with minority groups (1978, 1987, 1991). Ogbu researched minority education in the United States and abroad for approximately twenty-five years. Based on his original 1978 study and current research, he developed a cultural-ecological theory to explain minority school performance. Cultural-ecological theory has two main parts: one aspect of the theory focuses on how minorities are treated or mistreated in education, which Ogbu refers to as "the system." The other aspect of the theory is related to how or why a group became a minority in the first place and focuses on the way minorities perceive and respond to schooling based on their treatment. He refers to the second aspect of the theory as "community forces."

It is important to remember that Ogbu's theory is strongly constructed on how and why a group becomes a minority. For example, African American students are categorized as involuntary (nonimmigrant) minorities, people who have become a part of U.S. society against their will, usually due to having been conquered, colonized, or enslaved. Due to their involuntary status and response to mistreatment, minorities develop different cultural models of U.S. society. Ogbu defines cultural models as the ways that members of a minority group understand or interpret their world and guide their actions in that world. Ogbu blames involuntary minority students' poor school performance on the cultural models (or their interpretations of society) that guide their actions.

Ogbu and Simmons (1998) lay out four types of understandings/interpretations that negatively impact African American and other involuntary minority children's school performance—frame of reference, folk theories of making it, degree of trust of White people and their institutions, and beliefs about the effect of adopting White ways on minority identity. In brief, Ogbu has argued that involuntary minorities' first frame of reference is their social and economic status in the United States, and their second, the social and economic status of White middle-class Americans. Because they view their schooling and social and economic status as inferior to that of White middle-class Americans, their frame of reference causes them to be critical and mistrustful of the educational system (Ogbu & Simmons, 1998).

In summary, Ogbu's cultural-ecological theory attributes involuntary minorities' poor academic achievement to their interpretations and responses to racism and discrimination. Because involuntary minorities were held in the United States against their will, they mistrust White Americans and their institutions. As a consequence, involuntary minority parents and children have ambivalent feelings about the value of education as a means to success. Ogbu argues that involuntary minority communities, in turn, form a collective oppositional identity that is juxtaposed to "White" culture and language. Thus, according to the theorists, involuntary minorities' collective identity reject what it takes to achieve academically.

The strengths of Ogbu's cultural-ecological model are that to some extent it does incorporate social processes (his hypothesis on how students come to reject achievement), and it does view minorities as agents who consciously or unconsciously respond to their environment (the idea of forming oppositional behavior). However, the cultural-ecological model fails to look at the social context in which the students achieve or do not achieve, and it unremittingly operates on generalizations. Ogbu infers that African American students, as involuntary minorities, fail to achieve because of their ambivalence toward education and their collective oppositional response to mistreatment in larger society and the educational system. He states that involuntary minority students and parents withdraw physically or psychologically from the educational system because they are aware of their lower social and economic status compared to White Americans. Critics of Ogbu's framework note that African Americans, in particular, have been "involuntary minorities" for quite some time in the United States.; however, African Americans have not always opposed education. For instance, Vanessa Siddle Walker's (2000) research on segregated school systems between 1935 and 1960 demonstrates that African American communities do have a tradition of supporting education.

In fact, Siddle Walker found that many African American communities between 1935 and 1960 with segregated schools formed a collective identity that supported school achievement for the uplift of the race. Ogbu's theory causes minority students to be viewed as simply reacting to an abstract enemy called racism. Thus, readers are left to believe that underachievement is an anomaly attributed to the internal beliefs of the individual or his/her culture. As Siddle Walker advocates there is a need for more research that looks at strengths of the Black community and focuses on its resiliency.

Another weakness of cultural-ecological model is related to its assumption that involuntary minorities' parents and students hold ambivalent attitudes about the value of education, which generates poor school outcomes. Mickelson's (1990) survey-based research found that Black and White students hold abstract and concrete attitudes about education. Abstract attitudes pertain to such beliefs as "education is the key to success," whereas concrete attitudes reflect student experiences that education may or may not have led to success. The survey discovered that all students, regardless of gender, race, or income level, held abstract attitudes about education. Actually, Black students embraced the link between education and mobility even more than their White counter-parts did. However, Black students and working-class students held more con-crete attitudes about education; thus, they were more pessimistic about the rewards of education than White and middle-class students. Therefore, concrete attitudes help explain more thoroughly how social context affects achievement. The cultural-ecological model attributes low achievement to parents and stu-dents, but Mickelson (1990) demonstrates that achievement has more to do with students' experience with social inequality. Low-income and minority stu-dents know that education may not yield the same results for them as it does for other groups.

Even though there are alternative views, like those that Siddle Walker pro-vides, to Ogbu's oppositional theory, many research studies support Ogbu's findings. Using cultural reproduction theory, Foley's (1990) ethnographic study in a small Texas Mexican American town called "North Town," examines schools as sites for popular culture practices that reproduce social inequality. His study found that through sports, social groups, and classroom practices, students were socialized into their respective gender and class roles. He also found that youth who aspired to become socially prominent learned new com-munication styles and ethics that were reflective of the dominant class in the United States. In particular, he found that the more successful and socially ac-ceptable students exercised a style of communication and impression manage-ment techniques that were portrayed by the school as the ideal. The less socially accepted or academically successful students, who were usually minority, low-income students, and/or Mexican American, did not adopt the practices of con-formity, restraint, or acceptable communication styles. Those students who had adopted the practices of the dominant culture shed their own racialized identi-ties and embraced the meritocracy ideology. However, most of the minority students resisted conformity. Foley's (1990) findings are consistent with re-search on urban Appalachian girls (Borman, Mueninghoff, & Piazza, 1988) and ethnographic research on U.S. Mexican youth (Valenzuela, 1999). Thus, Foley's and others' findings are congruent with Ogbu's in that they, too, determined that low-income students and/or minority students were least likely to adopt certain school practices that are conducive to school achievement. On the other hand, as articulated by Valenzuela (1999) in reference to U.S.-born Mexican youth, "They oppose a schooling process that disrespects them; they oppose not education, but schooling" (p. 5).

Signithia Fordham's research (1988, 1996) builds upon Ogbu's cultural-ecological theory. In agreement with Ogbu (1978, 1987, 1991), Fordham also argues that collective identity affects the school experiences of minority stu-dents. Fordham (1988) conducted a two-year ethnographic study at a predominately Black high school in Washington, D.C., that studied the attitudes and behaviors of high-achieving and underachieving students. Fordham found that high-achieving males and females adopted a "racelessness" persona or detached from the Black community.

Drawing from the findings of the research study, Fordham concludes that African American students are harmed by the fictive-kinship system of the Black community (1988, 1996). Fordham asserts that the collective ethos of the fictive-kinship system is not in alignment with the individual ethos of the dominant culture; thus, students are nearly guaranteed to fail. They fail when they maintain a strong identification with the Black community. The researcher even claims that some students purposely sabotage their education in order to avoid being perceived as "acting White." Finally, in agreement with Ogbu, Fordham suggests that African American students' success or failure actually lies in the attitudes and behaviors of parents and the Black community. Because schools reflect the values and ideologies of the dominant culture, it is suggested that African American parents and the Black community as a whole does a disservice to Black children by promoting a collective identity.

Other studies have contradicted Ogbu's and Fordham's findings on the harm of the Black community and the fictive-kinship system. For example, Lee's (1992) overview of the New Concept Development Center (NCDC), an independent Black institution in Chicago, describes its mission as promoting collective responsibility. Its primary mission was to prepare African American children to assume future roles as political, intellectual, spiritual, and economic leaders in their communities (Lee, 1992). The overview explains that their mission would be accomplished through implementing African-centered principles such as acknowledging the importance of the child, community activism, knowledge of African history and world history and the individual's social and intellectual responsibility to the community (Lee, 1992). It was reported that after leaving NCDC, alumni go on to attend prestigious public schools and are enrolled in gifted programs. Also, the author boasts that one study showed that NCDC and other independent black institutions, on average, students achieved at or above grade level (Lee, 1992). Lee's report supports other research that illustrates that collective identity alone does not account for school success or failure.

Furthermore, Fordham's theory on the tension between the collective ethos of the fictive-kinship system and the individual ethos of the dominant culture is limited because it is embedded in binary thinking. The primary binaries that influence Fordham's thinking are White/Black, individual/community, rationality/irrationality, and success/failure. More specifically, in educational and social science research, African Americans tend to be compared to or viewed as simply reacting to White culture; Black people are consistently viewed as a collective identity, whereas White people are assumed to be only concerned with the "individual"; Black folks' behavior is typically viewed as emotional and irrational, because it only seems rational to "perform" what it takes to succeed; and success is always discussed juxtaposed to failure, which is anything that does not appear to be the norm or status quo.

Other researchers and/or theorists have extensively discussed the intrinsic problems with Western society's infatuation with binaries (Blakey, 1997; Giroux, 1997; Villenas, 2000; Foucault, 1984). First, what Fordham and many other theorists fail to realize is what is customarily labeled as success/failure (achievers/nonachievers) is largely predetermined and socially constructed by the dominant elite through the idea of norms. Foucault (1984) states, "In a sense, the power of normalization imposes homogeneity; but it individualizes by making it possible to measure gaps, to determine levels, to fix specialties, and to render the differences useful by fitting them one to another" (p. 197). Then he proceeds, referring to the examination, "it is a normalizing gaze, a surveillance that makes it possible to qualify, to classify, and to punish" (p. 197). Fordham and many other researchers are directly or indirectly serving the purposes of those in power by legitimating their modes of classification.

In Opposition to Binaries

Also, Villenas (2000) criticizes the practices of researchers who "manipulate and commodify" racialized identities "vis-à-vis majority culture" (p. 76). A practice researchers knowingly or unknowingly participate in, when they consistently engage in analyzing Blacks as constant reactors to White culture. In that type of theoretical framework, there only exist Blacks and Whites, and Blacks are who they are due to their treatment by Whites. Last, Blakey (1997) speaks against the manner in which Whites are usually not seen as having or embracing a culture, whereas African Americans are only a culture. Enforcing Blakey's argument, researchers like Fordham fail to discuss how White individuals, as also a part of a larger culture, respond (consciously or subconsciously) to Black students and other minority groups' communities. In short, binary thinking causes researchers to ignore or overlook complex relationships and the multiple variables that may shape African Americans' school experiences.

Sociologist Jay MacLeod's two-year ethnographic study in the Clarendon Heights projects looks at social reproduction, oppositional identity formation, and students' belief in meritocracy. MacLeod (1987) argues that most studies merely focus on the role of schools as contributors to social reproduction, thus ignoring other areas of socialization, like the peer group, family, and work relations. Borrowing from Giroux, he declares that oppositional behavior is not self-explanatory and needs to be linked with the subject's own explanation and it needs to be contextualized. Therefore, he sets out to study the peer group, work environment/situations, families, and school environments of two low-income teenage groups called the "Hallway Hangars," who were mainly White, and the "Brothers," who were mainly African American. In brief, MacLeod (1987) reports that the Hallway Hangars did not believe in the dominant ideology of meritocracy, and their oppositional behavior, inside and outside of school, was consistent with their beliefs. The Brothers, on the other hand, strongly believed in meritocracy and attempted to do well in school and stay out of trouble in their neighborhoods. Their parents and family members also stressed the importance of education as a means to getting out of the projects and to get ahead.

Nevertheless, in the end both groups of teenage boys ended up in the secondary labor market or the "underground economy." Their socially reproduced class positions were results of race and class discrimination in the schools and the larger workforce. The low-income and minority students at their school were usually tracked to the lower-tier curriculum regardless of their efforts and beliefs in meritocracy. Therefore, oppositional behavior and belief in what it takes to make it does affect school performance, but social forces also affect low-income and minority students schooling experiences. MacLeod's ethnography is more nonsynchronous than most other research studies in urban settings related to education, because he provides us with alternative research questions that rely less on binarism such as: How do low-income White students in urban schools experience schooling? What role do families take in educational attainment? How does the neighborhood environment affect education? What role do schools play in preparing students for long-term success? Why is it that Black students who do believe in meritocracy still struggle in school? And does the larger social structure, like the workforce, reward students differently for academic achievement?

An ethnographic research study in a Black middle-class suburb in Chicago demonstrates that individual, community, and larger social structures intertwine to determine what students receive for their education. Pattillo-McCoy's (1999) study reveals that despite beliefs in meritocracy and viewing their parents and other community members' success the high school graduates in that community nevertheless faced barriers to social and economic mobility. After high school graduation, many of the young (and some older) adults found it difficult to obtain work or sufficient income. Some of the young adults in the neighborhood were also affected by negative peer and community behaviors. The researcher explains that many middle-class African American communities faced the same problems as low-income minority adolescents, for racial segregation patterns keep Black Americans isolated to certain areas of cities. Therefore, there is constant contact between low-income and middle-class African Americans. This study reminds educational researchers to consider the interconnectedness of individual agency, community forces, and larger social structures and, in addition, the aforementioned effects on students' school experiences and outcomes. The study provides an example of how low-income minority students are not isolated groups that only have contact with other people who have dismal outcomes in U.S. society. African American students' frame of reference reaches beyond the ghetto.

Arguably, Michelle Fine (1991) offers a more holistic picture of the barriers that urban public school students endure, which are usually related to their race, class, and/or gender. She, too, finds that raced, classed, and/or gendered students face barriers inside and outside the school building that impinge on their aspirations. Fine's book, *Framing Dropouts: Notes on the Politics of an Urban Public High School* (1991), integrates analysis of individual attitudes and behavior, policies and politics of the school environment, community actions and behaviors, local and societal issues, and economic, social, and historical trends that affect urban residents and schools. She uses qualitative and quantitative data to observe the differences between low-income minority students who remain in school and students who leave school before obtaining a diploma.

Fine (1991) considers the factors in the students' school environment that might support underachievement or, in this case, dropping out. For example, Fine cites statistics that show that low-income minority students are likely to be discharged or suspended at a far greater rate than other students. High suspension rates strongly correlate with students leaving school, she notes. Besides those "push" factors that are related to high school dropout, it was also found that high school dropouts were more likely to possess a critical consciousness than students who remained in school. More specifically, it was found that the dropouts are more ambivalent and hold contradictory notions about the role of education in social mobility, which is congruent with Ogbu's and other researchers' findings. The students who left school, for example, told stories of people they knew who were making it without an education, and they shared stories of people they knew with an education who were not doing so well (Fine, 1991). Their stories are similar to Ogbu's and other researchers' theme of low-income minority students' sense of ambivalence about the value of education.

Additionally, the dropouts shared stories of oppression and discrimination related to their race, class, and gender in the school system and job market. On the other hand, those students who stayed in school hold a deep belief in meritocracy or a belief that education is the route to social and economic mobility. Also, the more successful students tend to distance themselves from their low-income minority peers. Distancing attitudes and behaviors are evidenced in that successful students usually associate themselves with higher-income groups, more stable family structures, and more socially accepted values. In addition, these students are more likely to explain the apparent signs of social inequalities in their neighborhoods as conditions or circumstances that individuals brought on themselves. In fact, reports Fine, they rarely critique the U.S. class system, and they more often consider themselves middle class (1991). Last, graduates are more likely to disconnect from their kin, community, and racial identities. However, the dropouts usually maintain contact with their kin, community, and racial identities. Also supporting Ogbu's findings, graduates are more often raised by foreign-born parents (Fine, 1991).

Another important feature of Fine's study is that gender is at the center of her analysis along with race and class variables. Not only does she consider how the interaction of race, class, and gender produces unique school experiences for minority girls as a result of societal gender role expectations, but she also considers how the interaction produces different life outcomes outside of school, without or without an education. For example, she cites statistics that show that African American women who leave school are more likely to be poor than White males, White females, and Black male dropouts (Fine, 1991). In spite of her methodology, her findings still support other researchers' findings about the students who fail to achieve and those who go on to graduate. However, as Miron (1996) declares, reform efforts have not been very effective for most public urban schools. Maybe reform efforts have not taken place because many researchers are asking the wrong questions; their methodologies are limited, or their interpretations are focused in the wrong direction at the outset.

For instance, imagine if the title of Michelle Fine's book were Framing Stay-Ins, then we might have asked: Are all minorities who stay in school not aware of race, class, and gender oppression? Do all successful African American or other minority students simply ignore their group's oppression? Do all minority students who do well in school necessarily believe in meritocracy? How do parents and community members positively influence academic achievement? Finally, how can researchers incorporate all that we know from previous research about what affects education, including restructuring in the economy and neighborhoods, social and institutional barriers, community influence, and individual agency to promote more research with a focal point on buffering adversity?

The Resiliency Literature

Resiliency studies ask questions pertaining to the motivation and persistence of students. Research on resilience is more likely to ask the following question: What resources do students at high risk have to support educational achievement? Because resilience research begins with different questions, they tend to yield alternative interpretations and answers. For example, an alternative finding to all of the above theoretical frameworks is Carla O'Connor's (1997) study that looks at the positive side of collective struggle. In the study, of forty African American adolescents, of the high-achievers, six of the students were found to be resilient. The six students (including two females) were viewed as resilient because they were aware of how race and class (and in two cases gender) affected their education and career opportunities but nonetheless were high achieving and optimistic about their life chances. As the above research points out, strong awareness of race, class, and/or gender inequality place most students at risk of underachievement or school dropout. Thus, the six students are considered resilient because they do acknowledge that education does not necessarily lead to social and economic mobility.

O'Connor points out that their social type diverges from Ogbu's cultural-ecological model, theories of school resistance, and research that shows a relationship between high academic performance and the embracement of the achievement ideology. As mentioned before, those studies reveal that the recognition of social barriers by students produces pessimism and disengagement or resistance to education, but O'Connor's reflections on the six resilient students allow researchers to explore the factors present in their lives that prevented them from physically or psychologically disengaging from school.

Specifically, in O'Connor's study, compared to other high-achieving students in the study, the resilient students do not wholeheartedly believe in the dominant ideology of making it and are race, class, and/or gender conscious. The resilient students discuss institutional racism in the educational system and within the workforce. In contrast, other high-achieving students believe that institutional racism exists in the workplace but that educational equality has been achieved. Also, it was found that the resilient students explained in more detail exactly how social class affects social opportunity and mobility. In particular, they speak of how money offers more affluent students social, economic, or occupational opportunities with less effort than those without money. Likewise, the more resilient girls specifically recognize sex discrimination in the workforce, the subordination of women in the home, and society's view of women as inferior to men. These students are resilient despite their knowledge that the odds are against them (O'Connor, 1997). Ogbu and the other researchers previously cited would have more than likely overlooked these students due to generalizations, central tendencies, and metanarratives.

Another contradiction to the literature is the positive role of the Black family and community in O'Connor's study. For example, the resilient females' consciousness raising was established through contact with females in their homes and communities. These findings are consistent with other research on African American girls. Two studies found that more resilient girls have strong relationships with their mothers or other female adults who taught them about issues of gender and race (Cauce et al., 1996; Davis and Rhodes, 1996). Through the behavior and attitudes of adult women in their lives, the resilient females learned that women should struggle against gender, race, and class subordination (O'Connor, 1997). Even more, all the resilient students have adults in their lives who educated them on race and class (and/or gender) oppression, and told them how they themselves fought against it.

Not only did the adults talk to them about it, they also showed them how to stand up against discriminatory practices. O'Connor reports that the resilient students provided stories of parents or other kin whom they witnessed challenge racist actions such as a parent who confronted a teacher's racist behavior. The adults taught them how to defy the system. In fact, O'Connor reports that the resilient students had "insight into human agency at the personal and individual level but also a basis for interpreting Black individuals and collectives as agents of change" (1997, p. 621). At the individual level, the students are aware of people like themselves who are successful despite social barriers. Moreover, they can imagine themselves engaging in practices that would allow them to get past external constraints to social mobility. Last, the resilient students in the study also internalized the belief that through collective actions of protest and resistance, marginalized individuals like themselves could transform the structures that oppress them. Interestingly, the resilient students are cognizant of educational inequality but take advantage of education as a starting point and vehicle to combat injustice.

Finally, we learn from O'Connor's alternative methodology (of extracting co-narratives) that consciousness raising alongside strategies to combat inequality may lead to resiliency. Also, O'Connor shows that collective identity does not necessarily produce negative dispositions toward school. In fact, collective identity can enhance students' educational aspirations. In addition, it demonstrates that African American female students, in particular, may learn from adult women to resist race, class, and gender subordination. Methodologically, we learn the importance of co-narratives, the exclusion caused by metanarratives, and to acknowledge as well as support individual and collective agency.

Many researchers have called attention to the need for new theoretical and methodological approaches to researching urban education reform. Smith (1982), Ladner (1987), and Leadbeater and Way (1996) have written about the urgent need for more research efforts that specifically target African American female students. Although failure and traditional ideas of achievement dominate most of the educational literature in this area, more studies are beginning to look beyond the notion that students are simply victims (either they give in or give up) of schooling. For example, some researchers are beginning to look at resiliency-fostering factors that buffer negative outcomes. Unfortunately, current literature on resiliency does not acknowledge the interaction of race, class, and gender, or the influence of individual agency and social structures on African American female students' educational development.

Rigsby (1994) argues that resilience has its origins in American ideologies of individualism and mobility striving. Current conceptualizations of resiliency reflect values of, and assume access to resources characteristic of, White middle-class families. Resilience themes emphasize that everyone can and should strive to get ahead, which implicitly implies leaving others behind. Theories of resilience also assume that there are no structural impediments to getting ahead, ignoring the impact of race, gender, culture, etc. Finally, resilience theorists imply that disadvantages that affect one's chances of success are individual and can be overcome with individual effort. I argue here that this narrow conceptualization of resilience does not work for African American female students.

Researchers tend to define and conceptualize resiliency in similar yet different terms. For instance, some of the terms synonymous with resilience are positive coping, persistence, adaptation, and long-term success despite adverse circumstances (Winfield, 1994). In short, as defined by Ashford, LeCroy, and Lortie (1997), resiliency is the ability to recover from or adjust to problems, adversity, and stress in life. For African American female students, stress could be related to racism, sexism, and classism in addition to the normal stresses that adolescents experience as a result of biological changes.

Resilience is sometimes also defined in relation to risk factors. Based on this definition, risk is a statistical concept that is better applied to groups than individuals (Masten, 1994). African American female students, for example, who live in low-income neighborhoods with high crime rates and low high school completion rates are considered to be a high-risk group.

Literature on resilience points out that educators, families, and communities are able to strengthen protective processes and promote resiliency when students are faced with external risk factors. The presence of positive interventions by a significant individual, school, or organization at critical moments in a student's life can counteract risks and vulnerabilities (Winfield, 1994). Unfortunately, current literature fails to identify gender and culturally specific fostering factors. It may be important to assess the cultural and gender composition or background of those intervening factors (e.g. faculty or staff of color).

The following list lists the characteristics that Henderson and Milstein (1996) report as those that researchers and educators have traditionally acknowledged as environmental protective factors that promote resiliency in the lives of students. The following factors are characteristics of families, schools, communities, and peer groups that foster resiliency:

1. Promotes close bonds
2. Values and encourages education
3. Uses warmth and low levels of criticism
4. Provides access to resources for meeting basic needs
5. Sets and enforces clear boundaries such as rules, norms, and laws
6. Promotes sharing of responsibilities, service to others, and "required helpfulness"
7. Provides access to resources for meeting basic needs
8. Expresses high and realistic expectations for success
9. Encourages prosaic development of values and life skills
10. Encourages goal setting and mastery
11. Provides leadership, decision-making, and opportunities for participation
12. Appreciates the unique talents of each individual

Taylor's (1994) research and review of the literature conducted with Black students and their families shows the following patterns that promote school resiliency:

1. Parents who are involved in their adolescent's schooling stress its importance, and inform students of racial discrimination tend to produce more competent students.

2. In poorer families, support from extended kin reduces parental psychological distress, in turn benefiting adolescent competence and adjustment.

3. And in at least one study, intellectual skills were found to be protective factors that help form strategies for sustaining academic performance.

Unlike the other studies on school resilience, Taylor's research does consider race and class influence on development. For instance, Taylor argues that adolescents of color have learned to define for themselves rules of adaptation pertinent to their survival in an unjust society. African American adolescents adopt culturally relevant values, attitudes, and behaviors to help guide them in decision making. Taylor cites Ogbu and other researchers to prove that resilience and adaptation are common among African American adolescents.

Taylor demonstrates that in spite of economic disadvantage and racial barriers, African American adolescents often master developmental tasks. However, Taylor also overlooks the impact of gender on education experience and development in the lives of African American female students. By failing to acknowledge the interaction and influence of race, class, and gender, researchers overlook what may be unique in the resilience of African American female students. In order to make a significant impact on urban education reform, researchers have to study resilience contextually and broaden the conceptualization of resilience, thus it becomes more inclusive. Without attention to race, class, and gender, we are likely to make educational policies based upon the experiences of European females and African American males.

How do researchers begin to include African American female students in resiliency literature? First, researchers have to analyze them in relationship to their race, class, and gender and from a strength perspective. These researchers have to understand and acknowledge race, class, and gender oppression in our society. They have to examine previous literature on the Black female, reinterpret the research findings into current conceptualizations of resilience, and reconstruct definitions of resilience. We need to look at these bodies of literature to unfold what we think we know about African American female adolescents' education, then close the gaps in this area need to be identified. With these steps, researchers can begin to include African American female adolescents in urban education and resilience literature.

Feminist researchers have already pointed out the racist and gender biases present in Erickson's model of development (Fine, McCormick, & Pastor, 1996). According to Erickson's stages of development, successful identity achievers are those adolescents who have solved an identity crisis by acquiring autonomy and independence. However, women develop "in-relationship" or what is called social individuality. Social individuality derives from women's resistance to oppression, such as racism (Fine, McCormick, & Pastor, 1996). As Fine, McCormick, and Pastor (1996) pointed out, women begin to resist when young: "Women often begin a lifetime of resistance as social individuals working to influence the interactions that take place in their homes, schools, and communities" (p. 19).

Furthermore, an important task of development for all African Americans is learning how to retain a sense of Black cultural identity in a Eurocentric world. The values and attitudes of Afrocentrism center on group sameness rather than on the individual as in Eurocentrism. African American students must learn to incorporate both Afrocentrism and Eurocentrism into their lives. This dual consciousness can become a source of tension, unease, and even shame in the presence of racism. For African American females, gender is an additional struggle in the process of socialization, because they have to face racism as well as classism (Cauce et al., 1996). Therefore, support from the family, community, and school buffers negative experiences.

Low educational attainment among Blacks is attributed by some people to poor cultural values or by others to racial discrimination in the educational system. The importance of families has not been truly emphasized in research on society. Families are usually not the focus of research, which tends to focus on the economy, policy, or history as sources of problems in education. Also, as McAdoo (1998) asserts, research on families has traditionally derived from negative paradigms that yielded negative results.

When including African American females in resiliency research, researchers have to ask "What role does the family play in promoting resilience?" How can researchers shift paradigms from studying the Black family with a deficit model to a strength-based model? McAdoo calls for researchers to first change their conceptualizations of the family to include the dynamics of a more diverse family composition. One of the biggest challenges facing African American children, is growing up without the resources found in two-parent families. Many African American children live in nontraditional families. Only 25.9% of African American children live with both parents, compared to 37.8% of Latino, and 56.4% of White children (McAdoo, 1998). Related to the increase in single-parent families is the number of African American children and their families who live in poverty. In 1991, 29% of Black children resided in families living below the poverty level (McAdoo, 1998).

Research shows that many African American children and their families survive under adverse conditions. In "Homeplace: A Site of Resistance," bell hooks discusses the importance of the family for women during the civil rights movement. The family was a place where women and their families could connect with each other and reaffirm their sense of collective pride and spirit. The family was also a place where women helped build a revolution within their communities (Fine, McCormick, & Pastor, 1996).

Researchers have found common patterns of coping that have contributed to resiliency in many African American families today—supportive social networks, flexible relationships within the family unit, a strong sense of religiosity, extensive use of extended family helping arrangements, the adoption of fictive kin who become as family, and strong identification with their racial group (McAdoo, 1998; Bagley & Carroll, 1996). The extended family can include parents, grandparents, cousins, nieces, nephews, etc. (Bagley & Carroll, 1996). Because studies prove that family-related reasons cause many minority girls to leave school, resilience studies should focus efforts on what supports from the family, extended and immediate, help to balance home and school responsibilities for young women.

One question to consider is what role the family plays in helping minority students cope with life stresses? In a study of 1,000 African American military families, family time was strongly associated with promoting well-being among family members and minimizing stress (McCubbin, 1998). More specific to African American girls is a study conducted by Gonzales, Hiraga, and Cauce (1998) on mother-daughter interactions among African American and Asian American adolescent students. In the study maternal support was positively linked to grade-point average, and negatively linked to behavior problems. Also, mother-daughter conflict was positively related to behavior problems. Those African American females who reported high maternal support and low conflict also reported higher grades and fewer behavior problems at school (Cauce, Gonzales, Hiraga, et al. 1996).

Another thing that resilience studies should consider is who in the family plays a major role in encouraging school success for minority female adolescents. Research has shown that mothers play an important role. Because African American women face racism and sexism in their everyday lives, they learn to adapt to multiple referent groups and pass this character trait on to their daughters. Black mothers teach their daughters how to retain cultural identity while accurately assessing their environments in order to create a variety of sources of positive identities and self-concepts (Cauce et al., 1996). The role of the mother in promoting positive coping seems to be essenitial to minority female students self-development.

Even more important to resiliency research than which person plays a role in buffering life stresses is the manner in which resilience is fostered. Resilience research will have to point out strategies that successful students use in the fight against oppression. Ward's (1996) research on intergenerational transmission of race-related resistance strategies passed down from Black parents to their adolescent child, illustrates the families' role in buffering adversity and promoting resilience. The study included sixty Black families, who participated in open-ended semistructured interviews in which they were asked to interpret the nature of the socialization process in their own voices and on their own terms. Ward reports that there exists a sense of individual and personal self-worth in the development of self-esteem for many African American girls. Family close-ness was also important to overall self-esteem. In addition, parents revealed that key to their child's socialization is learning when to attribute lack of success to individual effort and when to attribute it to social forces. The family system plays a major role in helping students maintain self-esteem in the face of race, class, and gender oppression.

In a study on resistance, Ward (1996) also found two strategies that parents utilize and pass on to their daughters. The first, resistance for survival, is a short-term solution that can be counterproductive to self-confidence and posi-tive identity formation in the long run. This strategy is called "tongues of fire" or truth telling, in which words are bold, unreserved, and "in-your-face" honest. The other strategy is resistance for liberation, which serves to empower girls through confirmation of positive self-conceptions as well as strengthening con-nections to the community. This is truth telling that promotes positive recogni-tion. According to Ward, this strategy ultimately helps a girl experience constructive, critical affirmation of herself and the collective by encouraging her to think critically about herself and her place in the world. Black mothers' ex-periences and evaluations of racism and sexism have contributed to the building of positive coping strategies in the face of adversity for their daughters.

Researchers do have to recognize that some Black mothers may not have learned to cope with adversity or are still coping with life circumstances. There-fore, it may not be in the best interest of the female student or resiliency re-searchers to focus solely on mothers. Resiliency studies should also gather information on the role of other adult women in the lives of African American female students.

Some studies have already begun to focus on the role of other women. One study found that other women such as aunts, adult sisters, sisters-in-law, older friends, and neighbors were considered by many urban girls as people who in-fluenced their achievement (Sullivan, 1996). Fictive kin, for example, are non-kin who have been welcomed into a family to assist in caring for children (Davis & Rhodes,1996).

In the lives of many African American girls, resilience is fostered by indi-vidual family members, family-like individuals, and even more important, other women.

What role does the Black community play in fostering resilience? Can Afri-can American female students' communities be culturally relevant protective factors? Communities, community organizations, and individuals within ado-lescents' communities can play a major role. Factors that place adolescents at risk can be buffered by external assets in community systems as well as internal assets. Traditionally, the Black community has been seen as a hindrance to a child's development (i.e., a cultural deprivation model). Very few studies have looked at the strengths that the Black community may possess for its members and the children in the community, in particular (some studies have focused on church communities).

For example, Ianni (1996) claims that although adolescents share some needs in common, adolescents' needs are structured by where and how they live. Even though many of them live in neighborhoods rife with poverty, unemployment, and high crime rates (Wilson, 1996), African American boys and girls have been successful at utilizing resources in their environments that support school achievement. Community systems can buffer the negative outcomes of adversity. However, Black females will experience poverty, unemployment, and crime rates differently from other adolescents in a high-risk neighborhood. Thus, resiliency studies have to recognize gender as a variable in resiliency building at the community level.

Because they experience stresses differently, the way African American females cope will also look different. McCubbin and colleagus (1996) describe community resources and supports as all persons and institutions that an individual may use to cope with stressful situations, including friends, schools, churches, medical, and community services. Social support, in particular, has to be considered as one of the primary buffers or mediators between stress and health breakdown according to McCubbin and other researchers. Researchers might question the extent to which communal social support enhances resilience building in females of color.

In *Educational Resilience in Inner-City America*, Wang and Gordon (1994) point out three characteristics of communities that foster resilience—availability of social organizations that provide resources to residents, consistent expression of social norms so that community members understand what constitutes desirable behavior, and, opportunities for children and youth to participate in the life of the community as valued members.

On the other hand, when we include gender, race, and class in this analysis, the characteristics will inevitably look different. For instance, we might adapt them to read: availability of social organizations that provide cultural- and gender-specific resources (e.g., childcare); consistent expression of social norms for desirable behavior (e.g., abstinence or condom use); and, opportunities for girls to participate as active societal/community change agents (e.g., opportunities for leadership skills). The conceptualization of resilience will be changed, once multiple identities (oppressed) are added to the analysis.

Although the focal point of recent research has been on deficits of the Black community and the neighborhoods in which urban schools are located, the Black community has a tradition of providing educational opportunities for minority female students. Studies involving Black organizations prove that there has long been a history of community organizations helping Black folks achieve education goals and increase outcomes.

The importance of community support in the lives of African Americans continues today. Numerous studies find that many African American girls understand the importance of community support in their everyday interactions. The American Association of University Women (AAUW) in 1992 found that African American girls, in spite of lower academic achievement, have higher self-esteem than their White counterparts. A longitudinal study conducted with school-aged girls found that some Black girls reject achievement out of a sense of self-esteem, while other girls develop a biracial identity (one that embraces White and Black culture) so that they can comply with the "white demands of the educational system" (Orenstein, 1994, p. 160). It is through a strong identification with their communities that many Black girls learn coping strategies to deal with stressors and achieve educational goals despite such stressors.

Some researchers attribute some Black girls' high self-esteem to a dual consciousness. Martinez and Dukes (1991), for example, studied a group of seventh through twelfth grade African Americans and Chicanos in a school setting. They found that African Americans and Chicanos have lower levels of self-esteem than Whites in the public domain, but they have higher levels in the private domain. Black girls possess a "private" self that reflects their standing in the community and a "public" self that involves their interaction with the larger society, including the school environment (Orenstein, 1994). Researchers acknowledge that resilient Black girls' self-esteem and identity is retained through close contact and interaction within the Black community.

Although the Black community has always served as an important resource to African American families and their children, a "community" mentality has been most critical to the development of Black females' multiple identities. Robinson and Ward (1991), for instance, described a mentality of "resistance for liberation" in which Black girls learn that their struggle is not individual but collective and are encouraged by their communities and school systems to work toward social change. Therefore, resilience is fostered through codependence between the Black girl and her community.

Gender- and cultural-specific resilient research involving African American female students should consider the influence of female adults in the immediate family or in the community in encouraging consciousness building. As O'Connor and others have found, the most competent and resilient minority female students possess a race, class, and gender consciousness. Resilient females will have a knowledge of multiple oppressions while simultaneously employing strategies to fight against such oppression. Notice that it is not enough for females of color to simply have an adult present in their lives as in traditional resiliency models. More important to resiliency is a "community mentality" that forms strategies for resistance that the adult offers.

Other studies have confirmed the important role that adult women in the Black community play in fostering resiliency in the lives of adolescent girls. Research shows that resilient adolescents show an ability to find an adult in addition to their parents for support (Davis & Rhodes, 1996). For instance, mentors have served as additional adult support for Black female adolescents. Mentors are defined as teachers and guides who provide information and advice in decision making. The mentor role is focused on future outcomes of the adolescent (Sullivan, 1996).

In a study of pregnant and parenting minority adolescent girls, it was found that adult women from the adolescent's neighborhood or who share cultural experiences enhance girls' ability to appreciate the positive aspects of their social support networks, cope with problems in the family relationships, and pursue activities related to their career goals (Davis & Rhodes, 1996). Specifically, the study found that adolescents with mentors were less depressed than those without mentors, and mentor relationships provided girls with a context for understanding relationship problems. This study finds that "natural" mentors or adult women from the adolescent's neighborhood who share similar cultural experiences are more important and beneficial in the long term for minority girls.

A study by Sullivan (1996) also notes the importance of natural mentors in the community. Sullivan conducted her research with urban adolescent girls who were considered to be at risk for dropout or early pregnancy and found that nonparental adult women served as inspirations for success. Adult women such as aunts, adult sisters, sisters-in-law, older friends, and neighbors were among the women who many urban girls cited as people who influenced their achievement. The study concluded that important and sustaining relationships with women are characterized by women's ability to listen, understand, and validate the knowledge, experience, and feelings of the adolescent.

Sullivan describes the type of relationship between nonparental adult women and adolescent girls as relational (muse) as opposed to mentoring (instrumental), which assumes deficiencies in the adolescent. In the relational (muse) model, both adolescent and adult possess vulnerabilities and strengths and value the contributions of both partners in the relationship. Mentoring relationships are important to all girls, but relational model relationships have acted as buffers to stress in the lives of many Black female students. The success of relational relationships may be due to the adults' ability to identify with the adolescents' community, culture, and gender.

Community-based organizations and neighborhood support agencies are another necessity in Black girls' lives, for psychological stress strongly impacts development and educational success. African American females are likely to experience depression as a result of rejection and ostracism, societal exclusion, and negativity derived from racism and sexism (Bagley & Carroll, 1996). Also, because a large number of African American families face a variety of mental health challenges such as violence, incarceration, teenage pregnancy, substance abuse, barriers to achievement, single parenting, unemployment, and discrimination, community resources are very important (Bagley & Carroll, 1996). Resiliency researchers might want to investigate whether resilient African American girls are more likely than other students to access community-based social support resources such as mental health services.

Most Black families seek out alternative resources instead of mental health services to battle psychological pressures in their communities. The Black church, for example, has always served as a means of support for youth and their families. Bagley and Carroll (1996) report that churches today provide different types of services to African Americans. For example, one church in New York sponsors citywide oratorical and essay contests for children in order to promote education. Another church in Chicago sponsors health screenings for hypertension, diabetes, and other ailments. This same church also holds health education and exercise programs for its senior citizens.

Additional studies also suggest that religious institutions may positively influence female attendees' behaviors. Although not all researchers agree, studies do show that Black and Latino/a adolescents who attend religious services may have stronger supports to enforce positive behavior norms. For example, a study of 875 Black adolescent females between the ages of fifteen and twenty-one found that girls who had never become pregnant and those who had an abortion attended church more frequently than adolescent mothers (Murry, 1998). Another study emphasized the importance of professional and spiritual help for overstressed adolescents and found that changes in adolescent participants' spiritual and personal development were significantly and positively related to changes in families who sought professional and spiritual guidance (McCubbin et al., 1996). More studies need to be conducted with African American female adolescents to learn how religious institutions contribute to educational resiliency.

In addition to adult, mental health, and spiritual support, Black female adolescents depend on positive peer support in building educational resiliency. Researchers might ask the following questions: What is unique about peer relationships between African American female students and their peers that encourage school success? Should resiliency models encourage peer relationships as a means to counter adversity? To what extent have resilient minority females utilized their peer group?

In studies with other populations, close friendships have been shown to satisfy adolescents' desire for intimacy, enhance interpersonal skills, sensitivity, and understanding, and contribute to cognitive and social development and psychological adjustment (Way, 1996). In Way's (1996) study of how urban, poor, and working-class adolescents (eleven Black females) perceive their close friendships over time, both boys and girls expressed intimacy rather than independence and autonomy in their relationships with friends. The girls in the study were more successful in finding and maintaining supportive relationships during their adolescence. The findings from the study suggest that strong positive peer relationships serve as systems of support. More studies are needed to look at the role of the peer group in fostering resiliency. Thus, it is important for communities, families, and schools to assist in promoting long-term positive relationships between Black girls and their peers.

In *Getting What We Ask For: The Ambiguity of Success and Failure in Urban Education* (1994), Payne asserts that reform is possible only after researchers construct better approaches to studying urban populations and their schools. Payne argues for more longitudinal, qualitative, and multivariate analysis and claims that better reform initiatives will come about once researchers move away from traditional deficit models. *Teaching Black Girls* does this by looking at Black girls and urban schools from a strength perspective.

Furthermore, *Teaching Black Girls* looks at both cultural and institutional practices that affect resiliency. Rigsby's (1994) argument that "resilience research, like many areas of social science, needs serious attention given to theory building that focuses on understanding the causal structures and processes that give meaning and direction to social life" (p. 91). For example, structural influences like institutional racism, sexism, and classism work simultaneously to influence the behaviors and experiences of African American female students. Therefore, a multilevel theory of educational resilience will be constructed to assist in understanding the behaviors that relate to the relative successes of individuals and groups.

In *Teaching Black Girls*, resilience is constructed and reconstructed to examine the complexity of the situation in urban classrooms. We will review some of the daily choices and occurrences in the girls' lives that present a challenge to positive educational development; however, readers will also be exposed to the support systems that the girls rely on daily during the good times and bad times. The next chapter sets up the background for the ethnography and the setting of these girls' stories. Finally, in chapter 4, readers will be introduced to Nicole, Zora, and Yssis. Readers will share the high and low moments in these young women's lives, and we will witness how they respond to those people and events around them. Subsequently, we will see how they are shaped by their environment and how their environment is shaped by them.

Chapter Three

The Construction of Social Inequality in a Midwestern City

The human condition has so far been a fundamentally unequal one; indeed, all known societies have been characterized by inequalities of some kind, with the most privileged individuals or families enjoying a disproportionate share of power, prestige, and other valued resources. (Grusky, 2001, p. 3)

Nicole (all names and locations have been changed) would be my first home visit and interview. Her house was located on the southwest side of Haven. The directions she gave were "Come down the hill, until you get to Parnell Street. Then make a right onto Parnell, drive three blocks, and my house is the big green house on the corner." She gave very accurate directions.

Driving into Nicole's neighborhood was like driving into an old black and white movie. Although the street is a two-way, only one car at a time can proceed because of the number of parked cars on the street. Most of the houses are old and look like they have never been renovated. The paint on most of the homes is faded or peeling; shabby curtains or blinds hang from the windows, and many homes have no grass in the front yard. Hanging out on the corner and in front of these shabby homes were teenage boys. Some of the young men were noticeably engaged in illegal activities such as gambling and drug trafficking. In fact, I believe that they were not attempting to hide their activities but wanted to advertise their business.

Finally, I arrived at Nicole's home and parked my car in front of the house. On her particular block, there were no children playing, no adults coming and going, and no teenage boys hanging out. I found in a later interview that most families choose to keep their kids in the house, instead of exposing them to gang fights, shootings, or drug dealing. Compared to some of the other homes on the block, something about Nicole's family home gave it a sense of warmth. It was a large house compared to the other homes on the block, and it was once painted a nice bright green. Also, it looked as if someone was taking care of it by adding yard decorations and mowing the lawn.

A note taped on the window next to the front door read: "Knock on the back door." Nicole's grandmother is an "old school" Black mother, who does not allow visitors or children to walk through the living room. The living room is reserved for guests on special occasions (although we never witnessed those special occasions). I went around to the back door, and my city girl defense mechanisms kicked in quickly. Because of my drive through the neighborhood, I was a little worried about going into someone's back yard that I did not know. Having spotted the young men on the street corner, I feared a teenage boy might jump from out of nowhere or answer the door and become harassing (it has happened to me before during social work home visits). Another fear, based on media stereotypes of the inner city, was that a wild attack dog would appear. Well, I had no problems with teenage boys or attack dogs.

Loud hip-hop music was playing, and there was no doorbell; therefore, I knocked several times before someone answered the door. Nicole answered the door and gave me a hug like we were old friends. She was obviously happy to see me. When she invited me in, I could smell perfectly seasoned greens with smoked turkey cooking on the stove. She told me that her mother, who had stepped out for a minute, had been cooking Sunday dinner. Nicole quickly showed me around the house, which appears bigger on the outside.

Then, she gave me a personal tour of her bedroom. Nicole was very proud of her bedroom, which had a full-sized bed in the middle of the room and was decorated with matching pink linen, an assortment of stuffed animals and dolls on the bed and around the room. Other items accentuated the quaint bedroom —a mirror, pictures of friends and family, and various other memorabilia. Her pride stems from the fact that many children in urban areas simply do not have the luxury of having their own bedroom. In addition, early in her life, family-related problems had kept Nicole moving to different homes. Thus, she learned to appreciate certain things like having a big comfortable bed to sleep in at night. Anyhow, Nicole's warm welcome, and the look, smell, and feel of her cozy house, made me feel right at home.

The Context of Urban Education

Space cannot and should not be ignored in critical approaches to teaching and learning. The places where students live have a significant impact on their self-esteem, level of confidence and the resources that they do or do not have available to them. Because Black girls' learning preferences are shaped by social experiences in their surrounding environment, urban educators need to be aware of, and arguably become experts on, the context of the historical experiences that have shaped their students' lives. For example, the research that provided the backdrop for this book took place in a city called "Haven." *Teaching Black Girls* would have been a different type of book, with possibly different outcomes, if the ethnography had taken place somewhere else. The African American families in Haven have been affected by social, political, and inequality for decades. It is important to trace the historical processes that have had a direct or indirect impact on students' life and educational experiences. By looking at these historical processes, we begin to understand that due to Haven's location and dense population, students and their families are able to see and feel immediately and often over the long term, the effects of political policies and changes in the economy on their lives.

Haven is a small city surrounded by small rural towns and communities that most people have not heard of even if they have lived in or visited the Midwest. Just before entering the city of Haven, during the daytime, drivers can see a hillside range to the right and left of the interstate, filled with tall beautiful evergreen trees. Looking straight-ahead, onlookers can see a view of the gray-looking Haven River, tall historical buildings, the infamous Acme headquarters building, and the Haven Bridge. My first visit to Haven took place at nighttime, and I was completely awestruck at the skyline and how it accentuated the landscape of the city. The lights and glow of the city after sundown remind visitors and locals of the city of Las Vegas right before your airplane lands in Nevada.

Because of its smaller population, and its location in the middle of rural farming communities, Haven cannot be compared to Chicago or the Windy City's suburbs. Instead, Haven is more likely, and more accurately, to be compared to Springfield or Champaign in Illinois. Like these cities, Haven has a similar population of 113,000. Unlike Springfield with its government ties and Champaign with its large university population, Haven has very little attraction for outsiders like educational researchers, the national media, or politicians. Haven's isolation has negative and positive consequences. In fact, when I think of Haven, I think of it as an isolated city that strategically maintains a small-town mentality, while simultaneously grappling with big-city problems.

A large segment of Haven's population is not fooled by the nightglow of the city. Many people living in Haven have only witnessed darkness and gloom. This brings us to the second question, "Yes, African Americans do live in Haven." African Americans comprise 14.8% of Haven's total population and constitute over half of Haven's public school system (U.S. Census Bureau, 2004).

Unfortunately, Haven has not been very receptive to the needs of its citizens of color. In the city of Haven, the Native Americans who once lived there are forgotten the Latino/a population have been deemed invisible, and the needs of individuals of African descent are ignored. The majority of African Americans are concentrated on the southwest and southeast sides of Haven, which contain most of the city's low-income and working-class population. African Americans native to Haven refer to this part of Haven as "down the hill," and European Americans refer to it as the "south end." It was brought to my attention that this area of the city gained its nicknames as a result of redlining in

Haven. Traditionally, Black folks were not allowed to live in any areas of Haven beyond Layfette Hill. Certain groups of Whites and middle-income Blacks have come to view the "south end"/ "down the hill" as a collective of neighborhoods, schools, groups of people, income levels, and attitudes that is separate and inferior to their own.

Metaphorically and geographically, the "south end" represents the downside, dead end, and abandoned side of Haven. During the height of industrialization (prior to World War II), the Haven River would have been a prime location for factories, shipping and receiving goods. But now, the river simply is a dead end for occupants living in the area (since I wrote this portion, riverfront remodeling has caused the eviction of low-income families from this prime real estate property). Currently, the area is composed of old abandoned buildings that used to serve as factories, truck stops, and storefronts during Haven's booming economy. Furthermore, the air in the "south end" always smells of stale beer during warmer weather days even though an old brewery has not operated in decades. Unfortunately, for many low-income and working-class Black folks, life in Haven only exists "down the hill." An important aspect of the ethnography was to observe how the political, economic, and social atmosphere of Haven has impacted the school experiences of African American female students who live "down the hill."

The purpose of this chapter is to look at the historical practices that have contributed to social inequality between Haven's African Americans and European Americans and threatened the educational resiliency of Blacks. It provides a historical overview of African Americans between 1940 and 1990 and shows how social stratification has become a defining feature of the city. Social inequality is defined as unequal rewards and/or opportunities for different individuals within a group or groups within society (Marshall, 1998). Social stratification research looks at the complexity, distribution, and persistence of inequality in society (Grusky, 2001). Drawing from historical data and social stratification literature, we find that traditionally individuals and families of African descent living in Haven have not received the same rewards and opportunities as other groups, and this inequality persists into the twenty-first century.

Sedimentation of Racial Inequality

In the book *Black Wealth/White Wealth: A New Perspective on Racial Inequality*, Oliver and Shapiro (1997) use private wealth at the center of their analysis to study racial/social inequality. Traditional measures of economic progress have looked at income, occupation, and education. However, Oliver and Shapiro "provide an analysis of racial differences in wealth holding that reveals dynamics of racial inequality otherwise concealed by income, occupational attainment, or education" (1997, p. 3). When wealth is at the center of analysis, the authors provide evidence that overall, African Americans have made little economic progress.

In brief, wealth is anything of economic value bought, sold, stocked for future disposition, or invested to bring an economic return; whereas, income refers to a flow of dollars over a set period, typically one year (Oliver & Shapiro, 1997). According to Oliver and Shapiro, there are at least three reasons why wealth is more important than income: (a) substantial wealth brings income, power, and independence; (b) significant wealth relieves individuals from dependence on others for income (freeing them from authority structures); (c) also, wealth is important because it is directly transferable from generation to generation. Unfortunately, the majority of African Americans are not enjoying the benefits associated with wealth that other Americans do, and this is mainly due to structural and social discrimination based on race.

Oliver and Shapiro have coined the terms "racialization of state policy," "economic detour," and "sedimentation of racial inequality" to explain the persistence of differences in wealth accumulation between Blacks and Whites. Even though the authors use the concepts simultaneously in their analysis of social inequality, this study is more concerned with the last of the three concepts, the "sedimentation of racial inequality." The focal point of this concept is how the cumulative effects of the past have "cemented" African Americans to the bottom of the U.S. economic hierarchy (Oliver & Shapiro, 1997). I argue that various historical sociopolitical processes have contributed to economic and social inequality between African Americans and European Americans in Haven. A history of institutional racism and societal discrimination has left the majority of African Americans in this small city cemented to the bottom of its economic hierarchy.

1940–1950: Migration, World War II, and Work. Because (for the first time since the mid-1800s) Haven's African American population more than doubled in this period, this study begins with the period between 1940 and 1950 even though African Americans have been present in the area of Haven since the early 1800s. Haven's African American population increased from 2,826 in 1940 to 5,777 in 1950 (104%), compared to a total population increase of only 6%. Another interesting statistic about this period is that the increase occurred after a decrease in the Black population between 1930 (3,037) and 1940 (2,826) (U.S. Department of Commerce, 1950).

The decrease in Haven's African American population between 1930 and 1940 and the increase between 1940 and 1950 reflect migration patterns of larger northern cities. Those decades are memorable for the Great Depression, industrialization, and World War II. Because the Depression left many workers without employment, many African Americans returned to the South or went looking for work in other areas. During the Depression, Black unemployment was disproportionately higher than White (Trotter, 1985). However, World War II provided revived economic, political, and social opportunities for African Americans in the northern Midwest. In 1961 interviews were conducted with 1,000 African Americans who came to Haven from the South regarding their reasons for migrating to Haven. Although it is not clear when they actually came to Haven, the study found that economic improvement was the main purpose for migration to the city (Garrett, 1973). Other reasons were the opportunity to vote, desire for social improvement, better educational opportunities, more justice in the courts, and the inability to continue tolerating the subordinate and restricted status accorded them in the South (Garrett, 1973). It is not clear if the reasons given are opportunities African American migrants specifically attributed to the city of Haven or if these are attributes African Americans associated with northern areas. Further research is needed as to why African Americans chose Haven specifically. For example, choosing to move to a city based on information from a relative is different from choosing to migrate to a city after reading a sign "Jobs in Haven" near a railroad station.

Furthermore, besides not knowing exactly when migration occurred amongst the interviewees, it is not known how many women were interviewed. As pointed out by Hine (1991), men and women migrated from the South for different reasons. In addition to economic improvement, women left the South in search of personal autonomy and to escape sexual exploitation and sexual abuse from both White and Black men. A more gender-specific study is needed to look at women's motivations for leaving the South to come to Haven, and how their move affected their family situations, employment opportunities, personal mobility, and individual freedom. Even more important, we need to know more about how women's experiences in Haven contributed to their view of opportunities available to their daughters. Mothers' positive outlooks about schooling, work, and social opportunities are important to a study on resiliency, since research shows that African American girls are more likely to name their mothers as their main source of support (Cauce et al., 1996).

More information is also needed on what types of jobs African American women and men worked at during this period. Interestingly, in informal conversation, when middle-aged Black folks are asked why their families come to Haven, most answer "Acme." Many individuals, of different races, associate Acme, Inc., with employment opportunities in Haven. It is known worldwide for tractor and other manufacturing and building equipment and locally for its major economic contributions to Haven and surrounding counties. The corporation boasts of its role and growth during the world wars. For example, the corporation reported a 53% sales increase in 1935 and added an additional 3,000 people to its payroll in that year. Also, the corporation points out that it played a significant role in World War II by manufacturing equipment for the war efforts (Nolde, 2000). In fact, the Acme Corporation reports that throughout the WWII the plant operated three shifts, six days a week. At that time, Acme reportedly employed twenty five percent of all those employed within a thirty mile radius of Haven (Nolde, 2000).

Unfortunately, African Americans in Haven did not capitalize on economic improvements at the Acme Corporation brought on by the war as assumed by past and present citizens in Haven. Reportedly, in 1941 there were no African American employees at the major corporation, and very few at other large industrial sites (Duren, 1992). Contrary to popular belief, Black women worked as domestics, and Black men replaced White men who went to war or those White men who found better jobs at Acme (Observer, 1992). Thus, African American women found themselves working in traditional African American female-centered occupations, and African American men found themselves in replacement positions and in those jobs that White men did not want to occupy. Furthermore, there had to be a strong possibility that after the war, Black men were fired in order to return White men to their old jobs.

Also, more than likely, Euro-American women were probably first in line to replace Euro-American males during the war. As an example, Acme reports that in 1943 approximately 85% of employees working in the aluminum foundry were women, and throughout the company, women made up nearly 30% of employees during the peak years of the war (Nolde, 2000). Nevertheless, African Americans did find work in other factories, industries, and the railroads. As one reporter stated, "because they were about the only factories that hired Blacks" (Duren, 1992, B–10), many Black men worked for the railroads, ABC Washing Corporation, Armour Packing House, and Haven Malleable Foundry.

In 1940, an investigation was conducted by Haven's Civil Liberties Committee to investigate the conditions of the urban African American population (Garrett, 1973). The study found that 40% of Haven's Black population was unemployed, while 32% of those employed held part-time jobs or WPA employment. Furthermore, the study revealed that applicants of color had been denied employment on account of their race. African American males were more likely to be employed as janitors, waiters, shoeshiners, or in lower-tier jobs, regardless of their educational background, training, or ability (Garrett, 1973). Garrett does not reveal what type of work women of color were engaged in.

Finally, the 1940s marked a mass fluctuation in Haven's African American population due to the Great Depression and World War II. African American men and women migrated to Haven with high aspirations and expectations; however, the group faced unemployment, temporary work or replacement work, or simply menial employment opportunities. African Americans in Haven endured poor housing conditions, segregation, and unfair treatment from the police and other service workers (Garrett, 1973). More information is needed on women's reasons for migrating and roles in migration and the types of job opportunities that were opened to African American females. We need to know more about how women coped with and viewed their own and their families' condition in 1940s Haven. As late as mid-1900 Black citizens of Haven were still at the bottom of the economic social hierarchy.

1950–1960: Housing, Employment, and Education. As explained by Oliver and Shapiro (1997), racial income differences are not enough to explain the racial wealth disparity that exists in America today. Researchers have to consider demographic and social factors that influence racial inequality, such as access to quality education, labor market experience, occupation, gender, sector of employment, work stability, and other indicators. Through this ethnography, I am beginning to witness the devastating effects of housing and employment inequality on a child's educational experience.

According to the U.S. Census Bureau data for 1950, African American men (3,118) and women (3,158) comprised 3.6% of Haven's total population (174,347). Haven was initially viewed as a place of new opportunities for African Americans leaving the South; however, the city did not necessarily meet all the expectations of its growing Black community. Many Americans evaluate their circumstances in life based on their living condition; for example, home-ownership is associated with attaining a "piece of the American pie." However, I would go even further and argue that many African Americans evaluate their lot in life based on employment opportunities and access to education for their children in addition to adequate housing. In 1950 did Haven city offer its growing African American population access to adequate housing, employment opportunities, and equitable education?

With regards to housing, the answer is "no." Black Americans in mid-twentieth-century Haven found themselves concentrated in overcrowded racially segregated neighborhoods. Haven's African American citizens were mainly concentrated in and segregated to the Carver Center Community area (Conver, 1957). The Carver Center Community area made up approximately 3% of the total area of the city of Haven, and it contained about 15% of the city's population. However, over 60% of that area was occupied by African

Americans (Conver, 1957). The pattern of high concentrations of Blacks in that neighborhood area is similar today, with a large number of students forced to attend overcrowded, dilapidated, and high poverty rate schools.

Redlining played a significant role in the social inequality in Haven. Bill Conver (1957), a journalist who researched "The Negro in Haven," described this section of town as a "badly crowded area of substandard housing (p. A-1). The author attributed Haven's residential segregation of Blacks to the under-standing between realtors and financing agencies to keep African Americans out of all-White neighborhoods. Conver's study found that, regardless of income level, racial discrimination forced African Americans to live in dilapidated hous-ing and poor living conditions. Poor conditions were caused by the aging of the homes, wear and tear caused by overcrowding, and the lack of proper mainte-nance by landlords. In addition, Black home purchasers were forced to pay in-flated down payments and very high weekly mortgages, which led to many foreclosures in the Carver Center Community area

According to Feagin (2000), housing discrimination is played out by a vari-ety of participants, including landlords, homeowners, bankers, realtors, and government officials. Segregation is enforced by the open hostility of White homeowners, occasional violence against Black families, and Whites deciding not to move into already integrated neighborhoods as well as the "racial steer-ing" and related discriminatory practices of the real estate industry (Feagin, 2000). In 1950 Haven there was no White violence against Blacks attempting to move into all-White neighborhoods, because there was never an opportunity for overt hostility. Realtors and financing institutions simply did not give Black citizens the option of choosing homes outside of the Carver Community Center area.

African Americans were not given equal access to employment in Haven. Feagin points out that housing segregation reinforces other types of racial ex-clusion, discrimination, and subordination targeting African Americans: "When residential segregation is extensive, job segregation tends to follow" (2000, p.159). Many African Americans charged Haven employers with discrimination in hiring, but employers claimed that non-White workers were either not edu-cated enough, skilled enough, or reliable enough to hire on a strictly merit basis, reports Conver (1957). A 1957 study conducted by the local Council on Human Relations looked at job discrimination in Haven. A survey was conducted that included thirty institutions of various types, including railroads, retail businesses, city, state, and federal employers. The purpose of the survey was to reveal the number of African Americans at each organization and to find out if Haven's employers were equally hiring equal numbers of Blacks and Whites. The Acme Corporation was the only respondent that did not come up with an exact count of their Black employees, but the remaining survey respondents accounted for 877 employees of African descent (Conver, 1957).

Conver found that African Americans had a variety of occupations, such as (at least one or more) doctors, teachers, carpenters, chemists, nurses, pharmacists, and dentists. However, most reported being employed as laborers, service and maintenance employees, clerks and typists, housekeeping and laundry workers, elevator operators, porters, janitors, foundry workers, truck drivers, firemen, and machine operators (Conver, 1957). Very few African Americans were employed in supervisory or higher positions. At the time of the study, the city of Haven itself employed approximately 25 African Americans. The 1950 census figures listed 100,494 people employed in the metropolitan Haven area; 2,444 of them (2.4%) were African Americans. In 1957 of the total employed (108,025), 2,592 were African American (Conver, 1957). Obviously, African Americans gained some access to traditionally Euro-American occupations since the 1940s. However, the majority of African Americans living in Haven were segregated in the lower-tier job market with little hopes of upward mobility. In this ethnography that looks at resiliency, we have to ask whether a sense of hope or despair has trickled down to current generations of African American adolescents and families in a segregated city. If hopelessness has not overcome the family and students in the study, then how is academic persistence and resilience fostered in a segregated environment?

As mentioned before, access to adequate education had to be an important measure of contentment for new Black Havens. As stated by Anderson (1988), "It did not take the Civil War, emancipation, or northern philanthropic foundations to acculturate blacks [to education] because blacks carry within their culture enduring beliefs in the value of learning and self-improvement" (p. 177). Access to free and appropriate education was probably as large an incentive for African Americans coming to the North as employment and personal freedom. Individuals and families living in Haven during the 1950s, more than likely, also held high aspirations and expectations of education.

Research has focused on the obstacles to quality education in the rural and urban South. For instance, public elementary school did not become available to the majority of southern Black children until the first third of the twentieth century, and, similarly, Blacks in the South were not widely affected by the spread of secondary public education until after the 1920s (Anderson, 1988). It is also known that in the late 1930s and early 1940s school facilities, teachers' level of education, and transportation (no service) for children of color in the South was inferior to White children's facilities (Davis, Gardner, & Gardner, 1941). Did African Americans in Haven find the access to quality education that they hoped for? We know that Blacks were segregated in overcrowded and underfunded school buildings.

The poor quality education in the South was due to "the belief that educated colored people were less amenable to the caste sanctions, less deferential, submissive, and dependent, and therefore a danger to the efficient working of the caste system," according to Davis and colleagues (1941, pp. 418–419). Thus, maintaining economic and political inequality was why White southerners did not support education for citizens of African descent. What would the motivating factor be for not extending a free and appropriate education to African American citizens of Haven? A more detailed study needs to be conducted to determine the average age and level of education of migrants from the South, and if the new arrivals had any initial expectations of Haven's educational system.

Oliver and Shapiro claim that there is a direct link between educational attainment and income and wealth (1997). Therefore, African Americans in Haven have been cheated out of income and wealth due to past (and current) educational inequality. Again, past discrimination has affected the current economic well-being of many Blacks in Haven. How did African Americans living in a small city strategically combat the injustices related to race and skin color? More information needs to be gathered on the relationships between Blacks and other groups, especially Whites, in Haven.

1960 – 1970: The Civil Rights Movement/The End to Inequality?

> The tradition of protest is transmitted across generations by older relatives, black educational institutions, churches, and protest organizations. Blacks interested in social change inevitably gravitate to this "protest community," where they hope to find solutions to a complex problem. Once the contact is made the newcomer becomes a link in the tradition. Thus the tradition is perpetually rejuvenated by new blood. (Morris, 1984, p. x)

This section begins with the preceding quote by civil rights historian Aldon Morris to denote the legacy of organized struggle by people of African descent in Haven. Members of the African American population in Haven have not simply been passive victims. In contrast, the city's citizens have a history of being active participants in determining their destiny. For example, after the Emancipation Proclamation in 1863, African American citizens negotiated for better educational opportunities and citizenship responsibilities (Garrett, 1973). Then in 1871 African Americans sent a petition to the Board of School Inspectors that requested that the Jim Crow school for Blacks be abolished and that their children be allowed to attend the regular district schools. The Board acknowledged the request and ended separate schools (Garrett, 1973). How legally desegregated schools affected the education of African American students in Haven is a question that has to be addressed here.

The modern civil rights movement emerged in the South during the 1950s, when large masses of Black folks mobilized to bring local and national attention to racism and discrimination. Mobilization efforts unfolded in the form of economic boycotts, street marches, mass meetings, going to jail by the thousands, and other forms of disruptive tactics referred to as nonviolent direct action. Morris (1984) refers to that moment in history as a period of "confrontation." The modern civil rights movement was different from past movements in that it (a) directly confronted and disrupted the normal functioning of groups and institutions thought to be responsible for their oppression; and (b) it was the first time in American history that Blacks adopted nonviolent tactics as a mass technique for bringing about social change (Morris, 1984). Changes occurred in local areas and across the nation due to the efforts of individual Black men and women who put their lives and their families' futures on the line. But the risk and sacrifice was made for the plight of the people.

Even though modern civil rights tactics did not emerge in Haven until the 1960s, the important thing is that there was a civil rights movement in the small city. By 1960 the African American population had grown to 10,157 (U.S. Census Bureau, 1970). However, African Americans did not have full access to employment, education, and housing. A 1960 report by the University of Illinois Institute of Government Public Affairs concluded that the Black population in Haven was "retarded" in respect to income. The study found among Whites and Blacks who live in the same area and have the same amount of education (8.6 years of schooling): 68% of the African Americans earned under $5,000; 26% earned between $5,000 and $8,000; and 6% earned over $8,000. In comparison, 54% of the Euro-Americans earned under $5,000; 32% earned between $5,000 and $8,000; and 14% earned over $8,000 ("Ministers," 1962).

The University of Illinois study also found that although 750 Black families in five Haven census neighborhoods made more than $5,000 per year; 76% found their homes were worth less than $10,000; and only 3% of Black homeowners had houses which would sell for over $15,000 (*Peoria Journal Star,* 1962). In addition, as in other U.S. cities, African American children were not receiving an education equivalent to that of other children in Haven. In 1962, African Americans constituted between 13,000 and 15,000 of the population, but only about forty African Americans graduated annually from Haven high schools ("Ministers," 1962). African Americans living in Haven in the 1960s found themselves to be trapped in the same inequitable social and economic situations as those in the 1940s and 1950s.

Individual African Americans and groups continued the tradition of demanding the extension of opportunities and responsibilities to Black citizens as well as White citizens and others. The most influential organization that helped advance civil rights in Haven was the National Association for the Advancement of Colored People (NAACP). In particular, people remember the organizing efforts of John Gwynn, who became president of the NAACP in 1961. He lead a picket at Mac-Hy market that did not hire Blacks, and later he helped gather crowds to picket, march, or sit-in at establishments such as Montgomery Ward, Central Light Company, the Haven Board of Realtors, Acme Tractor company administrative offices, Haven police station, Haven City Hall, and Haven public schools' administrative offices. Many of the participants of the demonstrations were students (though it is not clear if the students were in high school or college) (Duren, 1992).

One of the first incidents that marked the onset of the civil rights movement's presence in Haven was the sit-in at Central Light Company in July 1963. According to the demonstrators, of the six hundred employees at CILCO, only two Blacks had been hired in seven years. As a result of the sit-in, thirty-six demonstrators were arrested, and thirteen remained in police custody overnight. Those arrested were charged with disorderly conduct ("interfering with the normal conduct of business") ("Thirty-six Negroes," 1963). The nonviolent tactics employed by demonstrators and Gwynn prove that rallies were organized, pre-planned, and not simply spontaneous. As the chapter's opening quote explains, the leaders more than likely had contact with civil rights leaders in the South or had previous experience in organization and leadership (e.g., the church, civil organizations, or relatives). The results have been more minority hiring, an open housing ordinance, and attention to unequal school system. But, in reference to Blacks in Haven and elsewhere, as quoted in *Black Wealth/White Wealth*, (Oliver & Shapiro, 1997), "the status of black America today can be characterized as half full—if measured by progress since 1939—or a glass that is half empty—if measured by current disparities between Black and White Americans" (p. 25).

1970–1980: Desegregation, Integration, and Educational Reform Efforts.
African Americans in Haven have a long tradition of fighting against inequality and organizing efforts to improve their conditions. By 1970 Haven's African American population had grown to 14,500, nearly 11.5% of the total population (U.S. Census Bureau, 1970). The increase in numbers demanded that city officials take notice of the demands of its growing minority population. Most civil rights efforts have focused on moving forward school integration efforts and working to improve education for Black children. The problems

Africans Americans were confronting in Haven were not issues of desegregation but of integration.

First of all, as early as 1856, Haven had partially funded schooling available for children of color at Haven's first Black church and even allowed children of color to attend Haven School District 150 in the year 1871 ("Early history," 1998). Second, in 1954 the Supreme Court ruling on *Brown v. Board of Education* stated that separate educational facilities were inherently unequal. However, housing discrimination and segregation in Haven caused many African American children to attend overcrowded and underfunded segregated schools.

As in other northern cities, African American children were not receiving educational services similar to those received by Whites. Black citizens in 1965 complained that the schools with a majority of African American children did not receive bus transportation and did not have a sack lunch program even though the schools with a majority of European American children did have such programs. In addition, at this time there were no African Americans on the administrative staff in District 150, and only one on the cafeteria staff in all of District 150 (U.S. Commission on Civil Rights, 1977).

Haven Public Schools District 150 mirrored segregated school programs across the nation in the 1970s. As pointed out by Kelley and Lewis (2000), although Black children made up approximately one fifth of the total public school enrollment, almost two thirds went to schools with at least 50% minority enrollment in 1980. The citizens of Haven took legal action to alleviate school segregation in the mid-1970s. In October 1975 leaders of the Black community charged District 150 with discrimination against minorities, failing to abide with state desegregation laws, and the fact that many of the schools were not in compliance with state guidelines on desegregation (U.S. Commission on Civil Rights, 1977).

The year 1966 was when school desegregation initiatives actually began in Haven. Minority students were concentrated in nine of the city's twenty-nine schools, with twenty of these schools having White enrollments of more than 98% (U.S. Commission on Civil Rights, 1977). Undoubtedly, Haven schools were forced to rethink the city's commitment to desegregation and reevaluate whether African American children were receiving an education that was separate and, therefore, inherently unequal.

Actually by the time the city of Haven and School District 150 began implementing desegregation efforts in 1968, African American students made up 18% of the approximately 27,000 student population. Yet, minorities only accounted for 5% of the District's staff members. (U.S. Commission on Civil Rights, 1977). Haven was forced to acknowledge the growing African American student population, the unequal hiring of staff of color, and its segregated school system.

The school board attempted to solve its problems by the realignment of school boundaries and the use of the middle school concept, a building program for new schools, one-way busing, desegregation training and preparation programs for teachers and staff as well as increasing efforts to hire minorities, and improvement of the curriculum through use of multiracial materials (U.S. Commission on Civil Rights, 1977). These programs began in 1968 and had mixed approval from Haven citizens and civil rights leaders. Most African American citizens did not want to bus their children from neighborhood schools.

According to the report by U.S. Commission on Civil Rights (1977), some improvements resulted from the 1968 desegregation program. In the 1968–1969 school year, approximately 340 students out of 26,739 were bused, and the number of schools classified as segregated had decreased to sixteen from the previous year's twenty-five. By the 1971–1972 school year, the total number of segregated schools had dropped to ten, while the number of bused students was up to one thousand. More needs to be known on the African American high school completion and dropout rates in this period in order to understand the true consequences of segregation and integration.

Nevertheless, changes in state desegregation guidelines affected Haven's desegregation attempts. In 1972, the state's Department of Public Instruction found Haven School District not to be in compliance with state desegregation guidelines. In fact, by 1976 more than half of Haven schools were found not to be in compliance with state guidelines (U.S. Commission on Civil Rights, 1977). This problem was twofold: minority enrollment in Haven schools increased by 30% while White enrollment decreased by 19% between 1968 and 1975 (U.S. Commission on Civil Rights, 1977). It appears that in the city of Haven, in the mid-1970s, some Whites still were not comfortable with their children attending school with Black children.

Haven School District continues today to be in noncompliance with state guidelines on desegregation. African American teachers only comprise approximately 5% of the staff, although African Americans make up approximately 50% of the student body. Kelley and Lewis (2000) attribute the large number of African American children in public schools to White flight or the increased number of White children who now attend schools in the suburbs or go to private schools. A similar pattern is occurring in Haven, whose White middle- and upper-class families move away from the city into surrounding counties. Unfortunately, not a lot of research has focused on inequality within Haven School District. My current research does, however, look at low-income

African American girls' school experiences within the city. Nonetheless, still more research needs to focus on the history of African Americans within Haven schools. I provide evidence that educational opportunities still have not improved for many Blacks living in Haven, which compounds the problem of the sedimentation of racial inequality.

1980–1990s: Testing Inequality Using the Oliver and Shapiro Test. By 1990, African Americans made up 13.7% of Haven's total population (182,827) (U.S. Department of Commerce, 1998). Even though Blacks made up less than 14% of the total population, 44% of Haven County's Black population reported living below the poverty level (of those Blacks for whom poverty status was determined) in 1989. In contrast, approximately 10% of Whites reported to be living below the poverty level in that same year (U.S. Department of Commerce, 1998). Poverty-level status is an obvious indicator of the disparity between Black and White economic situations. Past and present-day discrimination has cemented a vast majority of Haven Blacks to the bottom of society.

Another indicator of the sedimentation of inequality is home ownership. Although laws and regulations established by the Federal Housing Authorities and other organizations disallow information that specifically inquires about Black homeownership, census information is a valuable tool in determining living conditions of African Americans in Haven. In 1999, the median home value in Haven was $49,200. My research found that in those census tracts predominately occupied by African Americans, the median home value was lower than those tracts predominately occupied by Whites. For instance, Tract 1 is 63% Black and the median value of home is $15,600. Tract 9 has the second-highest percentage African American residents, 74.2%. Its median home value is $32,500. The highest percentage of African Americans live in Tract 8, (86.4%), and the median home value is listed at $17,500. Not only do these numbers provide evidence of racial segregation in Haven, the numbers also support Oliver and Shapiro's (1997) argument that discrimination and segregation leads to the depreciation in value of homes in Black neighborhoods or homes owned by Blacks. Thus, for many African Americans living in Haven, homeownership will not necessarily lead to wealth or equity comparable to their White counterparts.

As pointed out by Oliver and Shapiro (1997), it is more difficult to analyze wealth disparities by race, because of the way we have historically collected financial data. However, income has become a "surrogate" of wealth (p. 30). Oliver and Shapiro point out that much is lost by studying income instead of wealth; however, for this discussion I use income data to show how historical racial discrimination practices in Haven have contributed to the sedimentation of inequality between Whites and Blacks in the city. There is a large discrepancy of per-capita income between Blacks and Whites. Even though African Americans are the second-largest population group in Haven, they had the lowest per-capita income by race ($6,765). Whereas, Whites ($15,130), Asian Americans ($14,461), and Latinos ($8,715) had significantly higher incomes than their Black neighbors (U.S. Department of Commerce, 1998). It seems that past discrimination in employment, housing, education, and earnings has led to "inherited poverty and economic scarcity" (Oliver & Shapiro, 1997, p. 5), which is reflected in life circumstances. Information provided by the U.S. Counties Census support the hypothesis that African Americans living in Haven are victims of the sedimentation of racial inequality.

Urban Education in Context

The preceding pages highlighted the experiences of African Americans in the small city of Haven and looked at the construction of the sedimentation of inequality there. In 1985, Trotter called attention to the need for research methodologies that linked African American experiences with industrialization to race relations, politics, and community development. Similarly, Oliver and Shapiro (1997)have discussed the effect of historical processes that lead to the sedimentation of inequality and large disparities between Black and White wealth. In Haven, few African Americans found themselves with access to industrial jobs; thus, protest and organizing on this issue more than likely complicated race relations, influenced grassroots politics, and encouraged Black community development. I want to study how this history has helped to construct the educational experiences of African American females. Even more, it is important to look at how parents convey a message of hope to their daughters under such circumstances.

African Americans came to Haven in search of personal autonomy and economic opportunities and to escape the hardships of the South. However, what they found was hostility, segregation, and discrimination. Not only did African Americans find themselves in lower-tier jobs, excluded from unions, living in overcrowded neighborhoods and in dilapidated housing, but they also found that their children were not receiving the same quality of education as White children. African American Havenites organized civil rights efforts to combat the injustices in the city, which have worked to improve the quality of education their children received.

Questions remain: How did women experience the interaction of racism, sexism, and classism within the city? What kinds of emotions had been experienced by those people of color who found themselves in hostile conditions, as a result of segregated working, living, and educational environments? By exploring these questions and similar ones we can begin to look at how historical practices in Haven have negatively impacted, socially and economically, students, families, communities, and schools today. Then we can begin to look at what supports to African American female students buffer the possible negative outcomes associated with race, class, and gender inequality.

Methodology

Scene I: Access and Entry

When his secretary told me to enter, the Director of Research, Mr. White (a fictitious name), was already sitting at a small round table, in the left corner of the room. On the table in front of him were the papers that I had submitted to his office. The papers described the purpose of the research, statistics on African American girls' educational outcomes, how long the study was to last, and the methods by which the participants were to be selected. Looking at Mr. White's white pale face, perfectly tailored suit, and the manner in which he had the papers scattered in front of him, I attempted to guess if I was going to be granted permission to implement the study.

Mr. White remained in his seat when I entered the room, and his body language did not change. He simply stared and shuffled around the papers in front of him. He did not think that I was important. I thought to myself, "Let the games begin!"

I have been taught that when someone enters the room, the polite thing to do is to stand up and properly greet the guest. I was also taught not to take a seat until I am invited to sit or to make myself comfortable. Mr. White did not stand and greet me; thus, I stood and waited until I was properly greeted and invited to sit.

Finally, Mr. White told me to sit down. "Have a seat," he demanded. Graciously, I sat. Then the game began with a series of questions and comments from Mr. White.

"I believe that it would be interesting to know why these students fail," he commented.

"Hmm. But, I'm more interested in how students succeed in spite of adversity," I retorted.

"Yes, unfortunately, the students do come from families that just don't seem to understand the importance of education."

"Yes, families do also play an important role in students' education, which is why I want to know what role the family, community, and school play in academic achievement."

Then Mr. White asked, "Why are you only talking with girls? I think it would be a better study if you talked to boys, too?"

"Here we go again. Black girls are never seen as 'good enough' or worth the time," I thought to myself.

Then, I put it in language that he could understand, "Actually, African American girls have one of the highest high school dropout rates, only second to Latinos." I realized that the general public was accustomed to the language of failure.

"Well, I have approved your study. However, first you need to get permission from the two schools' principals before proceeding with the study. Also, you are required to provide the district a copy of the final report."

I survived the White man in a suit by using language that most educators and policymakers have become accustomed to hearing, and by embracing patience with the system.

Scene II: The Principal's Office

In junior high school (now referred to as middle school), I spent as much time in the principal's office getting reprimanded or suspended as I did picking up an honor roll certificate or running errands for a teacher. Therefore, I was more nervous about approaching the schools' principals than I had been about confronting a White man in a suit. After some procrastination, I gathered up enough nerve to arrange meetings with the principals of the schools where the students would be recruited. The first meeting was with Principal Brewster, of Bluff Middle School (fictitious names).

Venus	Hello. My name is Venus Evans. I have a 10 a.m. appointment with Principal Brewster.
Secretary	Okay, have a seat and he'll be with you in a moment.

After working in the schools in various capacities, I have learned that principals are very rarely on time for meetings. They are usually monitoring the halls, in the middle of reprimanding or praising students, observing a classroom, in another meeting that went overtime, in the midst of conflict resolution between two students, or providing conflict resolution tips for staff members. Also, I know that establishing rapport with the school secretary is the key to getting important information and avoiding excessive red tape. An initial bad impression with a secretary could cut off access to important student files, demographic information, easy access to the principal, and other data that a researcher may not even think is necessary until the study has begun. Thus, I played down my irritation with the late appointment and my anxiety over meeting the principal. I took a seat next to a group of students, who were also pretending to be patiently awaiting the principal.

When Principal Brewster arrived in the office, the secretary said, "Mr. Brewster, Ms. Evans is here to see you. You had a ten o'clock appointment."

Principal Brewster was an overweight, middle-aged, African American man who had a very serious look about him. I wondered if the serious persona that he portrayed was for my benefit or for the students sitting in the office.

P.B.	Come right in.

I gracefully walked in and stood next to the guest chair that he had positioned next to his own desk and chair.

P.B.	Go ahead and have a seat. What did you want to see me about?

Most of the times in the schools, like in corporate America, the head secretary usually has the responsibility of setting up meetings and agendas for principals. Therefore, more than likely, Principal Brewster was not aware of the reason for my visit.

V.	I am a social work intern, receiving my master's from the University of Illinois [I thought that if I cited this big-name university, along with the degree sought, I would make a better impression]. As a part of our requirements, we have to conduct a research project. I have spoken with Mr. White, and he gave me permission to conduct the study as long as the principals of the schools agreed to go along with the study.
P.B.	What kind of study is it?
V.	I need permission to recruit seven African American eighth- grade girls. I want to talk to them about their school experiences and to find out what supports they receive from their family, community, and schools that support school achievement.
P. B.	What church do you go to?
V. (stuttering)	Well, actually I have not chosen a church home here in Haven…yet.
P. B.	I knew that you weren't from Haven. How did you get to Haven?
V.	Marriage.
P. B.	Who is your husband?
V.	Steve Winters.
P. B.	Steve Winters, the barber? He's a good brother. What's your name again?
V.	Venus Evans. I kept my maiden name.

P. B.   Well, Mrs. Winters, you have permission to do the study. You'll make a
                        great mentor. Talk to Mrs. Dee, my secretary, and she'll get you what-
                        ever you need. She can be your contact person here at Bluff.
                        But, let me tell you something. A lot of people come in
                        here with empty promises—don't let these girls down. If you tell them
                        three years, give them three years.

Those last words by Principal Brewster resonated in my mind throughout the three years of the ethnography. Many times those words got me out of bed, simply to make a phone call to the girls. It was also his last words that made me realize that his serious persona was not an act but a message to us "outsiders" not to use their students as "research rats" or as easy-access special school "projects."

Furthermore, I also included this scene in the principal's office, as an example of how many people, including the participants, their family members, school staff, and other folks in the community viewed me as a mentor. As a participant-observer of African descent who had "made it" (or who was "making it"), I was seen as a natural guide or counselor for African American girls. Likewise, those same folks who viewed me as a mentor and gave me permission to conduct the study felt they were contributing to my "making it" by helping me fulfill the requirements (the research study) I needed to finish my doctoral studies.

The Formal Setting

The students who participated in the study live in a racially (with less than 20% African American population) and economically diverse midsize city (approximately 113,000) (U.S. Department of Commerce, 1998), with over half of the school population being African American and low income (District 150, 1998). Participants were recruited from two majority Black and low-income schools. It is important to mention that at the time of the study, I was serving a nine-month internship as a school social worker in the students' school district. At the time the study began (fall 1998), one school's student population was 78.5% Black and 88% low income. The other school's student population was 80.3% Black and 91% low income (District 150, 1998).

At the beginning of the ethnography, thirteen students and their parents gave consent for participation. After attrition, five participants remained in the study. Reasons for attrition include leaving school before initial contact, high mobility, and no way to communicate with the student (to initiate the study), for example, no telephone service. Participants' ages at the start of the ethnography ranged from fourteen to fifteen, and they were eighth grade regular division and special education students. All of the students are from low-income and working-class families. The students had different family structures, including two-parent families, single-parent families, and households with extended family members. The final number of students (five) allowed for deeper relationships among the participants, their family members, and the researcher, subsequently offering a more engaged ethnography. Those relationships and shared experiences are reported in this book.

Insider/Outsider Strategies

During the gestation of this research project, the participants and I were in the midst of major transitions in our lives. Over the three-year period, the young women were making the transition from middle school to high school, while simultaneously coping with the biological, emotional, and psychological changes that emerge during the transition from childhood to adolescence and adolescence to womanhood. Like the young women, I was struggling with and coping with my own transitions. When the study began, I was a newlywed, new to a strange city, embarking on my first major research project, and beginning a nine-month internship as a school social worker. By the end of the third year, I was a first-time mom, a second-year doctoral student, and had become recognized as sort of a local community activist in the city that I had barely known just a couple of years before.

The location and the city where the ethnography took place and the communities where the students lived, worked, and went to school were more important to the study than I could have imagined. Originally I considered the city as "just" the site where the study was going to take place. However, it did not take long for me to understand how the setting of the study's social, political, and economic history impacted a child's education. Citizens' identities were constructed vis-à-vis their assigned spaces in this condensed town. For example, language like "up the hill" and "down the hill" mentally and physically established barriers between groups of people.

Physically, those "down the hill" attended the poorest schools, which had teacher shortages, poor outcomes on standardized tests, overcrowded and deteriorating school facilities, high staff turnout rates, high truancy, etc. "Down the hill" was literally marked by a decline in a major road that travels east and west. Those "up the hill," Black and White alike, are saved the bother of driving "down the hill," because we have our own shopping centers, major parks, schools, post offices, recreation centers, etc. Even those places on the southern end of town, like the city police station and major downtown corporations, can be accessed via alternative routes (e.g., interstate I-74) that lead one to believe that they have not actually traveled "down the hill."

Socially, assigned spaces had the potential of separating the races and the different class groups. Moreover, assigned spaces seemed to affect some students' self-esteem and outlook on life. Friends and colleagues of mine who live on the northern side of Haven "up the hill" noted that some students had never seen the northern part of Haven before. A friend informed me that once on a field trip with a children's organization, students were taken to the shopping mall (the only one in the city, which happens to be located on the north side). Reportedly some students actually thought they had left the city of Haven. Evidently, the students did not have access to or share the luxuries of other citizens living in Haven.

As a sister-outsider participant-observer, I did not ignore space, nor did I reinforce spatial barriers. In essence, I broke the unspoken social rules by traveling to the southern side of Haven to get the "official" story. Students and their families allowed me into their homes, community centers, and schools to hear their life stories. Besides upsetting local social norms, I also deviated from traditional researchers' rules, when I invited the young women participants into my personal space. Paradoxically, the social, political, historical, and economic history of the city that drew imaginary boundaries, simultaneously created a safe space for dialogue. I strategically used space to break down barriers while using it as a haven to facilitate discussion on shared experiences around issues of race, class, and gender. I will go into more details of how space was negotiated throughout the ethnography, for space allows for different fields of social relations to be explored.

As a participant-observer, it was my role to take note of the students' transitions. But as the "observer-being-observed," I also felt that it was my responsibility to share my own life transitions with the participants, and how I had experienced and coped with what they were now encountering. Some of things we discussed were simple but they seemed catastrophic to the students—coping with gossip, broken friendships, bumping heads with authority figures at school, preparing for high school, getting poor grades, or passing driver's education. Other things were more complicated and even caused me to rethink the burdens of being a Black female—early drug/alcohol use, broken promises by parents, teenage sexuality, and/or firsthand experience of death and violence. Other questions had more to do with me personally, such as "How was it being married?" "Did I enjoy motherhood?" "How did I afford college?" "Did I like White people?" During these situations, there was no doubt that my age (and/or my youthful appearance), the fact that I was a "girl," and that I was also African American created a safe space for dialogue. Unexpectedly, I became the mentor who does research. As an African American feminist researcher, I learned to be comfortable with this role and encompass it as a research strategy.

My mentoring role brought about the wonderful exchange of life's experiences in the form of stories.

In fact, the majority of the dialogue between the participants and me took place in the form of storytelling. Conversation with other women has always been a way for women, especially women of color, to share their stories of oppression (Madriz, 2000; Collins, 2000; Vaz, 1997). For example, the majority of the questions and problems mentioned above had no answers or solutions. However, I did have a "what happened to me when I was in that situation" story that I could tell in place of an answer. Also, the girls felt more comfortable telling me about their experiences in the form of stories instead of answers to close-ended questions. Their storytelling also offered me a bigger "slice" (Emerson, Fretz, & Shaw, 1995) of their life, which is what is most sought after in ethnography.

Storytelling is also useful for other reasons. Not only did it work for sharing stories in the field, but I also used stories to express what I "thought" I saw in the field. By admitting to "telling stories," I am admitting that ethnography is the researcher's interpretations and depictions of persons, events, and places (Geertz, 1973). When I was growing up, what ethnographers call "storytelling," we used to refer to as "telling stories." A part of postmodern ethnography is admitting that memory loss occurs in the field (Tierney, 2000), that researchers can only capture bits and pieces of life (Emerson, Fretz, & Shaw, 1995) and that ethnography is a "truthful cultural portrait" (Van Maanen, 1988). By definition, portraits are works of art; thus, a truthful cultural portrait is an artistic representation of culture. In ethnography, we used storytelling to share experiences, to gather information about stories, and to interpret stories. I would have never guessed that my brother's and sister's cries, "Mama, Venus is telling stories!" would come in handy in the research process.

As an African American female (graduate) student researching African American female students, I thought it was only natural that the students and other subjects of the ethnography would be interested in the "sister-outsider" who was interested in their educational experiences and life stories. I have to admit that I worked this interest and my hyphenated status to my advantage as a participant-observer. Living and playing the "sister" role, I was privileged to inside knowledge about the African American community and family. As explained by Delgado Bernal (1998), through past experiences, researchers of color are able to bring to their research a certain understanding of how and when to behave in certain situations, and why other people behave the way that they do in certain circumstances. For example, coming from a traditional working-class Black family myself, I knew that one rule of thumb (or survival) is that "children speak only when spoken to." I also know that one always respects her elders, because "you ain't grown" simply because you have reached a certain age or educational status. Adulthood is earned and not necessarily static, for wisdom reigns over book knowledge.

Therefore, as a sister participant-observer, consciously and subconsciously I always followed the lead of the adult present. Genuine humility is more than learned behavior; it is a part of my socialization and childhood experiences in a Black family. Because four out of the five students lived in female-headed households, usually my childlike demeanor surfaced in the presence of other adult women. Another example of the advantages of being on the left side of the hyphen, occurred when I had my twelve-month-old son with me on a home visit. Because I had personal issues with adequate childcare (or some would argue separation anxiety), there were simply times when my son became an initiated participant-observer. For instance, one time I had planned to simply pick up the student and go to another location to conduct the interview. However, upon entering the house, her mother asked me "How I was doing?" and began to ask questions about the baby. Well, I had not expected to spend that much time with greetings, and apparently the baby had not either because he became squirmy and fussy. Based on his behavior, "Mama" insisted that the baby was hungry. I, however, in a very polite manner insisted that the baby was simply a little squirmy from being in a new environment. Mama declared, "Naw, that baby hungry."

The baby and I ended up staying at the student's house for an extra hour while Mama prepared the food and fed the baby. The student and I did not do the interview that afternoon; instead I allowed the mother to take the lead. As a participant-observer, I actually learned more from the dialogue and actions that took place between me and the mother concerning my baby and the interactions that I saw and heard between mother and daughter while I hung out in the student's home. At that moment, I was not only an observer, for I had become an instant participant or family member. I was no longer just a graduate student doing research but a community member who was allowing the "village" to help care for me and my child. As a woman and "child" of the Black family, I knew when to listen, and as a student researcher I was learning how to establish rapport.

The "sister" status also afforded me the opportunity to blend right in in other ways too. Besides having the inside scoop on "what it means to be a girl" and an adolescent, the participants and I bonded on other levels as well. Being a part of the hip-hop generation, I was knowledgeable of the latest music that was getting air-play; I knew the latest styles of dress and what hair styles were in and which ones were out. Sometimes rapport was simply established by playing (whichever was more appropriate) rhythm and blues or rap music in my car or asking one of the girls how they felt about how a particular song portrayed women. To understand the music, one has to understand the language. Coming from a Black low-income and working-class community and attending a traditionally White institution, I had no trouble slipping in and out of Black English. The choice of language use occurred subconsciously and consciously but definitely appeared to affect the methods utilized in the ethnography.

As a participant-observer, I knew that the use of formal English comes with its own stereotypes and biases in the Black community and carried even more consequences among African American youth. For me, it was a double-edged sword during the research ethnography. The formal English definitely granted me access to the students, and the Black English (which really is my native tongue) had allowed the girls and me to be more relaxed during formal and informal interviews. Of course, our Black English conversational style made transcribing a little bit more difficult since my formal education never taught me to write in my mother tongue.

However, it is important to note that I usually did make a distinction between Black English and slang. Usually on more than one occasion, a student would accuse me of sounding "White." I think these accusations had more to do with me choosing not to use slang, for I was very conscious of not wanting to lose my identity as the responsible adult. As the adult and the researcher, interested in the young women's stories, I did not want them to consider me a peer. Trust is a major issue in the Black community, especially among women and adolescents, like many other oppressed and victimized groups. If the students thought that I was "just like them," I might have lost the status that comes with being perceived as a serious student and researcher (outsider), who is considered to be a person of integrity. Integrity was distinguished by whom I hung out with, the type of music that I listened to, how I dressed, and what words I used or did not use. There is no doubt that as a participant-observer, I learned to perceive and later record how I thought others perceived me. Outside of adolescence, I do not believe that there was ever a time that I was ever more conscious of how others perceived me.

Furthermore, in some Black communities, because employment opportunities are not always in abundance and/or money is not always plentiful, at an early age, citizens begin to learn and understand the meaningfulness of the barter system. The barter system is best described as a practice or an arrangement, usually made between individuals, for the exchange of goods and services. Logically, for African Americans, poor people, and women, the barter system is an ingenious means of survival or self-sustainment in a society that economically excludes or exploits us. Because the girls and I were socialized within this custom, we expected a little "give and take" as the research project unfolded. In exchange for information, stories, and the young women's time, they expected to be compensated and have their needs met as well. I also believed the young women should be compensated; thus, we employed an arrangement of our own within the formal research process.

Most times during or after interviews, the students and I had lunch or dinner at a restaurant of their choice. Only one interview took place at a restaurant, and most other interviews took place at my home (I decided against conducting formal interviews at a restaurant, because the loud background noise was not conducive to tape-recording conversations and the lack of privacy may have prevented more in-depth stories). It is also important to mention that in the beginning I conducted interviews in the reserve room at the library but later decided that the library sessions made the research project too impersonal. The girls and I were not connecting on a more personal level because of the long conference table between us, the four corner walls that appeared to be closing in on us, and the dull brown colors of the walls, table, and chairs. I was afraid the girls would perceive the study to be another psychological or social work evaluation. Thus, for several reasons, as well compensation, I conducted interviews and gathered stories at my home, in the mall, at restaurants, in my car, and in other more natural settings.

Outside of my mentoring role, I also became a public advocate for equal education for African American female adolescents and for all children in the city where the ethnography took place. Because I had worked, researched, and volunteered in various educational settings in Haven, I had hands-on knowledge of the history and current condition of schools in the city. Professional experience is another source of cultural intuition that brings a different understanding to research on the educational experiences of students. It may construct a different understanding than that of someone who has never worked in that field (Delgado Bernal, 1998). My knowledge was gained through the students' and families' reports, formal education, key informants in the community, and archival research.

In addition, flexibility as a strategy was vital to the kind of research reported in this book. Of course, flexibility is key to almost any qualitative research study. "Because working in the field is unpredictable a good deal of the time, the qualitative researcher must be ready to readjust schedules and interview times, add or subtract observations or interviews, replace participants in the event of trauma or tragedy, and even rearrange terms of the original agreement" (Denzin & Lincoln, 2000, p. 387). However, research with adolescents may require even more flexibility, due to time constraints, lack of transportation, maturity, attention span, articulation abilities, etc. For this book I worked with students who possessed different talents and abilities, and I was required to adapt my research-gathering tools to each individual's abilities.

For instance, at the onset of the study, the original plan was to interview the students twice a year in eighth, ninth, and tenth grades. The purpose of each sixty-to-ninety-minute taped interview was to adequately and promptly recording each student's school experience. However, after receiving feedback on the first set of interviews, I found that some of the young women thought the first interview was too long and boring! For students who were used to sitting in class for approximately forty minutes, the original interviews were simply too long. Furthermore, the students, and to some extent myself, felt uncomfortable with the tape recorder, even though it was purposely bought to appear small and discreet. I had to change the original plan if I wanted the students to stay interested in "our" book.

Instead of disregarding the participants' sentiments, I exercised some flexibility by adapting how, when, and where I gathered data. The new approach was to keep a first set of interviews (K–eighth oral narratives) but not to tape record interviews again until the end of their sophomore year in high school. How I would keep their school experiences fresh in their memory became my new concern. To tackle memory loss, I distributed journals to all five girls and asked that they record daily or weekly their thoughts about what was going on at home, school, or in the community. I even provided postage and envelopes to assist with correspondence and to remind them to write in their journal. The journal writing and letter writing did not work either. Only one student wrote in her journal (three pages), and no one responded to my letters. I did not give up, though, for I knew the girls were still interested in sharing their stories; they simply were not the sit-down-and-write-to-Venus type.

Plan C was to become a foot soldier for the sake of this study and similar ones. Because only two out of five girls had telephone service at home, the telephone was not a quick solution to my research problem; therefore, I was required to drive "down the hill" and do face-to-face visits. In the middle of the winter, in the blazing hot sun, with baby in belly (and later on back), I knocked on doors, visited schools, talked to relatives, ate with mothers, worshipped at churches, escorted grandmothers, shot the breeze with brothers, all to get "the story."

The most cumbersome feature of this method makes it the best method. In between interviews, I was required to write very detailed notes about what I heard, seen, thought, and sometimes even smelled. Even those times when it simply was inappropriate to write, I would have to run home and jog my memory. Nevertheless, in the same manner that the young women were required to become accustomed to my taking notes, they also had to get used to the tape recorder during times that I call formal interviews. In sum, flexibility was exercised throughout the ethnography and worked to the researcher's advantage and the students' benefit. Flexibility allowed for a richer ethnographic experience.

In Delgado Bernal's (1998) words, "cultural intuition is a complex process that is experiential, intuitive, historical, personal, collective, and dynamic" (p. 568). The insight that many researchers of color bring to our research stems from experiences in our families, communities, schools, and with the research participants themselves. My experiences as a female, adolescent, African American, student, and mother informed me of the need for flexibility in this type of study with these particular participants. From previous exposure with the African American community, I was able to adapt to not only to the environment (as done in traditional ethnography), but I also felt entitled to adapt to the needs of the community under study and those of my research participants.

For example, being that the study was longitudinal in design, flexibility and changes were allowed. Other notable benefits of a three-year ethnography were that it allowed for the establishment of rapport between myself and the participants, and it assisted in the recovery of memory loss. On a lighter note, sometimes students simply "forgot" that we were supposed to meet; well, with three years we had more than enough time to reschedule missed appointments. Other times, students would inform me that they forgot to tell me a "story" of something that happened to them, so either they would call me on the phone or simply wait until the next meeting to tell me the bit of information that jogged their memory the last time we swapped stories. I must mention that there were also threats to implementing a three-year ethnography. The main problem was that it was very difficult to keep track of and keep the interest of adolescents over time; thus, there is the threat of "losing" your participants. I lost one student to the lack of interest; she simply would not be available during established interview times. Another student, I simply could not locate her whereabouts (neither could her relatives). Therefore, I literally lost two students within the three years of the study.

Nonetheless, I argue that a longitudinal study is necessary to a book on resilience, for resilience is not static, but a process. It is my role as the researcher to attempt to take a snapshot of resilience at its various stages of development. Resilience is the ability to adjust to or recover from adversity or stress over time (Winfield, 1994). In other words, human beings do not recover from challenges to their physical or mental well-being overnight or within a time frame. A three-year ethnography, like this one, increased my chances of being able to observe how a student learned to cope over time.

Not only did I observe how resilience is constructed, deconstructed, and reconstructed, but I also observed the participants' rites of passage through life.

Following students from their eighth-grade year in middle school to the end of their sophomore year in high school, I had the opportunity to witness how students developed emotionally, physically, and intellectually. A prime example for this claim is that most of the students learned to interact with me as a researcher. Over time we developed friendships, I witnessed the students increase their communication skills, and over time they became adept at articulating their experiences and emotional reactions to certain situations. The findings in the original ethnography provide much insight into how families, communities, and schools can utilize gender- and cultural-specific practices that foster educational resiliency for many African American girls.

Chapter Four

Introducing the Co-Narrators

Nicole's Story: Blurred Boundaries

Nicole was the kind of interviewee who talked from the time the tape recorder began to the time the tape stopped and any possible time thereafter. In fact, she would call me sometimes in between scheduled visits to tell me more interesting stories. Nicole was definitely a young woman who wanted to tell her story. She was a student researcher's dream interview, because she did most of the talking with little prompting by me. As Nicole's story will reveal, she has come to celebrate the gift of voice, a gift that was unveiled by the support of her family, community, and school.

When I first met Nicole, she was fifteen years old and in the eighth-grade. She was in regular division classes, while receiving tutoring once a week at home. From the beginning of her eighth-grade school year to the end of her sophomore year in high school, Nicole made the honor roll list most grading periods. Nicole lives with her two older brothers (sixteen and eighteen years of age) and her maternal grandmother, whom she refers to as her mother. Nicole and her family have a long relationship with the school and the neighborhood in which she resides. They have lived in the same house for nearly thirteen years, and both of Nicole's brothers attended the same middle and high school she attended. Low mobility is fundamental to a student's school success, which is not common in a neighborhood where the school mobility rate is nearly twice that of the state's rate (District 150, 1999).

The Community

Even though Nicole has lived in the same house for over a decade, her immediate neighborhood offers little solace from the stress and strain of everyday life. Throughout the oral narrative of her educational experiences, Nicole described her neighborhood as a nonsupportive place. In fact, Nicole's neighborhood appears to be such a negative place for children that her grandmother usually does not allow her outside the house. When Nicole reported this, I thought it was simply an adolescent exaggerating about parental control. However, I found that the most resilient girls were not allowed outdoors very often to interact with their neighbors. I do not believe that Nicole's grandmother's strict rules about outdoor activity really concerned Nicole, for she also does not view her community as a safe haven or a place with adult role models anyway. For example, when I asked Nicole if she knew anyone in her neighborhood who went to college, she responded, "Please, no one!" (Interview I, p. 13). Her cynical response indicates her awareness of and low tolerance for the lack of role models in her community.

I observed that Nicole had a low level of trust of boys and girls at school and in the neighborhood. In general boys were thought to be only interested in talking girls into having sex too early, which increased the risk of pregnancy and school failure; whereas girls were associated with gossip and rumors, which put Nicole at risk of conflict and suspensions at school. Anyhow, she does not consider her friends as a source of support. As a matter of fact, before high school Nicole wanted to meet new friends and begin anew.

An important component of educational resilience is not only being able to identify positive sources of support but also being able to identify those persons or things in your life that do not serve as protective factors. From Nicole's standpoint, her current peer group was working against her instead of for her. Also, her friends did not seem to be on the same educational path as she was. It appears that Nicole was beginning to evaluate in her eighth-grade year what it took to be successful in high school.

Furthermore, Nicole stated during interviews that her community was of little value to her and had not assisted in her educational accomplishments. These sentiments appear to support other research studies findings with African American girls, which concluded that successful students were more likely to detach from the Black community (Fordham, 1996). Yet, from personal experience I knew that this was not always true. Therefore, for quite some time I pondered the question "Do the most resilient students withdraw from their (majority Black) communities?" The answer is "not necessarily."

Community resources and support include friends, schools, churches, medical, and community services (McCubbin, 1998). From other forms of observation, I knew that Nicole displayed some sense of connectedness to her community. For instance, once Nicole and I were sitting in front of my front yard "just chillin'," when Nicole asked me, "Where all the Black people at?" The neighborhood where I lived was a mostly White, middle-income neighborhood. Therefore, Nicole's comment revealed some type of comfort and connectedness to the Black community where she resided.

Moreover, because community resources expand beyond the people available to you in your immediate neighborhood, I had to reevaluate my original conclusion that Nicole (and the other girls) had withdrawn from the Black community. Then, I realized that Nicole worked and worshiped in the very community that she reported having no hope in. For example, Nicole attended church on most Sundays and had worked at various organizations in her community. Although Nicole was not involved in any activities at church, she does report having an aunt at church who influences her schooling. According to Nicole, her aunt talks to her often about school (Interview I, p. 12–13).

Like her aunt who attends her church and talks to her about school, I found that for Nicole, her work in the community was also usually associated with her future goals. For example, Nicole has worked at different organizations tutoring, supervising, and mentoring children.

> I worked at the Boys and Girls Club, T. school…I worked at the Boys and Girls Club, as a tutor (excitedly). Them kids there bad. That's the ghetto side. I didn't even like going. I mean you have to have patience for them kids. Your patience just have to be up there, and my patience…I got paid for it, so I had to make my patience get up there with them. So, it was straight, working there. And, I know when I was little them teachers didn't, because how much I was running in and out. And, I believe what I know, they should know. It was cool. (Nicole, interview, spring 2001)

First, Nicole's description of her work at the community organizations supports the hypothesis that many of the activities she engages in usually have to be related to school. For instance, Nicole appreciated working with children, because one of her goals is to become a teacher. Furthermore, the passage also shows that Nicole does have a sense of connectedness to her own neighborhood. Her sense of connectedness is unveiled when she refers to the location of her place of employment being on "the ghetto side." Evidently, Nicole has established invisible boundaries between her neighborhood and adjacent neighborhoods. Because I have volunteered and worked at that same organization, I can report that her place of employment is approximately only two miles from her home. Of course, the actual distance does not manner, for what a person perceives to be real is more important. For Nicole, the side of the community where she lived was safer than the side where she worked. In relation to educational resiliency, the above passage demonstrates that Nicole is very adept at utilizing those resources that are most useful while abandoning aspects of her community (e.g., negative people) that do not assist in meeting her educational needs.

Interaction of Race, Class, and Gender

Talking to Nicole, I grew to understand why she was so hard on her surrounding community. Many of the negative aspects of her community had directly or indirectly affected her family and school "self" at some point in her life. For instance, early in life Nicole faced hardships that affected her physical and mental development and, thus, her educational development as well. For Nicole, life was hard as early as kindergarten.

It was kind of hard when I was in kindergarten, because my mom, we got tooken from her, and all that kind of stuff. So, it was kind of hard for us. For me, because I was the baby, in kindergarten. It was hard. We would like go to the courthouse almost everyday. They come pick us up from school and stuff. (Nicole, interview, fall 1998)

As Nicole's educational narrative reveals, sometimes challenges with adversity begin early in life and may have an early impact on a student's schooling experience. Nicole's narrative also discloses the fact that many children take on the burden of adults' choices and consequences. Because Nicole possesses the shared identities of both pupil and daughter, these supposedly separate worlds are going to interact. Like previously, in the next conversation we can see how supposedly separate worlds interact or sometimes unintentionally collide.

So, who were you living with after that [after she was removed from mother's home]?

Well we lived…they took us away. Wait, at first my grandmother had my oldest brother. So, he ran away. He was like ten, and he ran and stayed with my grandmother. Me and my other brother stayed with my mom. Then, like when the bus came one day, they couldn't find my mom or nothing. So, we got on the bus, and they took us from school to DCFS [Department of Children and Family Services] and brought us to our grandmother's house. So, now we live with my grandmother. (Nicole, interview, fall 1998)

Once these separate spheres begin to interact, it becomes even more difficult, and I will argue, not even necessary, to try to distinguish what role each separate entity played in contributing to the student's level of stress. I argue that it is not necessary to try to pinpoint whether the family, community, or school caused stress, for even as we hear (or read) how Nicole tells the story, we notice that she does not dichotomize her stressors.

Nicole has endured other challenges to positive development that may have threatened educational resiliency. Research shows that minority children and students from low-income families are more likely to experience medical problems that affect positive educational development (Canino & Spurlock, 1994). In first, second, and third grade Nicole was required to receive special help at home, because of pneumonia and other upper-respiratory problems.

Based on the conversations between Nicole and me, it is difficult to determine what may have caused Nicole's long-term medical problems. Researchers in the medical profession and social science have not been able to determine if low-income and minority children's health problems are caused by environment, stress, access to adequate healthcare, etc. (Canino and Spurlock, 1994). The fact of the matter is that Nicole did have medical problems that affected her early childhood education and her socio-emotional development.

My mom [referring to her grandmother] always told me…My mom told me, you know I don't know how I came out, but I sick and stuff. But, my mom told me that the doctors said I would come out slow. I didn't come out slow, but I didn't come out like regular babies. When I was nine or ten, I didn't talk to nobody. My mom said she didn't think that I knew how to talk, because I didn't say nothing. She said that I didn't say "na-na." She said she'd ask me something, and I'd just go on about my business. (Nicole, interview, spring 2001)

In Nicole's voice we begin to learn how she understands the challenges that she faced early in her life. From her statement, "I didn't come out slow, but I didn't come out like regular babies," we begin to observe that she resists being labeled or categorized as abnormal. However, she does acknowledge that she did not have the same start as other children. Research studies have examined the consequences of children being aware of social inequality in our society and school (Ogbu & Simmons, 1998; Fine, 1991; O'Connor, 1997), but none has looked at the positive outcomes that may occur when students accept their disadvantages while embracing their differences.

Researchers do need to consider how developmental delays impact positive educational development, but we also need to take into account student agency. In other words, what happens when a student acknowledges she had different obstacles to overcome from others but rejects the idea of deficiency? How do embracing differences while rejecting assigned deficits contribute to processes of resiliency? These types of questions complicate our desire to focus on deficiency and failure instead to begin to expose the complexity of stressors, stress buffers, and the student's perceptions of both.

Nicole's ongoing conflict with her biological father is an example of the complexity of stressors and the student's perception of the situation. After I asked her about the role her father plays in her life, she said, "I don't even want to talk about him. I don't have no daddy." According to Nicole, her father consistently makes promises that he doesn't keep when it comes to special occasions like her birthday.

Nicole's description of her relationship with her father is important for two reasons as it relates to resilience. First, it informs us how important relationships are between daughters and fathers. Research on African American girls points to the positive outcomes that are a result of strong mother daughter relationships (Cauce, Gonzales, & Hiraga, 1998), but little research has looked at the consequences of the strained relationships between daughters and fathers, especially in low-income minority families.

Second, Nicole's description of her relationship with her father brings to the forefront how the interaction of racism, sexism, and classism in our society plays out in African American girls' lives and its absence in the resilience literature. Although it is only Nicole's perception, she understands her strained relationship with her father as having to do with his preference for his lighter-skinned daughter rather than her darker-skinned self. In our society, there has been a long history of individuals praising lighter skin over darker skin, even within the African American community (Hall, Russel, & Wilson, 1992). Lighter-skinned individuals were seen as more intelligent, virtuous, prosperous, and attractive. When identifying possible stressors, the resiliency literature does not even touch on this issue. As an African American female student, how does Nicole's very self-conscious awareness of her darker skin affect her self-image? And how does her self-image affect her schooling experience?

Accidentally, I learned firsthand of Nicole's extreme awareness of "race" and complexion. Once we were at the grocery store, simply hanging out while I got some grocery shopping done. Nicole was pushing the shopping cart while I browsed the aisle when a middle-aged White woman forcefully bumped Nicole's arm. Nicole and I both anxiously awaited the woman's apology. Sadly, there was no apology given, and the woman continued in the direction in which she was going.

Although Nicole was visibly upset, she nervously laughed off the incident. Therefore, I thought that it was an opportunity to share with Nicole my theory about White folks and their feelings about their right to take up space. My theory goes like this, as I told it to Nicole: "White folks feel that they have the right to take up space. Needless to say, they do not see Black folks as having that same right. Because they do not see Black folks as having the right to take up space, sometimes they do not even see us. Subconsciously, their racist attitudes lead them to purposefully or accidentally to bump into us without having to apologize for their conduct." At that particular moment in the grocery store, I thought that I had taught Nicole a very deep lesson on racial politics. On the contrary, Nicole turned to me and said, "You got a lot of nerves." My reaction was more or less, "Huh?" Then, Nicole said to me with the most telling expression, "I know you ain't talkin'; you just as White as she is!"

If I had not spent so much time with Nicole prior to this incident, I probably would have been taken aback by her comment. However, on previous occasions Nicole had told me how I looked White, which she attributed to my lighter complexion and my longer hair. Thus, the incident in the grocery store and comments made on previous occasions allowed me to assess just how much "race" meant to Nicole. For Nicole, "Whiteness" has as much to do with skin color as it has to do with one's ethnic background. Her ideals about White versus Black or light versus dark may be shaped by larger society, but they are reinforced by her own perceptions, her father's behavior, and now even my "teachings." Nevertheless, in Nicole's world, "race" is real, and it is attached to privileges and power.

Do you ever have contact with your other three brothers and sisters?

No. One of my brothers live in East St. Louis, and my other sisters are identical twins. We don't know where they are at. They don't try to call us or nothing. But, first we did have contact with them, but they don't even call us. But we know when their birthday and stuff like that is. My brother L., he stay with White folks. We went to court for him, my grandmother, to get custody of him and my twin sisters, but the White people took him from us. (Nicole, interview, fall 1998)

Unfortunately, Nicole has an understanding of her relationship with her family as "us" against "them." She reports, "the White people took him from us." From Nicole's perspective, her grandmother had no power, even as it related to her own kin. Nicole felt that White people (i.e., a Euro-American family and/or the court officials) took away something that belonged to them. Maybe Nicole's "us" against "them" mentality has contributed to her educational resiliency by strengthening her commitment to her family, whom she has noted to be her main source of educational support.

Before looking at the role of the family in promoting positive educational development, first we need to contemplate how social constructs like race, class, and gender are (re)enacted in the school environment. As previously stated, the family, community, and school are continuously interacting even though in research they are usually studied as isolated entities. In the preceding conversation, we begin to understand how Nicole's lived reality of "race" and her perceptions of White privilege coincide with her relationships at school.

When "Them" Are Your Teachers

Throughout middle school, Nicole experienced constant tension with teachers, and she viewed teachers as the cause of most of the conflict at school.

I'm on honor roll every time report cards come out.

You're an "A" student and teachers are still on your back?

Yeah. If they don't respect me, I'm not going to respect them. My homeroom teacher, Ms. Aspen, she straight. Most of these teachers be on their period. I think men teachers be on their periods too sometime. (Nicole, interview, fall 1998)

Even though Nicole somehow manages to get through school with high grades, the tension between her and teachers may cause a high level of undue stress. The above passage also highlights that Nicole does not view her teachers as respecting who she is as a person; therefore, she refuses to respect them. For Nicole, respect is mutual and earned. Also, the passage demonstrates the extent to which Nicole has internalized gender stereotypes but also reassigns gender-specific behavior (e.g., male teachers being on their periods too). Thus gender is behavior specific but not necessarily permanent, which may mean that gender does not limit her behavior.

Nicole, like many other urban adolescents, does not believe that her teachers are able to identify with most of the students at her school, not just with her. An "us" mentality is evident, but it initially appears to be a conflict resulting from age differences. However, because I grouped my transcribed interviews and journal notes by themes (e.g., tension with teachers, family support, etc.), I realized that age was mentioned as a factor in conflict with teachers only once. Other times, Nicole articulated race or cultural differences as the main reason for conflict between herself and/or other students and teachers. Because race/cultural differences emerged in personal conversation or in formal taped interviews, I had to ask Nicole, "Does race matter," as it relates to teacher-student relationships.

> I think Black teachers would treat us different from White teachers, because I think some of them prejudice at that school. Like this one teacher hate to see me coming. (Nicole, interview, fall 1998)

Nicole believes that the White teachers at her school are prejudiced against students of color and cannot identify with members of her peer group. Nicole believes there to be real differences between the ways in which Black teachers would treat students versus how White teachers treat students. In my interpretation, race is an issue for Nicole, but at the heart of the matter are cultural differences or the way people live. Race is a concept based on physical features, whereas "culture" has more to do with how people live day to day. Of course, in most cases "race" is traditionally not separated from "culture" in our society. At school, Nicole does not seem to separate race from culture.

> *How can the school help you with your educational goals?*

> That school can't help me. They sick in the head. They can't help ghetto people. They scared. Our principal and assistant principal are scary. (Nicole, interview, fall 1998).

At first glance, it appears that Nicole has abandoned the school as a source of support, because she has very little attachment to teachers and school staff. Nicole's lack of attachment may be related to real or perceived "cultural" differences. On the one hand, it concerns me that Nicole has internalized that there is a difference between "ghetto people" and White teachers, which means she has bought into a stereotype about who "ghetto people" are. Sometimes the term "ghetto" refers to a stereotypical "Black" identity associated with certain behaviors or attributes such as talking loud, cursing, listening to certain music, sporting particular hairstyles, wearing certain articles of clothing, living in a particular neighborhood, or more explicitly not "giving a shit" about what other people think and feel. This definition is more apparent by Nicole's comment that "They can't help us ghetto people. They scared." When I ask, "They scared of who?" Nicole replies, "They get cursed out every day" (Interview I, p. 15). I believe because Nicole generalizes students' negative behavior, who happen to be mostly African American and low income, she has bought into a stereotype associated with a group of people, belonging to a certain social class. Furthermore, because I have studied, worked, volunteered, and observed at the various schools in Haven and because I have talked to Nicole and many other girls like her, I am willing to argue that many of her teachers have also bought into this stereotype of "ghetto children."

Some teachers have an obscure perception of the students and families whom they teach. In turn, the school environment or a particular classroom becomes a controlled environment, controlling students' dress and behavior. Foley (1990) referred to methods employed by some schools to control low-income and minority students' unwanted behavior as "impression management," and Valenzuela (1999) called it "substractive schooling." I am sure that all schools to some extent control students' work and play, but this process becomes inappropriate and demeaning when teachers or school staff have obscured perceptions of their subjects.

However, a more political twist to Nicole's use of the term "ghetto" is that some folks in the African American community use it to refer to someone who has internalized and acts out stereotypical behavior. Nevertheless, one has to be careful of any single interpretation of Nicole's use of the phrase "ghetto children" (Interview I, p. 15), because "ghetto" is a very flexible word that has different meanings for different people in the African American community. For instance, from personal experience I know too that, more loosely used, "ghetto" can also refer to a shared African American cultural experience in Western society.

Most of Nicole's conflicts with teachers took place in the middle of Nicole's eighth-grade school year. By her sophomore year in high school, Nicole had less conflict with teachers and began to concentrate less on the racial background of her teachers. Nevertheless, the need for more African American teachers in the schools remained important to her, but it was expressed with ambiguity. As Nicole got older and had more exposure to more qualified teachers, she became more ambivalent about the need for African American children to be taught by African American teachers. Nonetheless, she held on to the perception of power and privilege being associated with Whiteness. She also understood the benefits of an African American female student having an African American female teacher, for Nicole longed for the one Black teacher (Ms.

Brown) that she left behind in middle school. She was the one person at the middle school that Nicole was attached to, and the older woman became Nicole's confidante.

Research shows that high-achieving African American female students are able to locate an adult in addition to their parents for support (Davis & Rhodes, 1996). Ms. Brown was a fifth-grade African American teacher at Nicole's middle school, who, Nicole said, helped her stay out of trouble with teachers, even though she was not actually one of Nicole's instructors. Unsurprisingly, Nicole named her as a mentor at her school. Ms. Brown was a resource at the middle school that Nicole sought out and utilized to her advantage, which helped her buffer stress at school. Unfortunately, Nicole had not had an African American teacher her first year of high school, which is probably why she continued to hold on to the memories of the qualities that Ms. Brown possessed as a teacher. But Nicole does not state that she does not like her teachers in high school or that her high school teachers cannot identify with African American students. She only implies that even now there is something missing.

In any event, Nicole had the privilege of a female African American teacher in her second year of high school. When I asked her if she liked her sophomore year teachers, the following conversation ensued:

> Oooh, we ain't even going there. I finally got…I got a black teacher. I sure do. Her name is Ms. W. Janice, my mom, grew up with her. She grew up with her on Sixth Street, and you know she ghetto just like us! She ghetto just like us. You know, she a cool teacher. It's time for play and it's time for work, and I mean it's time for work every day. (Nicole, interview, spring 2001)

Nicole spoke with excitement as she told me about her first African American teacher. It is in Nicole's description of the very essence of a "cool" teacher that it becomes clearer of Nicole's search for the ideal teacher to support her educational goals. Obviously Nicole was excited to have an African American teacher to fill a void in her educational experiences. She found more of a "cultural" connection as implied in the statement "She ghetto just like us" (Interview I, p. 4). From Nicole, we hear that race or the cultural background of a teacher does matter, but it becomes less important when the student feels she is being engaged or not cheated out of an education.

It could be argued that race does not matter to the student, that Nicole was not able to get along with her teachers in middle school because of lack of maturity or the stress in her life at that time. However, the following dialogue further supports the previous analysis.

Did you like your teachers?

I'm thinking they gon' be nicer in high school than they were in middle school. They wasn't. They had an attitude too (in a very low whisper). They were straight you know. They weren't them teachers. Let's just put it like that. You learn a lot more in high school than you do in middle school. Let's just put it like that.

As this dialogue shows, Nicole was more ambivalent about the relationship between herself and her White teachers in high school. More specifically, she was ambivalent about the type of teacher she needed to support her educational goals. She reported liking the one African American teacher at her middle school because the teacher talked to her and explained to her the difference between right and wrong behavior (Interview I, pp.8, 10, 14). Yet, by high school Nicole became more acquiescent concerning her teachers' attitudes toward her and other students, especially if she was "learning something." Thus, it has to be acknowledged that an African American female teacher may be a source of support for African American female girls like Nicole, but more resilient students of color may give up resisting control for the sake of receiving an adequate education.

School Support

At first, it appeared that Nicole had given up on the school itself as a source of support. In middle school she reported low attachment to her teachers, peers, and school staff, and in high school she was ambivalent about the low number of African American educators. Low attachment to the school environment is one of the biggest threats to academic success for students of color (Ogbu & Simmons, 1998; Foley, 1990; Valenzuela, 1999). I was even more concerned with Nicole making the transition from middle school to high school, because she was psychologically detached from the high school before she even got there. In our eighth-grade interview, I asked Nicole how she felt about going to her local community high school. Her response was "I don't want to go to M. I know that if I go to that high school, I'm going to get into it with too many people, because they be hatin'" (Interview I, p. 10). Nicole like many of the girls in her neighborhood did not want to attend the local high school. Two of the other girls whom I talked to about their school experiences did not bother showing up for registration; they are referred to as "no shows" at the local high school. Of course, most of these fears about the negative atmosphere of the local high school are based on the larger community stereotypes, media propaganda, and/or actual incidents concerning other friends or family members.

In high school, Nicole participated in three extracurricular programs throughout the school year. One organization that Nicole actively participated in was JROTC. Nicole claims that she enjoys JROTC because it prepares her for "real life." Nicole is very insightful about what it takes to succeed at school and in the larger society. For example, Nicole participates in the JROTC program because she likes to complete what she began; it gives her access to other positive youth; it teaches her discipline; and it is applicable to the real world. Even more significant is that Nicole initially became involved in JROTC because she wanted to use the army as a stepping stone to college. Although the military was not her first career choice, Nicole rationalized it was an available method to help her obtain free money for college. Her goal was to go to the military for "x" amount of years, then go on to college free of charge.

Not only does Nicole understand how to utilize various programs at school to help her reach her long-term goals, but she also recognizes the significance of support from the school staff. For instance, in the following conversation, Nicole and I are discussing her sophomore year grades.

You had really good grades this year. What helped you get those good grades?

I don't know.

You just smart (jokingly)?

Naw, I ain't gon say that, because I ain't smart. I'm smart, but I ain't that smart. I don't know, I think it's them teachers. Because people, you know, they be shy, and don't be asking the teacher. I'm the type of person, if I need help, I'm finna ask you. I ain't finna be shy or I'm gon' go to your desk and ask you. So, I think it's like the teachers really that help me. (Nicole, interview, spring 2001)

In the preceding dialogue Nicole (a) recognizes her own agency and (b) values the role that the staff at school plays in her educational accomplishments. Therefore, Nicole does not separate her success from what she does and what "them" teachers are able to do for her. In addition, for Nicole, the teachers and the staff at school also have to value her as a person. If a student feels valued or cared about at school, he or she is more likely to stay psychologically attached to the school (Valenzuela, 1999; Henderson & Millstein, 1996). As a sophomore, Nicole's value to the school was celebrated when she was deemed student of the month.

I was the student of the month (laughing). It was my birthday and they called me to the office, and told me I was the student of the month. You have to do something real good to somebody, and you have to share your feelings. I guess I had shared my feelings with the teacher, Ms. N., and told her how I feel. Because her mom had passed, and all the grief I knew I was telling her, you know what I'm saying, to help her feel better. So, I guess she felt I should be the student of the month. And, I got an award, I got a little rose, I got a $25 gift certificate. (Giggling) Why they say my name on the…when they said my name on the announcement, I swear I didn't know what I was thinking. I'm like, "What I do?" So, I'm walking in the hallway, and everybody like, "Congratulations, Nicole. Congratulations!" (Nicole, interview, spring 2001)

Another program Nicole participated in that may have promoted attachment to the school environment and buffered stress was her two-year involvement in a grief group at school. Nicole's great-grandfather, whom she called "daddy," died during her first year in high school. Accordingly, the school immediately stepped in to provide the support Nicole needed to cope with his death. Nicole actively participated in the grief group, and she admits that the grief group supported her "one hundred percent" even though she "broke down" every now and again (Interview II, p. 4). Also, the school did not abandon its goal of education first, which is why the students' participation hours were recorded to make up any missed work. Notwithstanding, the school knew that the student self could not be separated from what was going on outside of the school building. Therefore, we have an example of the school meeting both the needs of the student and the family. Furthermore, in her honesty about the limitations of her own agency, Nicole recognizes that resiliency is a human process and that even the most resilient students can "break down too" (Interview II, p. 4).

Finally, despite Nicole's on again-off again relationship with teachers and staff at her school, it does not surprise me that she has thought of becoming a teacher. She wants to be "a special teacher that help special children."

A special education teacher? Why you pick that career?

I have no idea. I don't have to be a special education teacher, but a teacher. I want to treat them the way they treat me, and see how they think and feel. (Nicole, interview, fall 1998)

Nicole wants to put to work her ideal of the perfect teacher. I thought Nicole was using "special" teacher to refer to special education teacher, but she was not. Nicole was simply speaking of the need for special teachers to assist special children such as herself. Therefore, I believe that Nicole is aware that there were special adults in her life at school who helped her cope with her special circumstances. It also confirms for me that Nicole believes that respect is reciprocal, which is why she wants to treat her students in a way that respects how they think and feel and hope they would do the same in return. Her comments reveal that children who have special circumstances require special teachers to help them reach their educational goals.

The Family

Nicole displayed low attachment to her neighborhood, peer group, and the staff at school, but she showed very high attachment to her family. Maybe because I grew up in a "nontraditional" family, being raised by my aunt and uncle with the support of other friends and family members, I was careful to allow the students to define for themselves who they deemed to be family. For many urban girls, the notion of family that we use in traditional social science and educational research is outdated. Similarly, the popular term "fictive kin" does not even do justice to the manner in which students, like Nicole, conceptualize who is their family. For instance, Nicole explained to me the intensity of a stressor she experienced her first year in high school and why it was so hard for her to cope at the time.

> My grandpa died. Actually, he was my father. He was there for me, through thick and thin. He was the first person that I said "da-da" to, the first person to buy me a bike (a hearty laugh). He was the first person for everything. (Nicole, interview, spring 2001)

Based on this conversation and similar ones, my method for observation and interpretation has been to allow the students to define for themselves who comprises family for them. Furthermore, I also permitted the participants to name what role they believe a particular person has played in their life and in their schooling process. Of course, both methods may get complicated in the writing process, but the resiliency process is complicated. Students' ability to deconstruct concepts like family and to reconstruct them to fit into their reality is a part of student agency.

Nicole continuously deconstructs and reconstructs the concept "mother." Nicole, like all the girls I spoke to, named her mother as the most significant person in her life and the one who has helped her "get this far" in school. She explains her grandmother's role in her education.

> *Who has helped you get this far in school?*
>
> My grandmother.
>
> *How has she helped?*
>
> Make sure I be at school every day. She doesn't have to tell us to go, we just go. Well, I just go every day. I don't care if those teachers talk about me. (Nicole, interview, fall 1998)

Many studies have noted that family support, especially maternal support, is strongly linked to positive school achievement amongst many African American girls (Cauce, Gonzales, & Hiraga, 1996; Ward, 1996; Sullivan, 1996; O'Connor, 1997). What is central to Nicole's educational story is that she completely redefines the traditional notion of family so that it fits her idea of family support. Referring to her grandmother, Nicole told me during an interview, "I got her legs. I think my legs like her legs. My smile, like her smile. I choose the same thing, what she choose. I don't know. I say, "Mom, you don't think I came out of you?" (laughing) (Interview II, p. 8). Obviously, Nicole knows that she is not her grandmother's biological daughter, but her comment does show how Nicole struggles with the traditional definition of "mother." Even more, the comment illustrates how Nicole has internalized a keen connection with her grandmother.

As important to this relationship between mother and daughter is that Nicole understands how fortunate she is to be a part of a family that has a strong commitment to the child. The most resilient students are better adept at recognizing their support systems (Winfield, 1994). Nicole not only recognizes her family's support, she is grateful for it.

> I love my grandmother with all my heart. I love my grandmother with all my heart. I'll do anything for that woman. When she sick, I'm sick. When I'm sick, she sick. I'll do anything for that woman. If she tell me to jump off a bridge, you better believe I'll jump off that bridge. I love her with all my heart. If it wasn't for her, I wouldn't be right here talking to you now. (Nicole, interview, spring 2001)

Because Nicole experienced so many hardships early in life and considers her grandmother to be her nurse and rescuer from that earlier life, Nicole literally attributes her life to her grandmother. Even more, Nicole conveys a high level of trust and respect for her grandmother. For Nicole, a mother's respect is earned, not something that is simply bestowed upon the woman who bore the child. In the following conversation, I ask Nicole to explain what she means by being "grateful" and surviving her childhood sickness. Notice how Nicole ascribes her recovery to her grandmother while simultaneously redefining motherhood as an earned role.

What do you mean by grateful?

> What it would be like without me. What my mom would go through if I'd died. How would it be, if I weren't there, looking at her, watching her. You feel me? Okay, like I said, I was taken in like 83 or 84. I'm glad that I'm with my grandmother, because the stuff that she doing now, I wouldn't want to be apart of that. I'm grateful that my grandmother came and took us and loved us like she do, and she do a good job. If it weren't for her, then we would be somewhere with them White people. We wouldn't be right here with her. We'll be somewhere else with them White people, where my brother at.

> So, me and my mom, my real mom, our relationship is nothing. It's like with all her kids, she love us, she know she did wrong, but she got to look at the fact that you can't

come into our lives now trying to play the mommy role. [My grandmother] been playing the mama role since 83/84, so you can't come and play the mama role. (Nicole, interview, spring 2001)

At the beginning of the above dialogue, Nicole refers to her grandmother as
mom. On the other hand, she simply refers to her biological mother as "she."
The objectification is due to the lack of respect. In fact, Nicole usually refers to
her grandmother as "mama." Nicole and I both sometimes in private conversations attempted to distinguish between her biological mother and her grandmother, simply for clarity. Of course, Nicole understands that "Janice King" is
her grandmother, but in her heart Janice is her mother. Being her mother is a
title that her grandmother earned and one that Nicole and her brothers bestowed up her, and it is a title and role that Janice embraces. Yet, Janice's high
level of commitment to her children (grandchildren) does come with sacrifices.
I captured a sense of these sacrifices in my field journal notes.

Went to visit Nicole today. When I first got to Nicole's house, she met me at the
door, talking on the telephone. She was simply lounging around in her pajamas. The
students had the day off school, and she was preparing for a weekend of basketball,
March Madness. Her mother came home shortly after I arrived. She had just gotten off
work. She wanted to rest and have a cigarette in front of the television. She was happy
to see me and the baby. In fact, before she rested, she made the baby some food. She
talked about how kind Nicole was and how proud she was of her. Nicole had gotten all
"A"s and "B"s this grading period, and had no problems at school with students or
teachers. Grandma asked me how it was being married. I explained to her that it had its
goods and bads for women, but yet we teach our girls that it is the highest honor—not
so. But I told her that I had a good man. She explained that she had never been married, but was in a long-term relationship for 39 years and broke it off because of the
kids. He eventually found a younger woman. She said she didn't care, because the kids
had been through enough without some man telling her how to discipline them or re-
strain their behavior. (Field notes, spring, 2001)

What does the above conversation between Janice and me have to do with
educational resiliency? On the surface, or as much as my field notes convey, the
conversation exposes my personal opinion about married life and the personal
sacrifices that Janice has made for her (grand)children. There is no doubt that
Janice empathizes with the hardships that Nicole and her brothers have been
through, and she has a high level of commitment to her children. For example,
Janice was not willing to stay in a relationship with a man who might have
threatened the well-being of the children.

However, this conversation at Janice's kitchen table, with my son sitting on
my lap and Nicole present may have served another function. The conversation
in the kitchen demonstrates how family members directly or indirectly shape the
student. Subjectification is the process through which an individual turns herself
into a subject, based on her own thoughts and conducts, as well as others (Fou-

cault, 1984). From my history with Nicole and her grandmother, along with the dialogue at the kitchen table, I am able to observe how Nicole is socialized into her gender role and turned into the "good" student.

For instance, Janice on several occasions prior to our kitchen table conversation has told me how proud she was of me. In short, she was proud of my academic and marital accomplishments. Because Janice considered me a mentor to her daughter, I was regarded as an example for Nicole. Therefore, at the kitchen table, Janice (the confessor) and I were giving Nicole a lesson on gender roles. The dialogue taught Nicole (the unknowing subject) life lessons about marriage, the importance of education, and a strong commitment to family (in fact, the traditional nuclear family). In Janice's eyes, I was a "good girl." Along with this good-girl status came the luxuries of having nice things, a good stable family (or man), and the freedom to make choices. Resiliency or sticking to one's goals leads to the things that many women in the African American community are not granted. At least that was the message delivered to Nicole that evening in the kitchen. Nicole got the message, which is probably why she sat there the whole time with her lips twisted.

On a more serious note, on several occasions, in our discussions, Nicole refers to herself as a "good girl" or a "bad girl." Nicole routinely dichotomized her behavior—you're either a good girl or you are a bad girl—and she constantly rationalized that there are consequences for being a "bad" girl. Even more, although she admits she had fun in fifth grade, she still referred to herself as a bad girl. Maybe to Nicole good girls do not have so much fun, especially in a school setting. Also, Nicole reports that she was required to take medication to help control her behavior. Undoubtedly, she has in-depth insight of the authorities' need to control bad-girl behavior. When I asked her if she was still taking medication for her behavior problems, Nicole stated, "No, I'm a good girl" (Interview I, p. 8). To quote Foucault, the "authority figures, be they confessor or psychoanalyst" (1984, p. 11), have done an outstanding job of controlling Nicole's thoughts and conduct. Whether there are "good" or "bad" consequences to her psychological state, they have obviously contributed to her educational achievement.

Although I can honestly write that Nicole is a very well-rounded young woman, she narrowly defines "good girl." To revert to the conversation at the kitchen table, subjectivity was played out by shaping Nicole's gender-role expectations. Again, how is this related to educational resiliency? Using my background, Janice was able to tie in the example of a strong commitment to education (educational resiliency) leading to a nice outcome (i.e., a good husband, material possessions, etc.) in the future. For Janice and Nicole, a good girl is an educated girl, and good girls become fortunate spouses (I think this is why Janice often emphasized a thirty-nine-year relationship she had with one man, which implied that she was "good" in that she was committed to a relationship). In Nicole and Janice's stories, we begin to ascertain a deeper understanding of the "how" in female caregivers' contribution to educational resiliency. It also clarifies the role that the student plays in her own subjectivity and process of resiliency.

Blurred Boundaries: Family, Community, School

Nicole's relationships, activities, and behaviors at home, in her social environment, and at school constantly interact to construct, deconstruct, and reconstruct resilience. Rigsby (1994) asserts that current theories of resilience overlook structural impediments to positive educational development. Structural impediments related to race, class, and gender biases in our society have been a constant threat to Nicole's success. Yet, Nicole has been able to cope and move forward toward high school completion. Literature on resilience points out that families, communities, and schools are able to strengthen protective processes and promote resiliency when students are faced with external risk factors (Winfield, 1994). However, most of the research on school resiliency has failed to look at coping over an extended period of time and has failed to look at how African American girls are able to succeed despite adverse circumstance.

Student agency is very important to fostering educational resiliency. Nicole holds positive feelings toward education and sees it as a means to change her current circumstance. Also, she actively participates in learning what is necessary to get ahead at school and in life. Nicole's belief in school and in herself is apparent as she discusses how she feels about high school.

> How I feel about high school? It's getting me somewhere, let's put it like that. It's getting me somewhere. I believe I can make it in the future. (Nicole, interview, spring 2001)

Although the words and emotions behind the words disclose her irresolute attachment to her school, Nicole, in spite of everything, believes in education and herself. Thus, school itself is a protective factor for Nicole. However, Nicole has been able to recover despite adversity, because her family, community, and school have been successful at blurring boundaries. Just as it is impossible to assess from what distinct area her stressors are initiated, one can't declare a particular protective factor. Because the interaction of race, class, and gender does not allow dichotomies, the boundaries of social, cultural, and political protective factors also should not be fragmented. More specifically, although the family, community, and school at some level have been a factor of stress in Nicole's life, all these (presumed) separate (state-constructed) entities have merged to facilitate school resiliency.

For example, in kindergarten, the school, DCFS, and Nicole's grandmother arranged a system for Nicole and her brothers to be safely escorted from school to home. Although this may be a contributor to stress, especially if Nicole did not understand why her family was being broken up, it still shows how the family, community, and school worked together for the welfare of the child/student involved. Even Nicole admits (Interview I, p. 3) that she liked going to kindergarten, because of the freedom she had at school. In other words, the school was a safe haven at an erratic time in her young life.

Another example of the family, school, and community blurring boundaries for the benefit of the child is the fact that Nicole has had a home tutor since the first grade. On medical advice, in first, second, and third grade, Nicole had a tutor come to her home, because she spent a lot of time in the hospital. DCFS paid a tutor to provide home instruction at no cost to her family. The school provided Nicole and the tutor with the curriculum that was needed for her to stay on track with her peers. In fact, Nicole continues to receive tutoring once a week at home. It is almost difficult to imagine the outcome if every student would be able to have the benefit of the family, community, and school working together and blurring boundaries.

In Nicole's case, her family took advantage of the resources that a community organization, DCFS, could provide to help the student succeed educationally. The community brought needed resources to the family and school in consideration of the "whole" child (the delivery of ideal social services), and, education moved beyond the school walls and went to the student and into the home of the family. What happens when one of these entities fail to do its part? Nicole explains it from her perspective:

> Well, I think I caught pneumonia and something else, and I almost died. I was breathing out of a tube and stuff. That was first, second, and third, grade. And, I know I got held back in second grade, because the tutor lady didn't never help me out. All she used to do was give me the work, and she'll go about her business. The same tutor from first, second third, grade, she still with me right now. (Nicole, interview, fall 1998)

Once the student perceives that one of the entities have failed her, as we hear in the preceding quote, it becomes a threat to her success. However, we learn from Nicole's stories that resilience is a process. It is a process for the student and for those environmental protective factors assisting her educational development, which is why Nicole is successful, even with the tutor who simply went about "her business."

How do you think your grandma influenced you to do well in school?

Actually, I had a tutor. I had a tutor since I was going to T. school. Her name was A.S. Write that down, A.S. I still got a tutor. And, she really helped me out, because I was young then, like ten, and I didn't know my ABCs, and I give her much respect, because if it wasn't for her, if I didn't have no tutor, then you know what I'm saying…I didn't know nothing. I didn't know my pluses. Then, she tutored me and she still do. DCFS pays $20 an hour, and she comes picks me up. (Nicole, interview, fall 1998)

Although Nicole makes it very clear that her grandmother is her main source of educational support, she also acknowledges the very important role that others, like her tutor, have played in her educational success. In fact, in the preceding interview she prompts me to write down her tutor's name, which shows that she highly regards her tutor as someone who has helped her do well in school. It appears that Nicole and others learned to work together instead of limiting their outlook to their own affairs. In the past, researchers and others have looked at the danger that may arise when state-/politically constructed entities, like schools or community organizations, impose on the individual or family and/or when the individual or family does not willingly work in conjunction with the school or the community. On the other hand, Nicole's stories help us begin to observe how the indistinguishable qualities of stressors (or the interaction of structural impediments) threaten success, but we also begin to understand how the blurring of boundaries along those same lines can promote persistence, adaptation, and long-term success despite adverse circumstances.

Zora's Story: Nature versus Nurture

It was a Saturday afternoon, and I had agreed to pick up Zora at twelve noon. Because she wanted me to come earlier at 11 a.m., I decided to be on time. This time, like many times, my son had to accompany me. When I rang the doorbell, a man's voice rang out "Come in!" I stalled before entering the house. "Come in," the voice yelled again. I walked in the screen door, for the front door was already opened. The inside of the house was dark and dreary as opposed to the outside of the house, which was landscaped with flowers and lots of greenery.

Outside, there are lots of plants and flowers and yard decorations. I know that her dad works in bricklaying and restores old houses, like a handyman. Their yard reflects his amateur landscaping (a joke between Zora and me). Inside, their living room walls were adorned with pictures and inexpensive decorative pieces. I spotted a black- and-white picture of her mom in her youth. She looked mean, almost like a gangster; she was not even trying to smile. From my view, the house decorations were old and inexpensive antiques, and there was a lot of green and brown in the house. I am sure that the house was a decorator's dream house in the 1970s.

I had only looked around briefly when I saw Zora's father sitting on the living room couch. I have seen him before working in the front yard, but we have never spoken. "Hello. Is Zora here?" Before he could answer, Zora and a baby boy in a diaper with corn rolls in his hair walked up to where I was standing. Because I came through the back door, I was standing at a lower level than they were. I would have had to climb about four steps to get to the regular house level (or go down a flight of stairs to get to the basement). Needless to say, I was in an awkward position when her dad asked me what my son's name was. "Stevie. He's named after his dad. You don't remember him from church?" I had attended Zora's church on several occasions as a visitor, since my in-laws are also very dedicated to this church. Other times, I went to the church during summer vacations to try and locate Zora.

Soon after Zora's sister joined us. It was her thirteen-month-old baby who greeted me. I asked Zora's dad if he knew the Winters family, and he stated that he did. Then, it must have clicked in his mind where he had previously met my son. Without thinking and out of ignorance I said, "You've probably seen him more than you have seen me." Zora's sister looked at me and shook her head as to say, "Don't get him started." It was too late to take back, because I got him started.

Her dad then wanted to know why the baby was going to church more than I was. I had a silly look on my face, because I did not want him to know why I did not go to church. He got off the couch, looked in the mirror, tugged at his suit jacket, rubbed his hands over his jeri-curl, and turned to me and said, "You better start going to church." Without another word, he walked out the front door and left to go to church. Zora finally finished getting dressed, and we left for our last interview together.

As the ethnographic description hints, Zora's family is very dedicated to their church. They are usually in church every Sunday participating in service activities, and they volunteer at church throughout the week. There was at least two times that I can remember tracking Zora down at her family's church, once during vacation school and another time after Sunday morning service. Her family's commitment to their community church contributes to Zora's resilience. Educational literature shows that religious organizations are sites of refuge that enhance resilience for many African American families and children (Bagley & Carroll, 1996). The encounter I have just described provides an example of Zora's immediate family's commitment to their neighborhood church, but also offers insight into her immediate family's rituals. These rituals have shaped her physical environment and her life choices outside the family context.

Outside of attending church activities, Zora's parents did not allow her and her siblings much time outside in the neighborhood; thus, reading provided an escape and an alternative leisure activity for Zora. Eventually, I began to recommend and share books with her that I thought would pique her adolescent interests like the novel *The Coldest Winter Ever* by Sister Souljah. Through book discussions, interviews, phone conversations, ice cream sessions, I learned things about Zora that better prepared me for our last formal interview together.

Initially, I had a difficult time learning about Zora's experiences with her family, community, and school. Zora only offered information on a "need to know" basis. She was a difficult student to interview, mainly because she was very reserved. I found, after transcribing her tape, that Zora made for a difficult tape recorded subject too. Not surprisingly, she was the first student to advise me to change the interview format, and she was the only student to return portions of her journal. Nevertheless, since our first interview almost three years ago, Zora's demeanor and appearance had changed considerably. My field notes reflect the change.

> As for her appearance, I thought that she was one of those types of girls who thought that other girls just "tried too hard." Zora came across as the tomboy type. It looked like she tried to do something with her hair; however, it just was not an in-style hairdo. On the day we met, she pulled her hair back in a short ponytail and appeared like she tried to do something with her hair, but she couldn't quite tame it. (Field notes, fall 1998)

However, on the last interview, I could see that Zora spent a lot more time attending to her appearance. In retrospect, I believe that I spent more time noting Zora's appearance than usual simply because in the beginning she did not impress me as the kind of girl who would overemphasize physical beauty; instead she was more concerned about her athletic abilities. Also, she had changed before my eyes. For instance, at our first meeting, not only did I take note of her appearance, but I also noted that she was very critical of her female peers and their efforts to conform to gender expectations.

> Girls just think too much. They just think that they too cute to eat. Like they scared to go into line. Like it's going to mess up their reputation. They the ones be starving. In gym, we suppose to sit on the floor in line, they think they suppose to sit in a chair. They need to quit.

Zora's captious response to eighth-grade girls' behaviors and the fact that it was the subjects on which she was most vociferous, led me in my mind to construct this perfect young feminist story. But what happened in the end is that Zora's stories taught me more about resilience as process in addition to the complexity and contradictions of human nature.

> I notice that Zora is beginning to put a lot of effort into her looks. She definitely sports the latest styles even though I can tell that she does her hair herself or a friend does it. The look is very creative but not very professional. Zora has really turned into a nice-looking young woman. She has grown a couple more inches; her hairdo is always in-style, and her clothes are always jazzy. Today she is wearing boot-cut khaki pants, black open-toed clog sandals, and a tank top, with a red Tommy jacket over it—sitting next to me reading Sister Souljah's book. I asked Zora if a lot of guys try to talk to her and other girls at school—she said "Yes!"
>
> She's about 5'5, 110 pounds, a reddish brown, very petite and slender, and her hair is always on point, compared to other girls her age. She could be a fashion designer, because she works with what she got. Even though she's aware of the latest styles, she knows what she wants out of life, which is an education. (Fieldnotes, spring 2001)

The Wonder Years

I took the preceding fieldnotes during our last formal interview session which took place on my family room couch. At the time, Zora was involved in JROTC, the Academy, and the grief group at school. The Academy is a college preparation course for high school students interested in the sciences, and the students conduct hands-on experiments in the classroom. According to Zora, she was the only female in her Academy class. Zora was also enrolled in algebra and physics and was thinking about taking geometry instead of trigonometry the next semester.

Like Nicole, Zora had been held back early in her educational career. In Zora's case, she repeated the first grade. As she informed me, "They thought I was slow, because I didn't say nothing when they asked me a question." Zora's memories about third grade further demonstrate her struggles with school and learning. "I hated third grade. My teacher was mean. We couldn't do nothing. I didn't like her because she was mean to everybody. I hated being in her class every day."

Research shows that children who have a negative educational experience, like repeating a grade, are more likely to leave school (Fine, 1991). Research also shows that African American children are more likely to drop out after such an experience (Smith, 1999). Regardless of her early struggles in school, Zora persistently strives to achieve in school. Even though Zora strives to do, she always falls short of the honor roll. Her comments as a second-year high school student display her frustration and concern with her grades.

> I'm always getting a "C" in one subject. In one subject, I'm always getting a "C." I bring the grade up, then the next grading period, I get a "C" in another one. I just got tired of studying. I'm like, I'm not finna be trying to work so hard and I'm not getting nowhere really. (Zora, interview II, spring 2001)

As Zora explained to me why she did not make honor roll the last grading period, I heard her disappointment. As a matter of fact, many of the conversations about her grades were filled with frustration. All the resilient students whom I talked with seemed to always worry about their grades. Despite ups and downs with her grades, Zora was very involved in school activities. Many times when I asked Zora what she liked about school, her answer was usually related to the "doing" aspect of school. For instance, when asked what she liked about that school in the fourth grade, she answered, "We went outside and jumped rope, threw snow balls. They used to always go in the girls' bathroom and fight. It was so funny. On Halloween, we had to sit in the library with a costume on because the teacher was telling us a story. It was fun being a clown." Zora was the type of student who liked to be active and engaged in hands-on activities at school. Regrettably, by middle school Zora disliked school because school had become less interactive in her view.

Seemingly, another major theme that emerged among the young women was the students' perception that school became more boring as they approached middle school. It appears that as students get older or reach the middle grades, teachers become more concerned with order and discipline whereas in the earlier grades educators may have students participate in activities, like costume parties, to help them associate learning and school with fun. The problem is that most students enter middle school at the ages ten or eleven, yet they are almost overnight expected to stifle their energy level. As a result, like Zora, most urban adolescents are at risk of becoming bored with school and may simply view their teachers as loathsome persons.

Of course, adolescence is strongly associated with defiance as children begin their fight for independence and self-identity. However, middle grade students may fail to perceive education as worthwhile if teachers focus more on discipline and punishment as opposed to creative and engaged learning. By eighth grade, it appeared that Zora and her peers had lost respect for their teachers.

Much of the tension seems to be related to her perception that the students "can't talk" and "can't do nothing" in the students' words. Zora, for instance, seems to be bored in the classroom and wishes for more autonomy. Speaking on her seventh-grade experience, students' rebellion in the classroom is captured in Zora's self-report in which she stated, "We didn't care what the teacher said. Just did what I wanted to do. We be gaggin' makin' fun of her" (Interview I, fall 1998). What are the consequences when students begin to question their teachers' competence and/or motives in the classroom? For example, I asked Zora how she felt about the grades she was receiving in eighth grade.

I didn't never have a hard time in math until in eighth grade. Getting "F"s, all "F"s.

Why do you think you are not doing well?

He just startin' to grade our homework. He used to complain about it. He used to just give checks. We didn't know if we did the homework correct or not. He should check it. Then, we get these tests. Last year, I used to get good grades on test, but this time…

How do you feel about your teachers?

Just kinda of funny actin', especially our history teacher. He can be nice, everybody like him, but he can change. He just be tryin' to show off that's what I think. Tryin' to let everybody know who he is or something. If he feel stupid he be tryin' to send you to the ACE room. (Zora, interview, fall 1999)

When students do poorly in school or in a certain subject, possibly the most resilient students do not internalize it as a failure on their part and continue to strive to do better. In addition, Zora's comments about her teacher "tryin' to let everybody know who he is" convey her perception that her (Caucasian, male) teacher occasionally takes advantage of his power in the classroom.

Notwithstanding her boredom in the classroom, Zora managed to stay involved in other activities at her middle school. She has participated in Girl Scouts, chorus, and many sports in school, and her favorite sport in eighth grade was girls' basketball. Yet, by the time she finished her first year of high school, Zora admitted not liking basketball as much. Unfortunately, Zora's boredom with school only escalated by high school, which she blames on the lack of activities available to first-year students.

Growing Pains

By the end of her second year of high school, Zora's level of participation at school had decreased significantly. The only extracurricular activity she had participated in by the end of her sophomore year was JROTC. Zora's sudden low level of participation in extracurricular activities in high school concerned me for two reasons. First, in middle school her high level of participation, especially in sporting activities is what I had originally thought kept her motivated and attached to school. Second, I was concerned because studies show that urban girls who participate in school athletic programs are probably not engaging in substance use (Gibbs, 1996) and are more likely to possess higher levels of self-esteem (Erkut et al., 1996). Extracurricular school activities, drug and alcohol abstinence, and high self-esteem are qualities consistent with most resilient students (Wang & Gordan, 1994). It was interesting that Zora was aware of her need to stay active and involved at school.

Even though Zora was apparently frustrated with the lack of activities at her school for first-year students, she remained attached to some extent to the school. She had a low level of attachment, though, because even after two years, she still wanted to attend another high school outside of her neighborhood. The high school she wanted to attend was located up the hill in a majority White, middle-class community, and it was not associated with some of the stereotypes of her present school. According to Zora, she wanted to attend the other high school, because it offered a health academy, a program of study that was more aligned with her aspirations of becoming a nurse. Although Zora has legitimate motives for wanting to attend the more prosperous school, Zora holds her own stereotypes about the neighborhood high school and her peers. In the following example, I was very honest about my fears of Zora becoming pregnant for some of the reasons discussed and not discussed previously. As a mentor, I felt it was my responsibility to Zora, her family, and school authorities to inform Zora that some of the behaviors she was engaging in, put her at risk of an unplanned pregnancy and possibly school failure.

I was telling somebody that a lot of girls don't finish school, because they got pregnant. Please promise me that you won't get pregnant.

I could do that shoo. I'm makin' it already. Man, it's so many people pregnant. I'm like, "Man, ya'll can't be tongue kissing" (laughing). My other friend, she just had a baby, the other day, and she wants me to be the godmother. She was runnin' around talkin' about she wasn't pregnant, everybody know you was. Now you then had the baby, now what you gon' tell everybody? "I didn't know." Shut up. If they at that school, if they ain't got no kids yet, they finna have one, or they already have one at home. That's how that school is. (Zora, interview, spring 2001)

Regardless of her own generalization of her female peers, Zora was very aware of media and public stereotypes of the neighborhood school and the students who attend the local high school. She was very upset that people stereotyped their community high school as a "bad" school, where people fight every day. She felt that the students were made to dress a certain way and wear identification tags around their necks because they went to school "down the hill" on the "south end." Furthermore, she spoke on her frustration with a school that treats the girls differently from the boys.

Like when we wear clothes and stuff. I mean it ain't nothing wrong with wearing a spaghetti strap shirt. It be hot in the school. You be burning up with some shorts, way down to here. You gotta have on a t-shirt. It is ninety degrees outside, why is ya'll playin'. "That is too revealing." Ya'll act like somebody finna come into the school and rape every girl or something. Everybody get to wear what they want at different schools. Why they always trying to enforce rules at M.? We gotta wear ID tags; don't nobody else gotta wear ID tags, but M. high school. M. high school. I think they do that, because we on the south end. That's why I'm tryin' to get away from that school, so bad. I don't care if I have to catch the bus every morning. I would do that. I hate that school, because of the rules. Their rules are so strict and stupid. You get a detention if you just a second late. (Zora, interview, spring 2001)

Using the pregnant body as a point of reference, Pillow (2000) explains how the female body is a "site of paradoxical social attention and avoidance" (p. 201). Like the pregnant body, the bodies of African American female adolescents have always been sites monitored, avoided, and scrutinized by those holding power. Whether the power holders are caregivers, slave masters (Davis, 1983), legal/political bodies (Roberts, 1997), or school officials, the Black female body has been the targeted culprit. Zora is conscious of her and her female peers' targeted bodies even though she does not name it as racism, sexism, and classism.

Hill Street Blues

What I like most about sharing Zora's stories is that her stories demonstrate the human qualities of even the most resilient adolescents. For example, the following is an excerpt from Zora's journal that discusses some choices and consequences that she experienced over a school year.

First I'm going to talk about my life, then school. As you may know or don't I'm in high school now. I graduate from Bluff Middle School. I'm 15 yrs old. About to be 16 yrs old next month. My life is not what you call a happy life. But it's okay sometimes. [I'm] going to talk about school. My first year at M. was alright. The beginning of the school year was not so boring. I did get lost for the first week. I know the school like the back of my hand. I am in J.R.O.T.C. I like it a lot. I also ran into my old boyfriend, too. I end up going back with my old boyfriend; we still go together. His name is Johnny. He one of my old boyfriends that isn't a dog if you know what I mean. It's hard to find a boyfriend like him now and days.

Now I'm in the tenth grade. I did run into a lot of people I thought was cool but turned out to be phony people. I have this friend; she been my best friend since the 6th grade. She starting to change a lot. I am too, that's what every teenager goes through. But, she not the same anymore. She does things that she knows isn't right. If I was to tell you, you would be shocked. Anyways, about me spending the night at my friend house was a misunderstanding. I ask my moms could I spend the night at my friend house for a night. She said I could but, I had to go to church the next day. I didn't go to church the next day. I stay out all night with my friends, my boyfriend, his sister, her friends, and his friends.

My mom was mad. She got over it. I was on punishment. I got in trouble for skipping school. I skipped one day. I kicked it with my boyfriend. He was suspended from school for 3 days. I had some fun. I got in trouble for that. That was my first time ever skipping school. I don't think I do that anymore. I will be on punishment again. That is the only bad things I did this year. Normal I don't be getting in to trouble at all. I just have to be hard headed sometimes. I get good grades in school. I never been in any really bad trouble. I never been suspended or had any Saturday detentions before. I not a bad girl. You can ask my mom; she tell you. My boyfriend is very smart, honor student, he's cute too, nice too. You don't want no boyfriend that don't know nothing. I know I don't. (Zora, sophomore, journal entry)

Zora's journal entry demonstrates that even the most resilient students engage in risky behavior, make choices that are possibly harmful to their schooling, experience complex and contradictory emotions, and encounter conflict with peers and adults. Even more, Zora's journal entry exposes her self-reflection, which shows that the most resilient students may be more in touch with their feelings, understand the consequences for their behaviors, think through what they expect from their peers and other relationships, and accept that individuals are different and constantly change. In other words, Zora's story screams, "I am human!"

Actually, many of the events leading up to our last interview remind me of the human side of resiliency and that African American female students of color are affected, like everyone, by things in their environments that can break them. Outside environmental factors many times exceed their boundaries and force themselves into the homes and hearts of even the most resilient students and families. My fieldnotes reveal how I accidentally crossed these boundaries myself.

> Zora told me that she wasn't asleep, but that she had heard some bad news: her biological mom had died. I asked her what happened. She said they had found her mom's body. She was choked up, so I told her I was sorry and that it wasn't a good time to talk. I told her I'll call or stop back this weekend. I think that I felt more uncomfortable about the situation. Therefore, I called her back; in the background I could hear her family discussing the death. I told Zora that if she needed someone to talk to; I'll be here, she can call. Call whether she wants to talk to me about this (the death of her mother) or something else nonrelated. She said okay, but her friend was visiting at the time. The conversation ended with her telling me to turn to the news. (Fieldnotes, spring 2001)

One day while enjoying the salty taste of chips and dip on my family room couch, Zora and I finally talked about her experiences in her family without the vagueness that dominated past conversations. For obvious reasons, I did not begin the conversation with the death of her biological mother. First, we talked about her relationship with Melba, her other mother. My first impression of Melba was that she was mean and too strict or uncaring. Zora basically dispelled that image. She does not think that she would be where she is today if it was not for Melba, for she (Melba) stays on her about her grades.

Who has had the most influence on you as far as doing good in school?

> She has, because she do not let you fall back on nothing. She'll try to put you on punishment or something, until you do good. Like she want us to be something. Mostly everybody in our family really ain't too much of nothing big. They just like, now it's our generation, do something. She not playing about that school stuff, she's not playing. I'm for real. If she didn't, I probably wouldn't even be worrying about school, like I am now. (Zora, interview, spring 2001)

The above passage illustrates that Zora feared but respected her mother's strict rules about grades. Melba, Mrs. Gaines, is actually Zora's biological mother's cousin. As she stated in her words, "My mom is my cousin, because that's my grandpa's first cousin." Zora's biological mother has had a long history of drug and alcohol abuse. Mrs. Gaines adopted Zora when she was very young. Zora's real mother has nine other children who live with different people, except Zora's brother (fifteen) who lives with her too. Zora sometimes speaks with some of her siblings who live here in Haven, but they are not that close, she admits.

Researching Home

Zora's biological mother was killed in early March, only a month prior to the second formal interview. Zora said the police had two suspects in mind, but they could not find them for questioning. Ironically, at the time of the interview Zora was not only angry with the suspects in the case but she also carried some resentment toward her mother. But before discussing Zora's strategies of coping, I first must reveal other aspects of the dialogue that took place that afternoon between Zora and me. I had to admit to myself that this would not be an open and honest helpful example of a feminist ethnography if I did not reveal my reactions to Zora's mother's death. In short, the conversations about her mother's death led to discussions about my own methods of coping with familial tragedy.

> *I know when my brother was killed, I had to take a day off school to go to the funeral. Then, I had to go back to school, on Monday, like nothing ever happened. And, it's like you wanna tell the whole world, like you should care. Why don't y'all care! Here y'all are with this easy life.*
>
> Yeah (with excitement, like she is feeling me). (Zora, interview, spring 2001)

There were distinct similarities between the savage murder of Zora's mother and of my brother, including how the media covered their killings and the police's handling of the two cases. We discussed those similarities along with our reactions and methods of coping with each. Then, we discussed how it was losing a mother and having to go on with life as usual.

> *My mom died when I was nine. And, that's the reason why I want to do this study. I can't be the only Black girl who going through all this shit, then have to get up and go to school on Monday morning like ain't nothing wrong. Was you close to your mother?*
>
> Yeah (sadly), I guess. But, I didn't really see her that much, because she was off doing her own thing, whatever. And, she was living with my sisters for a couple of months, and I would always go over my sisters' house on the weekend. Everybody say that I act just like her (laughing), like when I be talking and stuff on the phone. They say, you sound just like your mom. (Zora, interview, spring 2001)

Undoubtedly, the loss of her mother affected Zora at school regardless of the fact that they did not have a traditional strong mother–daughter relationship. Admittedly due to this unfortunate event, I was worried about Zora's commitment to school prior to this last interview. I was nervous, because I had learned from a concerned (or curious) classmate of Zora that her attendance had dropped significantly at school after her mother's death and that she had went through a noticeable personality change. Another student and I even came to the conclusion that Zora was pregnant. Upon reading this someone might think that our unsubstantiated conclusions are totally prejudicial and superficial. My presumption or paranoid thoughts derived from the assumption that when inner-city female students have a behavior or psychological change, other females, teachers, and mothers seem to automatically think, "Oh, God, she's pregnant." After study of the high school's copy of Zora's attendance record, I found that Zora had been absent from school and/or missed classes. I am ecstatic to report that Zora was not pregnant. As one might anticipate, her mother's death and the circumstances surrounding it had affected Zora's schooling experience. Mainly, she reported that she had trouble concentrating after the funeral and other family events.

Along with experiencing visible signs of depression, Zora missed over a week of school and reports that it was difficult trying to catch back up with her schoolwork. Telling her story of her struggles with her grades since March, I could sense her frustration through her body language as she whispered and repeated her words while rolling her eyes back in her head. It was as if she were talking to herself as she repeated, "I can't believe I got all "F"s." Zora blamed her mom (Melba) for letting her miss too many days of school. In addition to blaming her mother, she also blamed the school for not assisting her with her schoolwork once she returned back to school. Even though according to Zora folks at school did not assist with missed assignments, the school did attempt to provide support through their grief group. On the other hand, when I asked Zora if the group intervention was working, she responded:

> I just be sittin there, if they ask me a question, I be like I don't know. I didn't even know they had that group. Sometimes, I be thinking in my head that it ain't really happen. She still out there somewhere runnin around in the street, gon' pop up over our house, wanna eat sweets or something. It ain't took effect yet, even though I keep knowing in my head she ain't here (nervously). It just ain't getting there. I keep thinking, she still running around here somewhere. (Talking to herself) "Man, what's wrong with me (said with frustration)? She ain't here, what is you thinking she still here for!" (shouting with frustration). I'm like, yeah, I'm crazy. (Zora, interview, spring 2001)

Zora's comments prove that a specific intervention may work for one student but not for another. Remember that this same grief group worked to help Nicole cope with her (grand)father's death. The intensity of the trauma, the timing of it, and the individual affected by it may all affect the results that the intervention provides. Zora's comments also show that she is exhibiting signs of depression and anxiety as a result of her stress. There is no doubt that Zora was in the midst of coping with symptoms consistent with the early stages of surviving a tragic event. Because she was still in the beginning phase of coping, it was difficult to assess the significance of the support she received from the school.

However, it is easier to conclude that Zora's family may be adding to her stress. First, I have to assert that family is a broad and changing concept amongst individuals in the Black community. As rationalized earlier, the students were allowed to conceptualize family for themselves in our conversations. In most of the preceding dialogue, Zora exemplifies the construction and deconstruction of who is or what is family. Anyhow, from my point of view, the choices some of her family members make could potentially hinder her or be a source of support to her well-being. Like many other urban students, Zora does not look much to individuals in her community for support, but she does find hope in her family.

Have people in your community been trying to help you and your family?

Not really, only like family. My grandma, she was like, I ain't never really seen her. That was my mom's mom. I don't remember her. The only reason I do remember her is because when I was like one, we had moved from Chicago, so I was just meeting her like all over. I don't know none of these people. She was like real messed up. Our family, it's like it's a curse or something. Everybody in my family, like on my grandpa side, be going through the same stuff. All his kids was on drugs or is on drugs. I mean it's crazy. My grandma she doin' that stuff, my aunt, I'm like, man. My mom, she did, I don't know what she used to do, a little bit of everything. Well, somebody gon' have to break the curse, and they talking about my mom did. The curse ain't broke (angrily).

They talking about my mom broke the curse. I don't know, because "Y'all all still act the same." Still doing the same stuff, talking about "y'all gon' go to rehab," I ain't tryin' to hear that stuff. And, I be trying to tell other people, like when I see my friends or something, smoking (marijuana use) and all that kind of stuff, I be trying to tell them (refering to talking to them about trying drugs and later becoming addicted). But, they be like, "We ain't tryin' to hear that." How they gon' tell me? I'm like, "Y'all can start out doing little stuff, end up doing big stuff. Y'all gon' end up (pause) similar to what they is. I'm just trying to tell y'all, I don't wanna see y'all like that." They just think I'm crazy; I'm like whatever. (Zora, interview, spring 2001)

Overall, Zora presented conflicting feelings about her mother and how she died. For example, she detested the fact that her mother had so many children at forty. She also was angry that her mom was not taking care of any of her children, using drugs and alcohol, and was not very involved in trying to get her problems fixed. Maybe, like Zora, the most resilient students are better equipped at being able to observe, detach, and critically assess the negative behaviors of family members. Consequently, the resilient students' strategy is to abstain from the behavior or habits that were harmful to those around them.

Leadership and Resiliency

Undoubtedly, one of the most advantageous outcomes of conducting a longitudinal ethnography on educational resilience is that the human side of resilience is ultimately exposed. Educational resilience is defined as the likelihood of success in school and life, despite environmental adversities, as a result of early traits, conditions, and experiences (Haertel, Walberg, & Wang, 1994). Resilience refers to successful adaptation despite risk and adversity (Masten, 1994). Most theorists are likely to overlook or ignore the radicle of the construct of resilience as it relates to adolescents.

For example, resilience is defined as (1) the power or ability to return to the original form, position, etc., after being bent, compressed, stretched; elasticity (2) the ability to recover readily from illness, adversity, or the like; buoyancy. Hence, the term "resilience" is borrowed from the scientific observation of objects, raw materials, and animals and has been applied to the observation of human beings and social behavior. In the primal usage of the word, resilience is better applied to objects. From a Black feminist standpoint, after living through and recovering from a stressful or traumatic experience, the goal may not be to return to the original state, but to learn from experiences with stressors and to adopt a new state of consciousness.

A more recent definition of the term "resilience" by theorists encompasses the notion of an individual successfully adapting to stressful circumstances and conditions. But what happens when an individual moves beyond simply adapting (or modifying her original self) to fit into her social/physical environment? Instead, the individual makes meaningful observations of her environment and works to alter that which may be harmful to the self and others around her. Zora appeared to be this type of young woman.

When I was young, like Zora I wanted to be a psychiatrist. It is possible that young women like Zora and I chose our careers based on our experiences (in the same way that Nicole wanted to be a teacher). Maybe we wanted to "get into people's heads" (to use Zora's words) in hopes of figuring out the world around us.

So, you still want to be a nurse?

Uh, uh, a psychiatrist. I changed my mind, cuz I wanna get in people's minds. I been thinking about that ever since I got into high school. Thinkin…just wonderin…I be watching shows and stuff, when they be talking about psychiatrists and how be thinking fixing, like, them mentally challenged people. (Zora, interview, spring 2001)

I do believe that Zora wants or needs to have a deeper understanding of life and things in her environment. Her latest career choice may fulfill this need for her at the time of her mother's death and the irony and contradictions she witnessed in those affected by her mother's death. In relation to the processes of resilience, I believe that Zora still feels like there is hope in changing negative stressors and helping those who are affected by the stress and strains of everyday life.

Bluntly stated, Zora is a leader. And not only does Zora have a high locus of control, which guides her own decision making but she also likes to transfer her values on to others. As she articulated, "Others see something in me that they like" (Fieldnotes, 2001). Her observation is true, for others do seem to see something in Zora that they like. I have heard others talk about her kind and friendly personality, and I have also witnessed it for myself. As I wrote in my journal notes after our last interview,

> It is ironic that Zora feels she and her family are cursed, considering all the positive things about her. As we talk on the couch my fourteen-month-old son is hanging on her leg, and my overparanoid Chihuahua is sitting at her feet. They, too, are drawn to her spirit. It bothers me that she thinks she is cursed, because she is more likely to conclude that her life choices are beyond her control. I do hope that she finds the understanding she searches for, then she can learn that there are no curses, simply consequences. (Journal notes, spring 2001)

From her insight into her own life, her family, drug use among her peers, and school, I understand why Zora is a role model to others her age and younger. Not only do her peers see something in her that they like, but adults and teachers at school also observe Zora's tenacity. A key component of theorizing school resiliency as process is to look at how students come to their resilient status. Henry Giroux in *Pedagogy and the Politics of Hope* (1997) warns that "radical education theory has abandoned the language of possibility for the language of critique" (p. 120). In other words, Giroux points out that many theorists and researchers have failed to look at students' school experiences from a positive, strength-oriented lens. We have failed to forefront the possible good outcomes of a child's schooling experience. When theory is overly concerned with the "language of critique," warns Giroux, "schools, teachers, and students are written off as mere extensions of the logic of capital" (p. 120). It is no wonder that I had a difficult time finding research that would emphasize the importance of enhancing leadership qualities in African American female students.

Taking heed to Giroux's warning, I see the need to shift paradigms from critique to possibility to contemplate how the JROTC program has fostered resilience in Zora (as opposed to how JROTC may be (de)programming low-income students of color). Of course, her long-term involvement in the JROTC program alone lowers her risk of dropout, but how does it contribute to leadership skills?

I needed to know from Zora, what attracted her to JROTC, what kept her committed to the program. Mainly, Zora enjoyed the social and physical activities that were apart of the JROTC program. Remember, Zora was the type of student who needed to be active at school. She did not like to be confined and controlled in a classroom setting; thus, a program like JROTC kept her learning while moving and having fun. On the one hand, JROTC would be the perfect "disciplinary apparatus" (Foucault, 1984) for her in a school setting. Through strict physical and mental discipline, the young active Black female body is coerced into believing that her country has a genuine interest in her future and well-being; therefore, she, in turn, should have a genuine interest in protecting her country. In the meanwhile, she is promised and coerced by future monetary support, college funds, and perceived status that she may never encounter in the world that she knows now.

Yet, on the other hand, the JROTC program may have allowed Zora some control over her own body and environment. In her first year, Zora was a ranking officer in the program with responsibility over other students. After I attempted to explain to Zora that her role in JROTC was important, she explained that she had no idea that the JROTC staff would pick her as a leader. In fact, she thought that it was too early in her high school career to take on her leadership position. Her position is usually reserved for older students in the higher grades.

Why did they pick you?

They thought that I was a good leader or something, because I used to always try and practice and stuff, like for Color Guard.

So, do you think that you are a good leader?

I guess, I don't know (laughing). Other people think so. It's funny, how I be making friends with people who people don't even really like. I'm like, I don't know how I be making friends with people, who I know that other people ain't go be makin' friends with. I got a lot of friends like that. I'm like, "How do you hang around that person?" I'm like, maybe it's my personality. (Zora, interview, spring 2001)

As Zora further explained to me, she is dedicated to her work, which is why she has "rank." Maybe her own tenacity earned her that "rank," or quite possibly her "rank" cultivated her tenacity. Or, maybe it should not be an either/or question, and one should abandon the binaries in educational research. Finally, it can be argued that Zora possesses high educational aspirations, high self-esteem, and a high internal locus of control (subjectively speaking, of course), which all have been shown in child development research to foster resilience (Peng, 1994). It has also been shown that families, communities, and schools that provide leadership and decision-making opportunities for children foster resilience in students. In Zora's case, JROTC may be a strong factor in her character building, in turn, fostering educational resilience. More research is definitely needed on how programs or activities at school can help foster educational resilience in urban African American girls, like Zora.

Yssis' Story: Tough Skin

After taking a feminist studies class, I became interested in life histories and African folklores. Many of these stories were missing from my women's studies classes. In my quest for African knowledge, I learned about the Yssis, usually spelled Isis. Yssis was the most important goddess of ancient Africa, specifically, Egypt. She was also the sister/wife of the Egyptian god, Osiris, "Lord of the perfect Black," and the mother of Horus. As the African legend goes, after the murder and dismemberment of Osiris by his evil brother Seth, Yssis discovered the crime, recovered the pieces of the body of Osiris, and put them together again, restoring his existence and his power. According to the African story, Yssis admired truth and justice and made justice stronger than gold and silver (Welsing, 1991).

Tough Skin

When I went to the high school dean's office to retrieve Yssis' final attendance, grade, and behavioral reports, the deans referred to her as their "smart-bad girl." I nonchalantly corrected the deans and said, "Tough. Tough-smart girl." The deans only gave me a sour look and proceeded to print out a discipline report on Yssis that appeared to be a mile long. Her infractions included classroom disruptions, dress code violations, missed detentions, missed Saturday schools, etc. Actions taken against her included reprimands, letters sent home to parents, Saturday schools, detentions, and suspensions. Despite her high school disciplinary problems, Yssis was an above-average student.

Like most students, Yssis was not consistent throughout middle school but ended her middle school career with an approximate 3.0 grade point average on a 4.0 scale. High school only got better for Yssis, which is why her deans referred to her as their smart girl. At the end of her first year of high school, Yssis was ranked 50 out of 251 in her class, and had a cumulative grade point average of 3.25, better than a "B" average. By the end of her sophomore year, she was ranked in the top 15% of her class. Yssis had taken classes like geometry, Spanish, biology, chemistry, and world history. It definitely appears that Yssis was college bound.

In an effort to set up our first visit together, I had a difficult time contacting Yssis. Eventually, I found her mother at home. Her mother gave me their new phone number and informed me that her daughter was out of town visiting relatives but that Yssis would be back soon. By this time, an entire year had passed, and Yssis had already begun her first year of high school. However, luck was on my side, because at least I knew she had the same address. I had a phone number, I knew what school she was attending, and her mother seemed to be interested in my talking to Yssis about her school experiences. Yssis' mother, who prefers that I call her Beverly instead of Mrs. Montgomery, constantly boasts about her daughter's grades. Beverly has definitely had her trials and tribulations and her own share of stress and adversity in her life. Her struggles are written on her face and show in her physical demeanor. Although I know that she is in her early forties, at first glance she looks much older. Her looks are related to her health complications over the last few years, and her health complications are related to the challenges she has faced as a woman who has survived the temptations of urban life. Nevertheless, Beverly definitely is proud of her daughter Yssis, which is manifested in the fact that she does not hesitate to boast about Yssis grades. Beverly was the one who kept me posted on Yssis school performance, while Yssis was away on vacation.

In fact, Yssis was one of the students who liked to discuss the positive things about school. From early on, Yssis had a positive experience with school. She reflects on her experiences in the fourth grade:

> But, I remember…that's when I was like, really like trying to get into school more. Like, get my grades straight and stuff. I don't really remember all of it, but I remember that we used to always have fun in fourth grade. Recess is the favorite part of school, and stuff like that. I just couldn't wait for recess. But, I started getting gooder, better, grades. (Yssis, interview, fall 1999)

She was less critical about her peer group, teachers, and her own behavior than Nicole and Zora. It was interesting to me that Yssis was not very critical of her peers and teachers, considering that other students and the faculty at her school had described her as mean or "bad." After getting her version of the story, on why the deans in the high school office refer to her as their "bad-smart girl," I learned that Yssis has a temper. When Yssis does not agree with the reprimands or punishments taken against her for a demerit, she informed me that she gets upset and refutes the teacher. She stated that she believes the punishments for misconduct are sometimes inappropriate. I asked her if she had a lot of conflict with students at school, and she said, "If they don't mess with me, I don't mess with them."

I do not believe that Yssis is necessarily mean toward other students. I believe that she just wears an expression of toughness to avoid trouble. I believe that her reputed meanness is a protective facade against peer pressure or other negative influences at school. For example, it is difficult for a male student to approach you if he thinks that you do not have an approachable personality. Also, it is difficult for another student to draw you into the middle of conflict like "he say, she say," if he knows that you "don't play that." The Black child who is unwilling to stand up in her own defense is vulnerable to cultural and psychological alienation (Ward, 1996). Yssis has constructed her own psychological defenses that may be absent from the educational and resiliency literature.

Notwithstanding her perceived toughness and intimidating stature, Yssis was not the type of student who went out looking for trouble. Her philosophy was, "As long as they don't put their hands on me, I ain't thinkin' about them." Definitely Yssis may not be the traditional passive-good student that we read about in Fordham's (1996) or Foley's (1990) research, but her strategies seem to work in her particular setting. Fordham and Foley found that those students who conformed to formal and informal school social norms were the students who were more likely to be "high achieving." Yet, the fact that high school graduation is nearing for Yssis and that she is graduating at the top of her class highlights that Yssis' tough skin has served as a type of protective factor.

> I get along with the students, but it's a lot of fights at M. Like every day, it's like four fights. Sometimes it'll be like the same people. They'll like get suspended, then they'll come back and fight again. It's a lot of fights. It's like a lot of gossip going on around the school and stuff, but I don't even get involved in that, because I know they just trouble and stuff. (Yssis, interview, fall 1999)

Two important questions that Yssis' story raises are (a) Is "tough skin" a protective factor against negative influences in a student's social environment? (b) Is it possible for a student to succeed while challenging the unfairness or inconsistency in many urban school settings? As I have discovered, most of the current literature on school resiliency is based on conformity and ideal or traditional family living situations and is gender neutral. It fails to consider gender-specific protective factors, self-determination, and critical consciousness in students. For me, Yssis' story counters or deconstructs the traditional frameworks associated with school resiliency. For example, she is a girl, from a single-parent household and consistently defies authority, but she is also determined to become something better in life.

Self-determination is a major theme in the philosophy of independent Black institutions (Lee, 1992). Self-determination is the freedom to live as one chooses, to act or decide without consulting others. The idea that women, people of color, and/or folks from lower-income groups can control their own destiny is an oxymoron in our society. Therefore, it was not surprising that I could not find the idea of self-determination as a protective factor that fosters school resiliency in the resiliency literature. Key words that come close to self-determination in the resiliency literature are self-efficacy, hopefulness, and self-worth (Masten, 1994). Although self-determination may require all of these qualities, all the qualities will not necessarily result in self-determination.

Self-Determination

Yssis demonstrates a high level of self-determination. She displays such determination not only in her relationship with peers and school staff but also in the decisions she makes about her education. It is as if Yssis is determined to choose her life outcome regardless of the social barriers that are presented to her as a young female of color. From early on, Yssis and her family established a strong foundation to begin her educational career. For example, unlike most students in her school district, Yssis was able to attend one school, kindergarten through fourth grade, before she transitioned to middle school. Low mobility is a significant factor in school resilience, especially for African American families (Taylor, 1994). Even in the case of Yssis, mobility or a change in a family's living situation changes a child's perception. When I inquired about her family situation as a young child, Yssis reflected,

> That's when my older sister was.... We weren't living in the same house that we in now. We were living on Langley Street. It was just fun. We had everything. We had central air. We had a fence back then, we had like dogs and stuff. It was fun, because we used to go to church every day, church was like right across the street. (Yssis, interview, fall 1999)

Yssis' youthful determination may stem from the fact that she perceived that she had a good start in life. Unlike some of her peers, maybe Yssis had remembered a time when living was better or somewhat easier for the family and herself. It was apparent from our interview about her early childhood experiences that Yssis stayed involved in community organizations, which may have stimulated a connection to her neighborhood also.

> I was in 4H and stuff, and we went to the "Commonplace" for a while, down the street from my house. They did like tutoring there, summer programs.... They did everything there. We used to have fun there too. I went there, like, all through grade school and middle school too. I stop going there, like when I was in the eighth grade. (Yssis, interview, fall 1999)

As Yssis reminisced on her childhood activities, she spoke with a sense of eagerness, which insinuated life was a lot more active for her as a child. She also reflected on the roles that community organizations played in her schooling.

Do you think that being in like clubs, organizations, and stuff helped you out with school? Like tutoring and stuff?

Yeah (eagerly)! Like sometimes they'll be tutoring me, but then they'll like ask me to tutor like kids and that'll like get me a chance to see how it is to do stuff with younger kids and stuff. But, it helped me out a lot in school and stuff. They always said that I was too smart for tutoring, though. But, it helped me out a lot. Cause sometimes I didn't understand something, I could go ask one of the leaders, and they would help me out good. (Yssis, interview, fall 1999)

A major quality of resilient students is their ability to seek out those key resources at school or in their neighborhood that may serve as support systems (Masten, 1994). For example, Yssis is knowledgeable about the support systems available at school. As she explained to me, "They got before-school and after-school tutoring and stuff. And, you can go in anytime. They got study hall and stuff, and there's always somebody who can help you. It's always somebody there that if you don't understand something, they'll help you with it until you understand it." Obviously, Yssis has a high attachment to her school, which is evident in her knowledge of the resources available to her. However, an often-ignored quality of resilient urban students is agency. Wang and Gordon (1994) point out that in addition to providing supportive instruction, effective teachers foster resiliency by promoting self-responsibility for active learning. In Yssis' case, it appears that her teachers do assist and encourage her to take an active role in her learning.

Accordingly, self-determination does not imply that a student buffers adversity by her own efforts alone, but it does imply that she played an important role in her educational story. In other words, life did not just happen to Yssis; she is a main character in her life story. Furthermore, as articulated by Wang and Gordon, "when students become convinced that they are instrumental in their learning success, they work harder to overcome difficulties" (1994, p. 63). Yssis is cognizant of her role in her educational development as well as the important role that others play in her development.

Thus, self-determination as a factor in the process of fostering school resiliency includes being able to seek out needed resources while putting forth effort beyond the minimum requirement. In the following conversation, Yssis demonstrates how self-determination takes sacrifice and effort on the part of the individual student as well as requiring the support of others.

How can your family help you?

Well, I got a lot of smart people in my family, and like, if I just ask them something, they'll tell me, like if I'm having trouble like with some kind of math problem or something, they'll help me work it out or whatever. (Long pause) Cause this year, I took speech, and I was like having a lot of trouble with that, and my brother, he stayed up like all night with me, helping me prepare my speeches and stuff. And, I'm glad he did that. I probably would have got an "F" on that speech, because I didn't know what I was doing. (Yssis, interview, fall 1999)

Sites of Refuge and Struggle

In *Afrikan Mothers: Bearers of Culture, Makers of Social Change*, citing Francis Cress Welsing, Dove (1998) points out that the African American family as an institution under White supremacy is a survival unit. Further citing Welsing, she quotes, "The family is supposed to be a social institution that functions to support maximal development and protection of the young. However, under white supremacy, Blacks and other non-whites are not to be developed maximally; they are permitted to survive as functional inferiors, alienated from self and their own kind. The non-white survival unit is not permitted to defend itself or its young" (1998, p. 163). Using this statement, Dove analyzed African American single-parent families as both the site of oppression and resistance. In Yssis' case, her family has also served as a site of struggle and protection.

Yssis lived with her mother and an older brother; however, her immediate family is made up of her mother and two brothers and three sisters, and Yssis is the youngest child in the family. Yssis informed me that she has had an inconsistent relationship with her father since about the third grade. She was not very open to disclosing information about any family crisis, and certain things she simply let lie dormant in her memory.

Do you remember anything that was going on with your family between first and third grade?

Uh...uh (shaking her head no). I remember that's when my dad first went to prison. That's the only thing that I remember really. (Pause) A lot of times it was a lot of bad stuff going on at home. I don't really remember all that. (Yssis, interview, fall 1999)

After her dad went to prison the first time, prison became a revolving door for her father. Yssis admits that she has not been around him that much in her life. She also claims that her father's on again-off again incarceration did not affect her schooling. I think she was more concerned that it affected her emotionally at home than it did at school, but sometimes children do not understand that emotional stress in one social institution affects functioning in another. Yet her relationship with her father did cause some level of stress. When I asked Yssis if her father's absence affected school, she answered:

Not really, but sometimes.... Not really on school, but on different stuff, because I would like go into my room and cry and stuff, cuz my sister and brothers' dad would come over and stuff, cause my dad was never around, so.... (Yssis, interview, fall 1999)

In the school district where Yssis lives and where I researched, worked, and volunteered, it was not uncommon for students to have a parent or relative in prison. It was definitely a concern for teachers and staff at the schools, because we did notice that students brought a lot of their emotional baggage and stress into the classroom. Also, because the majority of the African American community in Haven is concentrated in a small area of the city, other students were usually aware of hardships that other families were facing. Other times it seemed teachers and other students only exacerbated the level of stress on the student by not being aware of the crisis the student was facing or simply not being empathetic of the child's situation. Because imprisonment of a relative was common in some schools, many people simply became apathetic. In most of these living situations, mothers or grandmothers were forced to take on the responsibility of childrearing. Thus, female caregivers also take on the primary responsibility of promoting positive social, emotional, and educational development.

Gender-specific support

Based on significant and long-term reliance on female caregivers, maybe urban girls learn to rely more with natural female role models at school and in their communities. For instance, Yssis did not appear to have as much tension with her teachers as Zora and Nicole did, until high school. She explained that her teachers "act different towards the Black people, then they act all nice to the White kids" (Yssis, interview, fall 1999).

It is interesting that Yssis, Nicole, and Zora attempt to avoid identifying their teachers as prejudiced or racist, but they do mention that their teachers treat White and Black students differently. Yssis even explained to me that she really does not know if having more Black teachers at her school would make her school any better. However, she said she would not mind having a Black teacher "just to see how it was." For Nicole, Yssis, and Zora, the racial makeup of the teacher was not as important as the perception of the teacher's level of fairness. Furthermore, the gender of an adult seemed to be more important to students than the race of a person. It may be due to witnessing the endurance and strengths of their female caregivers that many urban girls are more likely to seek out female-centered mentoring relationships and programs.

Yssis, like Zora and Nicole, also named her mother as the person who had encouraged her most to do well in school. Their identifying their mothers as their main source of support is consistent with other studies, which found African American girls are more likely to name a female caregiver as their main source of support and inspiration (O'Connor, 1997; Dove, 1998; Ward, 1996;

Cauce et al., 1996). On the other hand, other females in Yssis' community have also supported her educational accomplishments. She told me about a program she was involved in, in the fifth grade with her cousin.

> I was like in girls' club and stuff, with my cousin. We were like best cousins, best friends at that time. It was like, we would like read every Wednesday or something like that and we would go there and do all kinds of activities, make lists, and make other stuff. They had 4H club there too. (Yssis, interview, fall 1999)

This quote is significant for two reasons. One reason Yssis' words are important is because she found it important that she participated in a club exclusively for girls. She enjoyed the gender-specific program that focused on the educational and socio-emotional needs of girls. Also, the quote is important, because it gives a synopsis of Yssis' level of intimacy with her female relatives and peers. The fact that she remembers her girls' club experience in relationship to her bond with her cousin reveals how important family and peers are to her involvement in community organizations.

Her statements also confirm that most women and girls develop "in-relationship" or what is called social individuality. Social individuality derives from women's efforts to form resistance to oppression, such as sexism, classism, or racism (Fine, McCormick, & Pastor, 1996). In Yssis' case, her cousin's presence in the group assisted in her development of toughness. As she told me, her cousin was a source of protection from more aggressive girls or possible enemies. Obviously, her cousin's presence assisted Yssis in maintaining her tough standoffish persona.

Furthermore, maybe because Yssis started schooling with consistency and stability, she learned to appreciate consistency and familiarity by the fifth grade. She reported feeling more comfortable when she was allowed to spend more time with one (female) teacher. For example, in most middle schools, students are required to switch classes throughout the day. Yssis preferred spending time with one teacher for a given period of time. It allowed her to establish relationships with the teacher. In fact her grades improved as her relationship was allowed to grow with her female sixth grade teacher, she reported. Unlike other students, more resilient African American girls may have had the opportunity to form more intimate and long-term relationships with their teachers. Even more, maybe resilient students, like Yssis, Nicole, and Zora, feel more comfortable with female teachers, because they are used to developing "in-relationship" to other women.

Moreover, Yssis grew up in a family in which she witnessed her mother struggle as a single parent, and she attends a high school that has one of the highest teenage pregnancy rates. Consequently, she is very cognizant of her needs as an African American female. For example, not only did Yssis talk to me about her personal experience with puberty and the weight gain that sometimes accompanies it, but she also talked to me about the unwanted attention she was beginning to receive from boys. Like Zora and Nicole, she had a justified fear that getting involved with boys would impede her educational progress.

> And like…. When we first went there, they used to tell us like how older boys were going to try and talk to you and stuff (as you try to "sweet talk" you or talk you into a date), but don't fall into that trap, just focus on your schoolwork. And, I really like listen to that, because it's a lot of older dudes and they'll like, "Don't do your homework; come over here with us" (imitating the older boys talking to the girls). No! (Yssis, interview, fall 1999)

It appears that in Yssis' mind, like those of Zora and Nicole, members of the opposite sex threaten to block her progress of being the perfect student. Yssis admits also that she holds on to the words and advice of others who have warned her against getting involved with boys too early. Throughout the history of female development, boys have always been made out to be the enemy; older adults may be handing down practical advice in the setting where Yssis goes to school and lives. In the year that I began the research for this book, the Haven City/County Health Department reported that 16% of total births in Haven were to women nineteen years old or younger. During that same period, Haven ranked in the top-ten cities with the most residents living with HIV/AIDS. Yssis and other females had developed a practical method of avoiding putting themselves at risk for school failure.

However, supportive adults in Yssis' life do not stop at telling her what not to do. No, her adult mentors also inform her of what is important to do for success in school, like working hard to get good grades and not getting involved with boys. Furthermore, they reward her for her school accomplishments. Teachers reward her with good grades, but they also get her involved in challenging academic activities, like "Scholar's Cup" (an academic club that drills students on their knowledge in various subjects), and gives her praise and attention. Her family also gives her rewards (e.g., money and praise) and offers her the help that she needs after school hours (e.g., extra help with homework after school). Also, Yssis, like the other girls, found additional support outside of her immediate family.

> *Umm…. Do you have any mentors or role models?*

> I had a mentor, but she stop being my mentor in the eighth grade, she work at the Urban League too, that's how I got involved with them programs I was telling you about at the Urban League. But, every now and then, I'll see her and she'll ask me how I been doing, and about my grades and stuff, and she tell me if I need anything just come by her office or come by her house. (Yssis, interview, fall 1999)

Obviously, Yssis drives off of positive reinforcement from the adults in her life. She also has adults in her life who not only offer advice but also participate in hands-on activities with her like helping her with homework or getting her involved in organizations. Yssis' educational resilience may be fostered, because she does have an adult female mentor located in the community who also tracks her school performance. African American female adolescents who seek out positive relationships with other adults in their communities (other than parents) are more competent, because these relationships foster attachment, loyalty to parents and community, and independence (Cauce et al., 1996). Yssis' mentor may be significant in fostering resiliency, because (1) she connects Yssis to useful community programs, (2) is concerned with her school progress, (3) encourages Yssis to take initiative in seeking her out, and (4) appears to be easily accessible to Yssis.

Urban educators can learn from this very important symbolic relationship between Yssis and her mentor. Even though mentoring relationships have been shown to foster resilience, "muse" relationships prove to be more effective for African American female students. Mentoring relationships are more future oriented, focusing on who the girl is becoming, whereas a muse relationship is more reciprocal because the adult female serves to bring out the inner resources, potentials, and strengths of the girl (Sullivan, 1996). Two research studies found that young women of color and those who live in low-income families are more likely to benefit from and to seek out muses (Sullivan, 1996) and natural mentors (Davis & Rhodes, 1996) relationships. These types of mentoring relationships emerge from students' own social support systems like mothers, aunts, older siblings, and/or "other" mothers.

What is even more interesting is that Yssis named her sister, not her community mentor, as her role model.

> I really wanna be like my older sister, cause she like really like influence me to do stuff. And, she like work for the Red Cross, she a phlebotomist. I like wanna be like better than her, because she had like had a lot of problems with her boyfriend and stuff. I wanna kinda be like her, but better than her. Better than she was. She was a good role model. (Yssis, interview, fall 1999)

In muse relationships, students are more likely to be informed of the adult role models' accomplishments and faults (Sullivan, 1996). Thus, Yssis is able to say that she looks up to her sister while at the same time wanting to avoid some of the mistakes that her sister has made as a woman. As Yssis is knowledgeable of what it takes to get where her sister is and understands what to avoid along the way, she believes that she can one day have a better outcome than her older sibling.

Toward a Critical Consciousness

The manner in which I would like to consider self-determination (or tough skin) as a protective factor in the process of resiliency means that a student may be required to be decisive, exclusionary, and discriminatory. These are terms not traditionally associated with women. And they definitely are not words associated with the "good" student. Nonetheless, being very conscious and selective of who or what she associates with has worked for Yssis. In the beginning, for example, Yssis thought twice about meeting with me for this book, for she thought that it might take up too much of her time. In addition to the fact that she was not afraid to articulate her concern to me, it shows that she possesses a critical consciousness that serves as a protective factor. Yssis has made other critical choices in her educational development.

First, Yssis had to be conscious of the stressors present in her life in order to determine what she needed to do to buffer negative influences in her family, at school, and in her neighborhood. In the fourth grade Yssis was first confronted with peer pressure to do the opposite of what she needed to do to succeed in school. "All through school I made like straight "A"s. But, in the fourth, I started like slacken, because I was trying to be like all my friends and stuff," Yssis explained to me. She identified the problem and determined to avoid allowing others to prevent her from doing well in school. Yssis, like the other girls, often described the negative aspects of her immediate neighborhood, and how it lacked stimulation; thus, support for youth.

From my observations, I know that Yssis is conscious of the role that older adults play in the neighborhood as possible role models. She is also aware that a neighborhood should provide age-appropriate activities for its youth that may keep them out of trouble. Unfortunately, none of the girls have been able to find a strong support group amongst their peer group. Even more important, all the girls are conscious of the negative influences in their neighborhoods and try to avoid the neighborhood altogether by spending more time at school, in community organizations, and with their families. In conversation, Yssis describes to me the role that the school played in her achievement as opposed to her immediate neighborhood.

Do you think that your neighborhood and/or school have had a positive effect on you?

Yeah, it had a positive effect, because like, not really the neighborhood, but the school, they don't want you like talking negative, "You can't do this or you can't do that" (imitating negative talk). They want you to always think that you can do it, then they like, "Well, if you think that you can do it, then you can do it" (imitating positive talk from people at school). The neighborhood it ain't really like no.... You'll be like in a neighborhood, it's an older person will tell you like "You could be this or you could be that," but it ain't people like that around my neighborhood. (Yssis, interview, fall 1999)

Yssis is really adept at listening to positive reinforcement from those at school and in her family. In addition, her story informs us that there is a need for more positive role models in inner-city neighborhoods. As Wilson (1996) points out, the high mobility of successful African Americans into suburban areas has left many urban Black youth with very few accessible role models outside of their homes. With the lack of role models in the neighborhood, Yssis was determined to be an effective student for herself and her family. A critical consciousness is necessary to take on this level of responsibility.

For Yssis and the other students, one approach to measuring her own level of commitment to the responsibility of academic achievement was via grade reports. Yssis, Zora, and Nicole consistently stressed over tests, homework assignments, and grade reports. Yssis was very self-critical and conscious of her performance in a class as is evident when she reflects on her fourth-grade school year.

> *Okay, tell me what you remember most about fourth grade at that time, like your teachers, principal, your friends.*

> I remember my teacher. That was my favorite teacher in the fourth grade, and I was like sad when I had to leave, because I had to go to a different school. But, I remember... that's when I was like, really like trying to get into school more. Like, get my grades straight and stuff. I don't really remember all of it, but I remember that we used to always have fun in fourth grade. Recess is the favorite part of school, and stuff like that. I just couldn't wait for recess. But, I started getting gooder, better, grades. (Yssis, interview, fall 1999)

Maybe more resilient students like Yssis are more conscious of their student status and what it takes to get higher grades, and their role in deciding their future. As Yssis once told me, "It doesn't matter if a teacher doesn't like me. In the end, a bad grade only hurts me." She appears to always be conscious of her own presence or state of being, as in the preceding example when she makes a conscious effort to correct her own bad grammar, from "gooder" to "better" and when early in her education she made the conscious decision to improve her grades.

For many students, however, school is not fun anymore once students' sole focus is on measured performances and outcomes. The stress may cause even the most resilient students to become at risk of physically or psychologically withdrawing from school. By the seventh grade, Yssis had begun to experience the pressure of doing well, based on standardized tests and final grades.

> In seventh grade, that's when it started like getting harder (laugh). I was still making good grades then, but I had to work harder. I wasn't having fun that much, because I was always trying to study to get my grades up. Then eighth grade came and it was still

hard, because we had to take all those test and stuff. And, I was kind of scared cause I thought that I wasn't gon' like pass them and couldn't go to high school. (Yssis, interview, fall 1999)

It is possible that Yssis's and the other girls' focus actually does extend beyond immediate classes and tests and is more future oriented. They may be more focused on how the present affects future outcomes such as success in high school and later in college. Furthermore, it appears Yssis was conscious of what was needed to pass the tests and go onto the next grade, but she was also conscious of what she needed to do herself to pass the test. She made a conscious decision to study harder, to bring her grades up, and pass the state examinations. Needless to say, Yssis was ecstatic to discover that she passed the examinations and was promoted to the ninth grade. I have observed in classrooms in which teachers and staff have tried to motivate urban students to pass the annual standardized tests with superficial tactics, but they usually had little success. Maybe urban educators can learn how to motive students based on Yssis' story of resilience and motivating factors.

What keeps Yssis focused on her long-term goal to attend college and do something better in life? She is very conscious of what it takes to reach her educational goals. For instance, as she told me, her school is boring and has strict rules; however, she does not "wanna keep transferring to different high schools and stuff" (Interview I, p. 8). Somehow Yssis understands the importance of staying at one school and the route that some students take when school gets boring. As mentioned before, Yssis consciously internalizes the advice and experiences of others. It may be that she has learned to view what worked for others of her age and what did not. For example, even though Yssis has named members of her family, like her mother, as her main source of support, she also does not hesitate to critique their actions and behaviors that may impede on her goals.

What are some of your goals?

Ummm.... (short pause) To just graduate. I'm just trying to graduate, make something out of my life, because a lot of people in my family, they just like nothing. Just drink beer every day and stuff. And, I don't want to end up like them. I want to end up a better person, so I can do something with my life. (Yssis, interview, fall 1999)

It is interesting how Yssis uses her family as a reference point for how she is going to get to where she wants to go in life but also where she is *not* going to go in life. Maybe the most resilient students are able to recognize the strengths and limitations of their family members as sources of support. Maybe they are able to recognize what is holding those family members back.

Yssis' story also demonstrates further the complexities and contradictions that are raised in the process of constructing resiliency as the complexities and contradictions are witnessed in her statements here:

In your opinion, how do you think that your community, your neighborhood, could help you with your education?

I don't know.... Well, they do got a lot of programs and stuff around, but all the commotion around the neighborhood.... I think that we should move somewhere, like away from all this drama (slang for noise and commotion) and stuff, because it's a lot of drama around our house. People fighting everyday, arguing, saying stuff that kids don't even need to hear (nervous laughter). Kids be all around it just looking at it, they cussing and stuff, talking all this.... But, it is a lot of programs around the neighborhood that'll help you with your school and stuff. If you need to just talk, somebody always there to talk to you. (Yssis, interview, fall 1999)

At first, it appears that Yssis has given up on her community as a source of support. It is not that she has given up on her community, instead she has more or less given up on her immediate neighborhood. Yssis is very conscious of the lack of resiliency portrayed by individuals in her community. Thus, she has made a conscious decision not to be actively involved in her immediate neighborhood. On the other hand, she has not abandoned the resources that are available to her and other students. In fact, Yssis is probably more knowledgeable about the programs that support school achievement than other students in the neighborhood. Moreover, she may have been more motivated and had the courage to access those programs.

Tough Skin

In painting the portrait of Yssis as having a "tough skin" or at the least having a strong will, my intentions are not to perpetuate the Black "superwoman" image that is so prevalent in much of (White) feminist literature. Moreover, in the same manner that it is critical to resist signifying the Black family as the perpetrator of success or failure, it is just as critical to avoid exaggerating the tenacity of urban girls. Images in the visual media of urban girls are these lip-smacking, head-rolling, fast-talking, young dancing sisters, who confront hardship by being the loudest talker or the most agile dancer. Some feminist scholars are not too much more creative, they simply have the task of utilizing "validated" sources to back up their images of Black women. In feminist analysis, Black women who are asexual, hard workers, and the most spiritual are the ones who prevail.

The problem with the Jezebel urban girl and the "superwoman" mammy image of Black women is that African American women are forced into tight monolithic categories. Consequently, the dichotomized images of African

American women and girls present us with stoical or reactionary subjects, both of which are more applicable to robots than human beings. In an analysis on Black urban girls and school resiliency, it is crucial not to see resiliency as superhuman. When researchers see resiliency in this fashion, we fail to look at human agency as a resource. The risk we take is in looking at educational resiliency and school persistence as something mystical and supernatural.

What is unique and more vital to Yssis' stories is that even though she has received scratches and bruises along the way, she has also given bumps and bruises. Yssis is an outlier at school and in the educational research. In educational research those students who have positive rapport with adults in the school building, and with members of their peer group at school are more likely to be successful. Yssis, on the other hand, chooses not to have friends of either sex. Not only is she admittedly standoffish, she has also been described as an intimidator. Even more important to emphasize is the fact that the authority figures in Yssis' high school early on labeled her as a "bad" student. Yssis' social characteristics defy educational norms and ideas of the "perfect" female student: She has not given up on schooling, nor is she resisting schooling or yielding to the desires of boorish authority figures.

In sum, Yssis is a tough and determined young woman. She is not the type to let negative people discourage her from accessing the resources she needs to succeed in school. Also, she has been very adept at identifying and combining her resources at home, school, and in the neighborhood. For Yssis family is important, but community organizations are just as important. She is wise enough to know what works and what does not work to her advantage as a young woman who strives for excellence. At the conclusion of our last meeting together Yssis sums up how educational resiliency has played out in her schooling experiences.

> *Well, that's it. Anything else that you want to tell me, that you want to add. Your family, community, school…. How all of that works together?*

> Well, I was really influenced to get in the programs in the community, because I see my like older brothers and sisters and stuff getting in it. They was like always in the programs, so I always wanted to be in them too. So, when I joined it like, we had our whole family in the program, and we was like…that's when our whole family started making like good grades and stuff, cause some people in my family they like really having trouble in school, and they would drop out like in the eighth grade and stuff. When they went to the programs, they stayed in school, but I had a lot of people in my family drop out and I just don't wanna end up like them. (Yssis, interview, fall 1999)

For Yssis, family involvement in her education is important to her own engagement in school. Finally, her family is an inconsistent guiding light. She models their "good" behaviors and critiques their "bad" behaviors. In other words, she learns from their mistakes by using them as a reference point of what not to do and what not to become. More importantly, they seem to encourage and welcome her constructive criticism by pushing her to "become better than" them. Also, after Yssis learned about the origins of her name, she has researched more about the spiritual and political origins of her name. I believe that knowing the meaning behind her name has motivated her to live up to its spirit. Urban educators and teacher education programs can learn much from Yssis, Nicole, and Zora's spirit-filled stories of resiliency.

Chapter Five

Resiliency in Urban Classrooms

In this book, I have studied educational resilience by measuring and observing school persistence, and the strategies the girls' themselves had to employ to "make it" in school. In chapter one, I present the problem of current research on African American girls and urban education that tends to focus on pathology. Chapter two focuses on the current research on resiliency and the state of urban education and looks at how researchers can begin to include African American female students into current discussions of resiliency. Then, chapter 3 introduces readers to the social, economic, and political context in which the participants are experiencing schooling. Last, in chapter four, we meet Nicole, Zora, and Yssis. Their stories of agency help us begin to understand the elongated and sometimes ambiguous process of resilience. As mentioned earlier, initially five African American female students actively participated in the ethnography. Although five were interviewed at the beginning of the study, only three students remained in school from their eighth-grade school year to the end of the sophomore year. The stories of these three most educationally resilient students were presented in chapter four. I want to conclude this study on educational resilience with Terry's story.

Terry's Story

I saw Terry a few weeks ago as I was wrapping up the last few chapters of the book. We both were shopping at one of those major chain stores, where shoppers usually come in needing only a few basic household items but tend to end up purchasing more things than needed after being enticed by the bright colors and low prices. Then, it is only after we have gotten past the checkout cashier that we realize that we have extended our budget and allotted time in the store.

When I ran into Terry, I, too, wanted to be enticed by the glitz and glitter of the store while I stole time away from the writing of this book. In fact, I guess I was so infatuated by my unplanned shopping spree that I completely overlooked Terry, for she was the one who walked up to me just as I was reaching to grab my shopping cart and said, "Hi, Venus. Do you remember me—Terry?" Although I answered right away, "Of course, I remember you, Terry!" I was taken aback for a moment that an eighteen-year-old girl, even though I had not seen her in two years, would think that she was not worth remembering. I believe my quick response actually served to preserve or strengthen what little self-esteem she may have had left.

I was awestruck at Terry's appearance. The other girls in the study had blossomed into womanhood. They grew taller, gained weight, with spreading hips and thighs, and became more fixated on personal appearances. From my perspective, in Terry's case, her growth had become stagnate. Yes, she had gotten a little taller, but in her brown flower-patterned skirt, she appeared bone-thin. She also was wearing a black trendy scarf, neatly wrapped around her head, which seemed to only accent her ashy dark-complexioned face.

The new Terry standing next to my shopping cart in the midst of bright lights and bargain prices was a complete contrast to the old Terry I met, as a fifteen-year-old eighth grader. That Terry, with her pampered rich black complexion, was energetic and looked forward to beginning and completing high school. When I first met Terry, I remember thinking, "I hope no one takes advantage of her fun-seeking and risk-taking spirit." These thoughts resonated, because Terry used to boast about police raids and the violence that took place in her own home or her neighbors'. Even though the young woman standing in front of me wore a smile on her face, she did not appear to be very well taken care of, physically or emotionally.

Then again, in retrospect, I had to wonder if Terry had ever been taken care of, at home or at school. During my initial contact with Terry, I was amazed by the fact that Terry had lived in a house of four generations of African American women. Although Terry's mother seemed to move in and out of the house, Terry lived in a subsidized housing complex with her maternal great grandmother, maternal grandmother, and mother, along with other siblings and cousins. Her living situation made me reflect on and revere the resourcefulness of African American women. Yet, I still had to note that by definition, Terry could be categorized as a homeless student. Within social services, a homeless student is one whose family (or legal guardian) is currently without a dwelling of their own and/or a child who has not had a permanent mailing address within a given period of time (i.e., students who have moved twice or more within the last six months).

For example, Terry's legal guardian was her mother, but Terry lived on and off in her grandmother's home. Terry reported that she could not get along with her mother's live-in boyfriend; thus, she moved out of their house and into her grandmother's home. Furthermore, during the three years of the study, Terry lived in at least four different locations. In fact, by the end of the second year of the study (as a freshman), neither her grandparents nor I were able to locate Terry. Before she had become "lost data," I had learned that Terry had left school, as a first-semester freshman. On our last visit together her mother asked me to talk to Terry about getting back into school, when she didn't return following a suspension.

Even though her high school's administrative records had her listed as a "no show," members of her family informed me that Terry had started school at the local high school. They reported that Terry had been unfairly singled out and consistently harassed by authority figures at her school. According to one cousin Terry had left school after her high school dean accused her and the rest of the students of "smoking up their books that his tax dollars had paid for" instead of using them to study. It was the same cousin who also assured me that I would not be able to talk to Terry if she thought that I was going to attempt to talk her into going back to school. Needless to say, I never was able to track down Terry again to learn of her educational experiences. Thus, I never heard Terry's side of the story of why she decided to leave school.

Nonetheless, after hearing and witnessing small portions of the whole story, and meeting Terry for the first time of the beginning of her adult life, I had concluded that someone had neglected Terry's needs at some point during her educational career. In less than a minute into our brief encounter, Terry debriefed me on the highlights of her experiences over the last two years. "I had a little girl. Her name is Ranesha; she's one," boasted Terry. I congratulated the proud new mother on her baby girl and told her that I would love to meet Ranesha one day. Now Terry's daughter is growing up with five generations of African American women. Maybe she will have a more resilient start than Terry. As Terry disappeared into the overcrowded aisles, my mind gravitated back to the writing of this book.

Theorizing Educational Resilience

Questions about the "true" meaning of resiliency actively dominated my thoughts on the interpretation of resiliency. Why had I initially contemplated leaving Terry's story out of the pages of the book? Why do I choose to privilege some educational stories over others? What is my responsibility to the girls and their families in the writing of this book? Also, how do I report the pleasant along with the not-so-pleasant stories? How do I discuss individual agency alongside self-destructive behavior? How do I capture a slice of these young women's lives without exaggerating strengths and ignoring deficits? How do I acknowledge my own racist, sexist, and classist assumptions about schooling in America's low-income communities? In other words, how do I shift paradigms to reconstruct a concept that has been founded on White-Eurocentric, middle-class, and male ideologies of success?

There is little doubt that I may view resilience differently from most scholars and researchers. From a White male Eurocentric middle-class paradigm, resilience is not usually associated with women, workers, or people of color. Unlike many researchers, I am capable of witnessing resilience in a teenage mother who decides to leave school and seek out paid labor with the hopes of providing adequate childcare for her child. I am also able to witness resiliency in a group of women who live together under one roof in order to combine their resources. I am also able to view the long-term benefits of sticking with a hostile learning environment in hopes of improving one's life chances. From the time that I began to write this book, I have argued that I am observing and theorizing from a unique standpoint, which allows me the opportunity to view resiliency in its various states. Furthermore, I have argued that my positioning also allows me to understand the gender- and cultural-specific forms of resilience.

While not denying that the study of resilience is open to subjective interpretation (historically by White middle-class men), I do argue also that it is necessary to operatively narrow resilience for the study of African American female students. Other studies have looked at the resourcefulness of the Black family, the supports available to teenage mothers, and the strategies students use to survive a hostile school environment (Stack, 1974; King, 1995, Valenzuela, 1999; Foley, 1990; Fine, 1991; Pillow, 2000; Roberts, 1997; Guy-Sheftall, 1995; Dehyle, 1995). However, very few studies have focused on African American female students and educational resilience and those support systems that foster school resiliency. Therefore, for the sake of contributing to this small body of literature, I chose to narrow resilience down to its application to the school environment. I consciously made the decision to include those students who were educationally resilient, measured by school persistence, in the main body of this book. My intention in measuring resilience in this way is not to privilege some survival stories over others but to focus on alternative stories that have been sacrificed in past educational research to confront more pressuring issues like equal educational opportunities for adolescent mothers.

Situating Resilience

In congruence with postmodern opposition to metanarratives, I argue that resilience is gender and cultural specific as well as contextually bound. In the case of the young women who participated in this study, both the interaction of race, class, and gender and the historical, cultural, economic, social, and political conditions in which they live have affected how they experience schooling. Accordingly, the process of resiliency must also unfold within and as a result of the "space" in which they live and are educated. Thus, the process of resiliency that they experience is linked to their specific circumstances.

From the historical analysis portion of the ethnography, we learn about the sociocultural influences on the students' education. In the telling of their educational and life experiences, we witness some of the stressors that the students have encountered in their lives that have had a direct or indirect impact on their schooling. More importantly, we also learn of the support systems available to the most resilient students that buffer adversity and foster educational resilience. Once the relationship between stressors and systems of support is established and understood, we can begin to examine the unique process of resiliency that African American female students undertake. Figure 1 demonstrates the relationship between stressors and the supports that African American female students relied upon in this study. It also shows how as a result of the adversity encountered and the support systems available to students, they developed specific qualities that appeared to foster resilience. Those same resilient qualities have the potential of causing more stress on the student as well as reinforcing the goals and outcomes of their support systems.

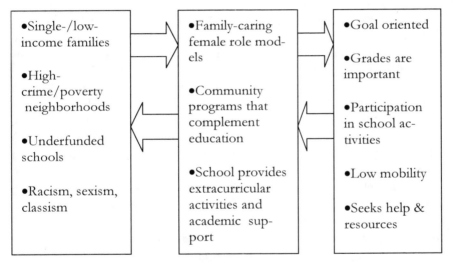

Figure 1. The impact of context on educational experiences: The bidirectional flow of stressors, supports, and qualities of resilience.

Again, all the students in the study live in low-income and working-class neighborhoods. They also attend one of the more high-risk schools, which is identified as such by its high dropout rate, high mobility rate, and the number of low-income students who attend the school. I found that the students do not dichotomize or order the significance of their stressors. Most of the stressors that the students experience occur at the intersection of their race, class, and gender. Consequently, these stressors have affected the young women's educational experiences. For example, four of the five students in the study experienced some kind of medical problem that impeded the schooling process.

Nicole reported that she was hospitalized for pneumonia and, as a result, required home schooling for the first three years of schooling. She also reported that she was diagnosed as having attention deficit hyperactivity disorder prior to entering middle school. Nicole and her mother were required to integrate their resources. In her case, the family, community, and school came together to help Nicole achieve academically.

Likewise, Zora reports that teachers thought she had a learning disability, because she had refused to talk at school for a period of time. Even though Terry (and the other non-educationally resilient student) was not considered "educationally" resilient Terry experienced an early pregnancy that affected her educational experience. Obviously, we cannot determine if a student's environment, income status, or biology caused any of her health conditions. However, other research has found a relationship between poverty and health problems and student deficits at school (Canino & Spurlock, 1994). Zora eventually thrived, despite the circumstances that may have caused her speech delays, but Terry did not have the support that was necessary to buffer adversity. On the other hand, all the resilient students were required to draw from family, community, and school support.

Other stressors that students have encountered are racism and classism in the larger community, police or government intervention in family affairs, violence and drug trafficking in their neighborhoods, hostile school environments, etc. Many of these factors have not only affected their individual (micro-level) school experiences but have managed to affect them on a broader (macro-) level. For example, the students in this study were affected by teacher shortages, and were less likely to have an African American female as a teacher. They were more likely to be educated by bitter White women, who found themselves with low pay, few resources, and teaching in an environment that was "culturally" different from their own. I can only presume that these were the "prejudiced" teachers whom the students described in their life stories. The most resilient students located resources that countered prejudicial behavior. For instance, Nicole found an African American teacher in her school building whom she felt understood her emotional needs. Yssis, for example, who had more trouble finding solace in the school building, located a mentor through a community organization. Zora, on the other hand, found solace in her own personality, by helping more troubled students.

To add stress, students also found themselves being restricted by policies that dictated what they learned, how they dressed, and how they behaved. For example, all the girls in the study complained of school policies that appeared to allude to the sexual messages in their styles of dress (e.g., girls were not permitted to wear sleeveless blouses or tank tops). Most of the girls alleged the racist and sexist policies serve to try to prevent sexual molestation or rape by controlling young women's behaviors. These policies target the potential victims' behaviors, and they assume there is going to be a victim. As we hear from the girls, many of the policies at their schools were put into place because the larger community views them as uncivilized heathens who need to be contained. Even more, they assume that the African American girls in the school building are Jezebels, who tempt potential rapists/victims.

Fortunately, the most resilient students in the study are conscious of how the images held by members of the larger community and society affect the rules and discipline policies of their local schools. What is even more interesting is that the most resilient students attempt to guard against "tainting" their own images. They strive to maintain the "good girl/good student" image by avoiding sexual relationships with boys and participating in the labeling of "those girls" who fit the "loose girl/bad girl/bad student" stereotype. These gender-specific resilient strategies have worked to the advantage of the resilient students.

In sum, all this stress bottled up in the students from the family, community, and school only causes more stress among the students. Therefore, at many times, it was even difficult for students to turn to their peer group for support. Only one of the three students expressed a high attachment to other students attending her high school (Zora). None reported spending time with peers in their immediate neighborhoods. In the case of the resilient young women, community organizations and extracurricular activities at school at least provided a controlled environment for the opportunity to foster peer relationships. All the girls had participated in community and school student groups. Anyhow, I argue that the stressors that the young women experienced throughout their educational career are related to their race, class, and gender and where they live and attend school. I also argue that these gender- and cultural-specific stressors required the most resilient students to draw on gender- and cultural-specific resiliency-fostering supports.

Resilience and African American Female Students

After reading the stories of the most resilient students, we are able to begin to answer the following questions: Who are the students who are more likely to stay in school? What factors contribute to students staying in school? When are the profiled African American female students at their most resilient? What are the historical, economic, and political conditions that affect their schooling process? And how do the most resilient African American female students cope with, resist, or buffer adversity?

I found that the most resilient students were those young women who received support from their family, community, and schools simultaneously. Because the young women's stressors could not be dichotomized, neither could their support systems. It appears that those families and students who were more adept at blurring the boundaries between family, community, and school were the most resilient. The more a student was able to utilize resources at home and in the community, the more likely she was to stay psychologically (measured by school involvement in extracurricular activities) and physically (measured by school attendance) attached to the school building. Community resources that assisted in educational development usually included after-school programs like tutoring, mentoring, and group-related activities. In most cases, community participation usually depended on its relevance to school. Participation in religious services was the exception. Most students attended church because they had family members who attended the church, and they felt it was the "right thing to do." Church appeared to be very important to all three resilient students.

Educational resilience often was also reinforced at the community level by programs that offered the young women temporary job opportunities during the summer or after school. Even in the community work programs, the most resilient students still preferred job assignments that focused on education or learning in some capacity (e.g., tutoring younger students or providing child-care). Most of the educationally resilient students associated internships or student employment programs with learning opportunities. For example, Nicole tutored children because she thought that it gave her the chance to see what it would be like to be a teacher who cared. Yssis made a decision to continue working at her summer job with children because it offered a college scholarship incentive to long-term employees. In this research study, I also categorized community resources, as those programs that offered some type of direct or indirect support to the student's family. For example, Nicole had received tutoring services in her home, which were funded by DCFS.

It is important to restate that in some cases lines were blurred between stressors and resources. For example, Zora and Nicole both received intervention services through DCFS, which may be categorized as potential stressors or distractions to a student's education and development. Postmodern tenets remind us that we must avoid binary thinking that would force us to order stressors and buffers, because the two may actually be working bidirectionally. Hence, the bidirectional flow of the arrows in figure 1. For example, looking at that particular analysis on resilience, I found that all the resilient students were very concerned with their grades. The student's overconcern with grades may actually produce more stress and strain in her life. In the same manner, school activities and academic curriculums (a support system), like JROTC, are supported by and reinforce inequality and subjugation (an initial stressor) is eventually accessed by the student who displays resilient qualities to support school achievement. Looking at stressors, support systems, and individual agency simultaneously reminds us that resiliency-fostering factors are dynamic in nature. In this particular study, the resilient African American female students and their families utilized community resources as a mediating entity as they negotiated a space of their own in the realm of education. The resilient students understood that community resources assisted in their educational development by providing networking opportunities (e.g., community mentors) and needed resources, such as paid work, gender-specific activities, tutoring services, or a safe space beyond their schools and homes.

Like with community resources, the most resilient students were keen on taking advantage of resources available to them at the school itself. For instance, all three of the educationally resilient students in this study at some point had sought tutoring in at least one subject. Moreover, the educationally resilient students were also more likely to participate in extracurricular activities that supported their long-term goals. Because all the young women planned on completing high school and going on to college, all three participated in JROTC, with the goal of receiving a college scholarship. Resiliency studies show that students who are involved in school activities are more likely to be academic achievers and to complete school on time; thus, these students early on had increased their chances of completing high school (Gordon & Wang, 1994).

Even though all the resilient students generally had a negative attitude about their schools' environment (staff and other students), most had positive feelings about at least one adult in their school. A positive feeling toward an adult in the school was usually a result of one-on-one contact, such as after-school tutoring. For example, Nicole, an honor roll student, stated, "Those teachers don't understand us ghetto children." Also, she is the student who felt there was a need for more African American teachers at both the middle school and high school she attended. However, this resilient student named her White resource teacher, which is similar to a tutor, as the one person who has helped her most at school. As a side note, Nicole also mentioned the emotional support that she received from an African American female in her school who was not a teacher. Therefore, research on gender- and cultural-specific resilience programs might emphasize that the race of a teacher is less important than the caring nature of the teacher, but students may be associating "caring" with race and/or cultural attributes of the teacher.

These findings on teachers' caring attitudes toward students are consistent with Valenzuela's (1999) work with Mexican and Mexican American students' perceptions of schoolteachers. As Valenzuela (1999) found in her research, the individual histories that teachers and students bring to classroom encounters necessarily influence the chances for successful relationship building. Still, in most cases, there is likely to be some room to maneuver—that is, if the situation is approached literally "with care." (p. 73)

Because caring relationships with teachers were not very frequent, the family members of the students also contributed to school persistence. Although all the students' families had experienced crises of their own at some point in their child's educational career, they were able to meet her educational needs. Most of their crisis situations were related to their social and economic positions in the city in which they lived. For example, Yssis' family had survived a divorce and incarceration of her father; Nicole's biological mother had lost custody of her children; and Zora experienced the death of her biological mother in the middle of her freshman year of high school. Ironically, none of the students lived with both their (biological) mother and father during the time of the study. Yet, all of the resilient students named a family member as their main source of support. More specifically, the young women named their female caregiver as the one person who has helped them "get this far" in school.

In my view, family support was the most dynamic in nature. Family support, in this study, defied almost everything I have ever learned in sociological theory about educational resilience. For instance, most hypothesize that those students who come from two-parent (heterosexual) families are going to be more competent in society. In this study, I learned that the most resilient or competent students were those students who felt love in their family. Although Yssis and Nicole admitted to having missed a relationship with their fathers, none of the resilient students felt that living in a single-parent household (or not with their biological parents) negatively affected their education. All three of the resilient young women felt that their parents cared about their educational accomplishments and wanted them to do well in school. More importantly, all the students reported that a family member helped them directly with some aspect of their schooling, like completing a homework assignment or studying for an examination.

Aside from emotional support (e.g., girls reported that mothers are "there for me when I need her") or financial support (e.g., providing housing or clothing), family support also included monitoring school participation (e.g., intervening with discipline problems at school or even punishing a student for not doing well in school). Nevertheless, very high attachment to a female caregiver was very significant in the resiliency process. For example, the forms of support listed above were more likely to come from a female caregiver, such as a mother, grandmother, or aunt. Although all five students in the research study named their mothers as their main source of support, the more resilient ones were more likely to draw on the resources available from the family, community, and school.

The resilient students felt that it was important that they receive assistance from community organizations, at school, and in their family. However, students were usually very specific as to what it was about the support systems that promoted educational achievement. Even though none of the students felt that their immediate neighborhoods were safe havens, they still believed that it was important for children to live in safe neighborhoods. Ysiss even felt that it was important to have older adult role models in the neighborhood to guide children's decisions. Also important is the fact that the resilient students suggested that community organizations should provide more educational programs that served to keep children out of trouble and to help them with their schoolwork. Finally, the resilient students also felt that the Black church was important to African American children. I believe that the students felt that church was important to their own development, which would help them get along better with their peers and teachers at school.

As for school support, the resilient students appreciated stern but understanding teachers. Again, I do not believe that the girls necessarily felt an African American female teacher could teach them more or any better than a White teacher. My hypothesis is that the students associated African American female teachers with being stern but empathetic to their needs and the adversities they faced in life. As pointed out by Lisa Delpit (1995), some African American teachers bring a teaching style to the classroom that is congruent with the parenting styles that some African American children are accustomed to at home. In this study, the students assumed that African American teachers had the potential to mix caring and sternness to provide an ideal learning environment. Moreover, the students welcomed those teachers, regardless of race, who were fair. In contrast to other ethnographies, this study found that even the resilient young women were in opposition to unjust school policies and discipline procedures. Oppositional behavior was displayed in "talking back" to teachers and other school staff, refusing to carry out a punishment, or simply choosing to ignore a school rule or policy. Unlike students in other studies on resistors, the resilient young women continued to attend school and soon enough decided to conform to what it took to graduate from high school. Their conformity was marked by their advocacy for more school programs and extracurricular activities that made education fun like schooling appeared to be prior to high school.

Admittedly, the students did not have many recommendations as to how the family could better support the needs of students like themselves. I believe they did not have too many recommendations because they had family members who were already displaying behaviors that they needed to succeed. However, this study found that relationships between maternal caregivers and students fostered resilience when students experienced a "muse" relationship with their mothers. As previously noted, muse relationships are more natural in nature as opposed to mentoring relationships, in which an adult guide is usually assigned to a student. With muse relationships, students are able to choose their own role models, usually someone who is from a similar background or community. Furthermore, muse relationships, like the ones that appeared to have been more worthwhile for the students in this study, teach girls life lessons by sharing from one's own experience. This study found that female caregivers, who were reportedly more open and honest with their daughters about their life experiences, produced stronger mother–daughter relationships. Even more, it was also found that regardless of other available mentors or role models, resilient students always named their female caregiver as the main source of support.

Individual Agency

Although support from the family, community, and school is significant in fostering educational resilience, students' individual intentions and motivations also play a significant role in school persistence. For instance, all the resilient students in the study looked forward to completing high school and eventually going on to college and obtaining a long-term career. In fact, the most resilient students had already developed a plan for their life course. For example, in the eighth grade, Zora's goals were to go to high school, get into the nursing academy, get involved in activities, graduate from high school, and go to college. Of course, not all of the girls' goals worked out as planned, but it is still important to mention that the most resilient students had some type of plan in place. Maybe their articulated goals actually served as a buffer to school failure.

Grades also appear to be very important to the most resilient students in the study. The most resilient students seemed to be always conscious of grade evaluations and usually strived to do better in school or in a particular class. I found grade evaluations to be a stressor for all the resilient young women instead of serving as a reward or positive reinforcement. Regardless of the level of real or perceived stress, the resilient students asked for help or sought out useful resources in their family, community, or schools. Despite their ability to seek out social and academic resources in the community, the most resilient students had low attachment to their community neighborhoods. Yssis, for instance, simply chose not to associate herself with any of her peers at school or in the neighborhood. Nicole and Zora's parents forbade them to hang out in their neighborhoods. Definitely, the most resilient students were not "social butterflies" in their immediate neighborhoods, by choice or by force. Notwithstanding their low attachment to their immediate neighborhoods, the most resilient students and their families were more likely to have a low mobility rate. Nicole and Zora have lived in the same neighborhood and homes from kindergarten through high school, and Yssis from approximately fourth grade through high school. Therefore, low mobility was also a supporting factor in the students' resiliency.

Another significant finding about the character of the most resilient students is that these young women were also very attuned to and vociferous about intimate relationship with boys, sex, and the possible negative consequences of an early unplanned pregnancy. The resilient young women rationalized from the experiences of others around them (e.g., peers, neighbors, or family members) that sexual activity was a potential threat to their educational and career goals. In other words, intimate relationships with boys and pregnancy were viewed as threats to their long-term goals that they were almost always conscious of and articulated often in their educational stories.

Also, it is important to mention that resilience is a process. The most educationally resilient students did not necessarily display the qualities listed here all at once or all the time. Just like any other skill, building relationships with adults, asking for help, and participation in extracurricular activities require skills that we are more adept or comfortable with at a particular time. For instance, some students in the study had to work on improving their school attendance, and others ended their participation in a school organization. Yssis, for example, had decided that she no longer felt comfortable participating in after-school activities at the Urban League. Similarly, Zora's relationship with a boyfriend interfered with her attendance record, and Nicole found out that her plans at joining the cheerleading team had to be altered. What is more important about these students is that they showed resilience over time, suggesting that educational resilience is a process, not a one-time technique. Instead, resilience is a means by which students are able to locate and identify their own strengths and the capital available to them from other people, places, and things in their immediate environment. The most resilient students had the ability, the support system, and the resources that are necessary to bounce back, recover from, and move forward from adversity.

Where Are They Now?

It has been a little over four years since the study with the five girls began. Because resilience is a process toward some type of goal, we have to wonder if the students in the study have reached what they set out to attain. As eighth graders, all of the girls were looking forward to going on to high school and graduating in four years. It has already been discussed that Terry's education was interrupted by the need to focus on personal responsibilities. More specifically, Terry, had to attend to the needs of her child. As for the educationally resilient students, Nicole, Zora, and Yssis, they are all looking forward to graduating from high school in less than six months.

I try to keep in contact with the students through surprise school visits, home visits, or telephone conversations. Nicole is still the energetic "mama's girl" whom I met more than four years ago, and her mother is still trying to cook for me. Nicole and her (grand)mother, after living in the same rented house for more than fifteen years, finally moved into a different neighborhood. The last time that I spoke to her and her mother, they were celebrating that Nicole had received recognition in the local newspaper for making the honor roll. Nicole was definitely going to college, but her mother was concerned because they "don't have a lotta money" that Nicole could not afford to attend a four-year institution right after high school. Also, her mother did not want Nicole to accumulate excessive debt from college loans. Her plan was to attend the local community college for two years and then transfer to the local university to complete two more years of study.

Unfortunately, Zora left her aunt's home and moved in with her sister but that living situation was only temporary too. The last I heard, she was going to move in with her maternal grandfather until she graduated from high school. I do know that Zora's attendance had suffered due to her moving to different locations and having to catch the bus to school. Actually, I had called Zora up to inform her that I had seen a dip in her attendance. She explained her living situation and promised that her attendance would improve and that she definitely was attending class to graduate with her class.

Yssis is busy as well focusing on getting into college. She was waiting to hear if she had been accepted into the local university's nursing program. Actually, she is not really interested in nursing, but it was the only career that someone had visited her school to speak on. The last time we got together she wanted to meet with me, because she was disappointed that her school counselors had not provided her with information on college majors and information on careers. She thought we could meet to discuss other careers and college majors. Although Yssis' preference was to attend college close to home to watch over her mother (and money was an issue), when we met we were attempting to do college searches over the Internet. She decided that maybe it was not wise to stay that close to home, where individuals may not necessarily understand the stress of college life. After contemplating the pros and cons of attending college in town, it was decided that she could at least learn what her options were for attending other state colleges.

Redefining Resiliency: Implications for Educational Policy and Urban Education Reform

Implications for Research in Urban Education

As previously stated, one of the most profound findings of this research is that the most resilient students were those young women and their families who were best at blurring the boundaries between the family, community, and school. One important aspect of this book was the theoretical framework and the methodology employed, which also blurred the boundaries between theory, methods, and practice. In chapter one, I introduced the theoretical framework and methodology used to conduct and write this research, post-womanist research. I proclaimed throughout this ethnography that my own raced, classed, and gendered experiences along with the reported stories of the research participants offered unique insight into the educational experiences of African American female students. At a time when qualitative methods and standpoint epistemologies are under attack in education research, it appears perilous to call for more gender- and cultural-specific research methodologies. However, I contend that by failing to acknowledge or ignoring the interaction of race, class, and gender as it affects the researcher and the researched, educational theorists, researchers, and policymakers will continue to yield deficit perspectives on the experiences of African American students.

In "Culturally Sensitive Research Approaches: An African-American Perspective," Tillman (2002) describes culturally sensitive research as those approaches to the study of education "that place the cultural knowledge and experiences of African Americans at the center of the inquiry and emphasize the relationship of the researcher to the individual or the community under study" (p. 6). As pointed out by Tillman (2000), culturally sensitive research approaches places the ethnicity and cultural experiences of the researcher and the researched at the center of the research process. In her article, Tillman (2000) points out that culturally sensitive research approaches are essential to understanding the experiences of African Americans in an educational context. Without such understanding, researchers will continue to contribute to a body of literature that focuses on deficiency (Tillman, 2000). I argue that post-womanist research is a useful culturally sensitive approach to the study of African American female students and all African American children's schooling experiences. Because of the framework and methodology employed, we are able to focus on educational resilience instead of school failure.

In her article, Tillman (2000) outlined a framework for culturally sensitive research approaches for African Americans. Culturally sensitive research approaches use culturally congruent research methods (uses qualitative methods and considers context), culturally specific knowledge (the researcher's cultural knowledge is considered), cultural resistance to theoretical dominance (challenges traditional claims of objectivity), culturally sensitive data interpretations (the cultural experiences of African Americans are viewed as valid and appropriate in analysis and presentation); and culturally informed theory and practice (knowledge gained is useful for educational change) (Tillman, 2000). Post-womanist research can bring us closer to these practices and objectives of culturally sensitive research methods in educational research.

As pointed out in chapter three, I use qualitative research methods and ethnographic approaches in this study; however, these methods are embodied discursive practices based on my knowledge of, experiences with, and respect for African American culture. Second, I also provide a historical analysis of the social, economic, political, and educational context in which the students live. It is not taken for granted that certain behaviors or conditions simply exist or occur in a vacuum; a link is made between past behaviors and events. Even more important, the post-womanist researcher places herself and her research participants, those who have been raced, classed, and gendered, at the center of her research agenda. Thus, it is obvious that I am a nonobjective being in the research process. Furthermore, as an outcome of my methodology, I served as a mentor to the students in the study; I have used the knowledge gained as a platform for the telling of the African American experience in the city where the study took place, and I become an advocate for educational reform locally and nationally. Therefore, I argue that post-womanist research is synonymous with culturally sensitive research approaches to the study of the school experiences of African Americans and is thus useful for the study of such students' experiences.

Implications for Social Work and Educational Practice

Besides this study offering implications for research in urban education, it also has implications for practice in social work, community organizations, and educational settings. My research suggests that due to their raced, classed, and gendered status in society, the African American female students in this study accessed support systems that were gender and cultural specific. First, the participants named "family" as the one thing that has had the most influence on their positive educational development. More specifically, the young women named their female caregiver as the one person who has had the most influence on their academic decisions. Furthermore, the educationally resilient students admitted to preferring educational programs that were gender exclusive.

First, these findings suggest the need to welcome female caregivers more openly and directly into the school building itself, and the need to foster stronger caring relationships between female caregivers and their daughters. Second, this research suggests that we need to reevaluate programs that spend large amounts of money on mentoring programs that tend to focus on outsiders as role models for young low-income African American girls. This research suggests that such programs may be a waste of time and money. Instead policymakers and program developers may want to focus on providing extra dollars to programs that target female caregivers or natural (family or community) mentors that help them meet their family needs or provide them with extra money to take a day off work to spend time with their female students at school or in after-school programs. As we know from this study with resilient students, family members are already involved in their child's educational development, but their efforts may not be visible or at the forefront. These findings suggest that there is a need for more community and school-based dropout/prevention programs that specifically target African American female students and their female caregivers, for these are the primary support systems that resilient students gravitate toward.

In addition, by conceding that female caregivers and natural mentors (e.g., aunts, older sisters, godmothers, community leaders, etc.) are essential to the positive educational development of African American female students, I also have to address another question that this research raised: Does "race" matter? Posed another way, do African American female students benefit from having an African American female teacher? It is difficult to argue from the findings of this research study that African American teachers are "better" for African American school children. However, the findings from this research study do provide enough evidence to demonstrate that the most resilient students sought out natural mentors inside and outside of the school building who were of the same gender and cultural (economic and social) background of themselves and their families.

According to Ladson-Billings (1994), African American female students may benefit most from those teachers who practice culturally relevant teaching methods: "the primary aim of culturally relevant teaching methods is to assist in the development of a 'relevant black personality' that allows African American students to choose academic excellence yet still identify with African and African American culture" (p. 17). In this kind of pedagogy, first, it is acknowledged that African Americans are a distinct culture group, with a unique historical experience in our society, and, second, these distinct cultural differences are regarded as strengths that are prerequisites to nurturing positive educational development (Ladson-Billings, 1994).

In this particular study, all of the students expressed the desire to have more African American teachers present in their school buildings. I use the word "desire" to signify the students' conscious or unconscious yearning for something (or someone) that is at the moment beyond reach but may be attainable in the future. One student in particular, the more vociferous, Nicole, directly voiced a need for African American teachers. I use "need" here to articulate that for Nicole at that particular time in her educational development, she felt there should have been a requirement to have African American teachers for African American children or that the school should be obligated to hire and retain African American teachers. However, remember that Nicole later retracted her earlier declaration of the need for African American teachers.

It is my belief that Nicole later retracted this need or requirement, because she, like the other students, realized that a teacher need not necessarily share her racial or ethnic background as long as he or she respected, acknowledged, and appreciated students' raced, classed, and gendered experiences. Thus, although this ethnographic study does support the desire of some African American students to be taught by African American teachers, it would be shortsighted to conclude that African American children must be taught by African American teachers. At this point in history, there are not enough African American teachers available to this group of students. Therefore, it would be negligent to directly or indirectly imply that African American female students have to be taught by African American female teachers.

On the other hand, I do understand the students' need and desire to be supported and motivated by teachers who are respectful and aware of students' cultural backgrounds. For example, all of the students in the study reported that they and their peers were experiencing racism and class discrimination from their White teachers and the larger White (and Black) middle-class community. The racism, sexism, and classism they experienced were most evident in reports of surveillance of dress, unfair disciplinary policies, non-caring teachers, and teachers with low expectations of students. Supporting the students' need and desire for teachers who are culturally competent is Nicole's wish for an African American female teacher who was "ghetto just like us." Nicole felt a cultural connection to this teacher who grew up with her grandmother and was from the neighborhood of Nicole and other students in the study. Ladson-Billings (1994) also described how Black teachers in de facto segregated schools were mainly from the Black community and lived, worked, and worshiped with the schoolchildren's parents. Nicole, and other students like her, may benefit most from teachers who have some type of connection to the African American community and/or teachers who are skilled at connecting their teaching practices to the relevancy of their students' experiences. Therefore, it is too complex of a question to simply ask if "race" matters, but we are beginning to understand that "culture" (and all that it entails) is very important to the educational development of African American female students and African American children in general.

I argue that these findings imply the need to recruit and retain more African American female teachers (or other individuals) who are empathetic of the impact of race, class, and gender on Black girls schooling experiences. Although I am not sure that empathy or "caring" (Valenzuela, 1999) can be taught, by admitting the need and desire for gender- and cultural-specific research, pedagogy, and curriculum, educators and social work practitioners may begin their own processes of contributing to educational resiliency. With my three-year-old son inquisitively sitting on my lap as I type this section, I can only hope that this need and desire are fulfilled expeditiously.

Implications for Urban Education Policy

One of the most significant findings of this research project is that the most resilient African American female students were adept at utilizing support from the family, community, and school simultaneously. All of the students had these various resources at their disposal in their own community, but only the most resilient students accessed the resources simultaneously. What can these young women's stories contribute to urban education reform and education policy overall? Their stories tell us that there is a need for more educational research and policies that take the "whole" child approach to school reform. In order for educational policies to be effective, programs and policies, at both the national and local level, must be implemented that simultaneously identify the family, community, and school as systems of support.

Traditionally, educational theorists and policymakers have attempted to dichotomize and delegate responsibilities to the family, community, or school for the education of African American students in urban areas. In the past, researchers and policymakers attempted to place the blame for school failure on students' families and their perceived lack of involvement or indifference to their children's educational outcomes. Other theorists have even pointed the finger at the behaviors and belief systems of the Black community for underachievement in low-income school districts (Ogbu & Simmons, 1998; Fordham, 1996; Wilson, 1996), and/or blamed the individual student for not being able to shed his/her Black identity for the sake of school achievement (Fordham, 1996). More recently, new educational policies, like No Child Left Behind (NCLB), are attempting to hold teachers and underachieving schools "accountable" for student success. The one thing that all of these theories and initiatives have in common is the focus on failure and underachievement.

In order to promote positive educational development and begin to focus on educational resilience, policymakers have to begin to recognize that all three entities are viable resources for African American students. However, in order for the family, community, or school to be feasible support systems, policymakers have to initiate policies and programs that avoid placing sole responsibility on any one entity. We know that that level of responsibility has not worked in the past and has only left our schoolchildren with the burden (Smith, 1999). Thus, to move forward in urban education reform, policymakers are going to have to be held accountable for making sure that all three entities have the resources (funding, staffing, etc.) that each needs to function on behalf of the child. Educational policymakers are going to have to promote more research and advocacy programs that serve to eradicate the boundaries that have traditionally been established between the home environment, community organizations, and school systems due to historical patterns of racism, sexism, classism, and heterosexism. We know from this research that when students are able to access available resources from all three entities simultaneously, students are at their most resilient.

Finally, we learn from this research and other research on families that the traditional nuclear family is quickly becoming a myth that appears to only exist in the minds of social researchers and educational policymakers. Although there has been a shift in the larger society as to what entails a family, many of our education policies continue to envision a biological mother and/or father as the head of the household. However, as we learn from this research, one's mother (or primary caregiver) can be an aunt, grandmother, uncle, great grandfather, etc. Therefore, there is a definite cultural lag (Miron, 1996) between our educational policies and social trends in larger society. If policymakers are going to welcome families as active participants in their child's education, educational reformists are going to have to allow the students and/or their families to decide what constitutes a family member.

Currently, our education and social work policies require the signature or presence of a legal guardian; however, the person a child lives with or draws support (emotional, financial, etc.) from may not be her biological parent and/or legally appointed guardian. As was discovered in this study, many of the resilient students reconceptualized "family" based on the roles and responsibilities an adult played in their life. Simply by assigning kin terms and responsibilities to adult family members (other than their biological parents), the most resilient students were demonstrating a form of creativity and coping that fostered educational resiliency. The oversight of policymakers of the roles and responsibilities that nuclear and/or extended family members' play in many students' everyday realities might isolate caring family members from community and school programs. For students to acquire positive coping skills and educational development, all three entities have to work collectively. Lastly, educational policymakers have to reconsider and accept what constitutes family as it relates to parental involvement in a student's positive educational development and outcomes.

In conclusion, I argue that a new and more inclusive gender- and cultural-specific look at school resilience has the potential of having a transcending effect on educational practice. For example, this new focus in resilience research can assist reformers in producing more gender- and cultural-specific dropout/pushout prevention programs. Local policymakers and school reformists are able to implement programs that meet the needs of African American girls, their families, communities, and schools.

Also, this new perspective may bring gender- and cultural-specific issues (e.g., concerns that Black feminists have traditionally addressed) to education discourse altogether. Resilience research has the potential of assisting policymakers in identifying the impact of race, class, and gender oppression on educational experience and outcome. Some researchers in urban education (Taylor, 1994; Anyon, 1997; Payne, 1984) have studied the impact of race and class discrimination on urban education, but very few have studied gender oppression in urban education. Even more important is the fact that little research has focused on the ways in which female students of color cope with and overcome many forms of gender, race, and class oppression and maintain resilience in the face of adversity.

Rigsby (1994) reminds us that resilience is contextually bound in time and place and culture. Multiple identities and multiple oppressions require that minority females draw upon unique gender- and cultural-specific systems of support. From past research on African American females, their families, and their communities, we are able to recognize resilience-fostering factors. We also realize the need for a more inclusive definition of resilience, and a need to reconstruct resilience. Finally, gender- and cultural-specific resilience research has the potential to help facilitate progress in urban education reform initiatives.

Chapter Six

Critical Urban Pedagogy

Once in a teaching evaluation, a graduate student complained that I was too hard on teachers. I like to believe that I am just as tough on the parents and Black leaders of African American students. Nevertheless, I think that sometimes it does appear that I am harder on teachers, and this may be the case. As a mother of an African male child, I have a personal stake in the improvement of education for all children. Because educators helped facilitate my emotional, social, and intellectual growth, I have very high expectations for our nation's teachers. I have witnessed through my own resiliency and from young women with whom I talk that teachers are very important to our development. Based on our reliance on teachers, it is always surprising to me when teachers say, "Those people forget that education is a privilege."

What we need to focus our attention and teaching efforts on is the verity that in the United States, education is a right. Also, I would add that most Americans even see education as a responsibility. My fear is that once we begin to consider education as a privilege, we threaten to choose those to whom we will allocate or withdraw the privilege. Honestly, it also offends me when White people indicate that they are allowing me or my children the privilege of attending school. My forefathers and foremothers fought for all children to have the right to a free and appropriate education in the United States. Education is viewed as a necessary constituent of a democratic society, and historically we are in the moment where teachers have to recognize and embrace these principles that many have fought and died for in our country. A rebirth of these democratic principles, along with emancipatory principles, will assist African American girls to attain social, educational, and economic resilience.

In earlier chapters, I suggested the tenets of postmodernism and Black feminism as useful lenses to begin to understand the educational experiences of African American female students. Post-womanism considers the interaction of race, class, and gender while also acknowledging the role that the family, community, and school play in fostering educational resilience. Also, post-womanism recognizes the significance of human agency in buffering adversity. As we learn from the resilient girls in this book, resilience is a process that is constructed and reconstructed throughout educational development. Resiliency is also participatory in that the individual has to have access to and be willing to access the resources that may be available to her at various stages of development. Furthermore, and more importantly, we have learned in *Teaching Black Girls* that resilience is a gendered and cultural endeavor that is affected by the social, political, historical, and economic context that the student lives in. A post-womanist gender- and cultural-specific research methodology raises the following question: Is it possible to develop post-womanist strategies for enhancing teaching and learning? Based on my conversations with resilient African American girls, it is possible to engage in critical gender- and cultural-specific pedagogy that benefits the student teacher and larger cultural community.

The postmodern embrace of differences brings forth the multiple vocular narratives of marginal groups like urban African American female adolescents. Furthermore, the tenets of postmodernism concede for those interested in educational and pedagogical reform to understand how knowledge, truth, and subjects are produced in language and cultural practices (St. Pierre, 2000). Postmodernism also allows us to comprehend the effects of human agency and subjectivities on educational experiences (McCarthy, 1988). Overall, postmodernism helps to produce theory and practice that help us understand how larger social structures and culture, the macro and micro, and the intersection of race, class, and gender affects educational experiences. Black feminism offers a critical pedagogy that promotes a concern with fighting against economic, political, and social injustice for Black women and other oppressed groups (Collins, 2000). Pedagogically, Black feminism would require that teachers and students examine how issues affect African American women in the United States as a part of a global struggle for women's emancipation. It also supports the idea of pedagogy working from a focus on resilience and strength. More importantly, Black women and girls are at the foci of pedagogy. Together Black feminism and postmodernism extend a critical pedagogy that ruminates over the intersection of race, class, and gender on the educational development of Black girls.

Cultural Connections

In my work with educators, school administrators, school service personnel, and preservice teachers, I have learned that many educators drive in from distant rural or suburban locations to teach urban students. Many of these teachers have a genuine interest in serving urban students, but most find themselves teaching in urban neighborhoods because there are no openings in their own community schools. At times, the outsiders experience culture shock after coming in contact with this different way of life. From my own educational experiences and discussions with hundreds of urban girls, I know that sometimes Black girls are the first group to encounter the aftershock of White and middle-class teachers' initial reactions to this different cultural context. How can I argue that Black girls immediately feel the burden of urban teachers' burnout and stress? Because African American boys have been traditionally labeled and handled as behavioral (and criminal) problems, our urban schools have systematically figured out how to get rid of boys immediately. The fear and abomination of African American males have tracked them into self-contained special education classes, detention, in-school suspension, out-of-school suspension, alternative schools, expulsion rolls, and prison. The point is that there are many institutional "alternatives" readily available to teachers who feel overwhelmed by a male pupil, and the teachers' actions may never be questioned, because such actions are becoming the norm in many public urban schools. Of course, teachers do not rid their classrooms of all the males, but they may have eliminated (or threatened) those who are less bearable and have managed to cope with those students who are more tolerable. In fact, if one has ever worked in a majority Black public school, they would have noticed that many urban classrooms have a revolving door. Meaning, even the tolerable students are constantly being sent in and out of the classroom to the principal's office throughout the school day.

The shock of teaching in an urban context that is different from what the teacher may be accustomed to is sensed by the Black girls in the classroom. Not only might the Black female student look different, express herself differently, dress differently, worship differently, and behave differently from her teachers, but she may also think differently. For example, when I was in fourth grade my family relocated from the inner city to the south suburbs of Chicago. (Ironically, by the time I entered eighth grade, that same community became mostly African American.) At my new school, I was immediately placed in the lower-tier classroom. I do not think that the teachers knew or cared that prior to my family's move, my siblings and I had always been in gifted education classes. I worked hard to be removed from the lower-tier program and eventually was placed in the upper-tier group. Despite my academic achievements, I had been labeled by my White female teachers as a "big-mouth," and my name remained on the board on most days for speaking out of term, talking too much in class, or insubordination. Throughout the rest of fourth grade, and all through junior high school, my name usually remained on the chalkboard. And, even though I had a love–hate relationship with the principal's office, I still managed to graduate at the top of my eighth grade class. I never gave up my commitment to prove myself to those White teachers.

It was not until recently, after hearing so many Black girls' cries of "Why won't they just leave me alone" that I realized that teacher–student conflict was not just my story. Black girls feel like they are the targets of many teachers' stress and frustration. It may be that Black girls do not fit into the tight gender categories constructed for White middle-class girls. Often I hear teachers, White and Black, describe urban girls as aggressive, loud-mouthed, mannish, and brash. These are stereotypical descriptions that have existed since slavery. Most have been propagated by the media, based on the perception of the emasculated

African American male and the non-feminine African American female. It is true that most urban Black girls live in families where mothers and grandmothers, by choice or unplanned circumstances, are community leaders, workers and mothers, financial planners, and primary breadwinners. Although the majority of Black families do believe in the traditional nuclear family, the majority of African American women are single parents. Consequently, many Black girls are sent the message early that at any moment they can become the head of household. Therefore, watching mothers perform their gender as leaders, activists, workers, financial planners, etc., Black girls are taught to have a voice and to speak up just as often as boys.

In middle-class White culture, girls are socially constructed as silent, docile, inactive, congenial, and frivolous. Urban Black girls do not fit this Victorian prototype perpetuated by European-American culture. Moreover, their realities do not allow them to be trivialized. As a social institution, schools contribute to socializing girls into their gender roles, and society benefits from keeping girls in these restricted roles. Thus, what appears to be insubordination may be due to a cultural disconnection between Black girls and their White and middle-class teachers. Like my adolescent school episode(s), the resilient girls I spoke with were also forced to cope with the stress and strain caused by this cultural disconnect between teachers and urban students. Nevertheless, we all admit to thriving with the help of our teachers, but it was with the support of a certain type of teacher, who operated within a certain type of classroom, who adopted a certain approach to teaching, who proved to be more significant in our road to resiliency.

Is Multicultural Education the Answer?

Given their complex realities and multiple identities, African American urban girls may benefit more from a multicultural approach to education. An approach to educational practices directed toward race, culture, language, social class, gender, sexuality, and disability (Grant & Sleeter, 2003). Black urban girls are affected by larger American culture while also being a part of a history that has sculpted a distinct Black and urban culture. It is also this same Black urban culture and social experience in America that has helped shape how Black girls perform their gender. These unique histories and multiple identities have helped to facilitate the construction of distinct language patterns, rituals, beliefs, and conducts. Undoubtedly, African American girls will benefit from educational practices that understand and emphasize the interaction of race, class, gender, and context on educational development. Besides, it is not mere coincidence that most of the resilient students I talked to for *Teaching Black Girls* at some point received special education services due to a medical, social, or learning difficulty. Whether these diagnosed special needs are valid or not, all urban girls can benefit from educational practices that understand ability differences and learning preferences in urban communities. With the coupled goal of fostering educational resiliency and acknowledging differences, a multicultural approach to teaching and learning would move us to the beginning of understanding the multiple identities of African American girls who live in urban areas.

However, multicultural education is only part of the response to more effective and responsible ways of teaching Black girls. I began with a discussion on the usefulness of multicultural education, because many individuals are educated in and are familiar with multiculturalism. In fact, most teacher candidates and veteran teachers have come to expect topics of discussion in their higher education classrooms and professional development programs that focus on multiculturalism. Granted there are some who do not wish to understand or see the usefulness of multicultural frameworks, most teachers have come to accept it as a reality. Most teachers are pedagogically and politically comfortable with current multicultural approaches to teaching and learning. To be comfortable implies a state of contentment and ease, physically and mentally. With the current level of social and economic disenfranchisement of African American girls and women in our society, there should be no teacher of urban girls who is at ease, undisturbed. As raced, classed, and gendered bodies, Black girls are at war in their own homes, schools, neighborhoods, and nations. Black girls, low income and working class especially, need teachers who are going to fight alongside them in this cultural battlefield.

Critical Pedagogy

Multicultural practice and curriculum is not enough because it is pedagogically and politically too comfortable. In the words of Hazel Carby (1999), "Multiculturalism has reacted to racism as if it were limited to a struggle over forms of representation—a struggle over images—in an attempt to disguise social relations of domination and subordination in which it is situated and reproduces" (p. 203). African American urban girls are in need of a more critical pedagogy that examines how individual and institutional racism, sexism, classism, and heterosexism complicate their daily existence, a pedagogy that extends beyond multicultural education to take into consideration the context in which students live, play, and work. Critical urban education, for example, does this. In addition, urban education, and all that it symbolically entails, is at the center of teaching and learning. Furthermore, a critical urban education goes even further to understand how these social constructs are produced and sustained by racism (Kincheloe, 2004). Critical urban pedagogy as a frame of reference for teachers recognizes that schools are social institutions that operate within larger historical and cultural contexts.

Many African American girls live in complicated situations inside and outside of the classroom. Urban Black girls become targets of racism, sexism, and classism from members of their own families, neighbors, and teachers and staff at the school. Not to mention how the larger society has profited from the negative images of urban Black girls. A critical urban education looks at resiliency and possibility while not ignoring the stress and strain that urban students incessantly experience. As articulated by Kincheloe (2004), "We advocate a curriculum that draws on the strengths of urban students rather than relying on indicators that point out only their weaknesses" (p. 9). Too often researchers, teachers, policymakers, school personnel, school administrators, and the general public hear only about those factors that place African American urban children at risk. In contrast, a critical urban education allows us to appreciate the abundance of resources that are available in urban girls' immediate context that may perhaps buffer adversity and further educational resilience in African American female students. A critical urban pedagogy also serves the purpose of preparing students to utilize those same support systems to question, critique, and challenge the injustices that they experience as urban girls.

In this chapter I am also theorizing and making recommendations for practice based on my own beliefs, experiences, and research with urban girls. I am also in agreement with Delpit (1995) and other African American scholars that African American children have "to play the game" or learn European philosophical beliefs and standards in order to challenge and debunk the system itself. Furthermore, I contend that Black students have to learn about their own people's history in America and abroad, and they need to know about the contributions that African people and women have made to all of humankind. This premise is tied to the frequently repeated adage, "If you don't know where you came from, you ain't gonna know where you are going." If African American children are to determine what their expectations are of a democratic society, they first have to understand the historical, political, and economic struggles and triumphs of their people. With such a well-rounded knowledge base, urban girls, families, communities, and teachers can work together to foster educational resiliency.

Teaching in Context

I want to use Nicole's words as a framework for building a multicultural and a critical urban education that is gender and cultural specific. If Nicole could speak directly to teachers, she would tell them first to leave her alone, to be caring, and ask for a teacher who is "ghetto like us." Fortunately, because I know

Nicole, and other Black girls like her, I know that her words should not be taken literally. For example, Nicole truly does not want to be left alone; in fact, she wants to be respected and paid attention to. Furthermore, she does not want a teacher who lives in the ghetto or even "acts" ghetto. She simply wants a teacher who understands the ghetto way of life, who will understand what it takes for Nicole to survive on a daily basis. Once the teacher understands how Nicole survives, she will also come to eventually empathize with Nicole and other students like her. Through genuine empathy and understanding urban educators learn what barriers urban girls encounter as students and social beings in their immediate contexts. Urban girls' schools are connected to the larger Black community, and they are constantly struggling to preserve this continuity. Yet, many classroom teachers are trying to cut this self-sustaining and communal cord. There comes a struggle between teacher and pupil, because the ghettoized communities have given resilient urban Black girls both life and breath. In other words, in their day-to-day lives growing up in urban neighborhoods they have developed distinct identities. Their identities have been created from the experiences of struggle and triumph, suffering and joy, rigidity and resilience. Once they value urban Black girls' unique identities, then teachers can choose to care about their students' current life conditions and future well-being. Since resilient African American girls simultaneously name their family, community, and school as sources of support, any attempts at critical pedagogy must be connected to larger social and political projects.

For educators who are truly interested in fostering positive relationships with urban girls, the first step is to learn about not only where they live but also how they live. Such a duty requires that teachers step out of their comfort zone and challenge their own assumptions and beliefs about the communities they teach in and in which their students live, learn, work, and play. The teacher can begin by researching simple demographic information about the school's community such as the racial/ethnic makeup, the average income level of residents, the number of single-parent households, educational level of residents, and average number of children in households. I would also recommend that teachers trace the social, political, and economic history of the school community so as to look beyond the uncomplicated quantification of human beings' livelihood to a broader look at how African American urban life is constructed over time. Of course, a teacher's time is limited, and it is difficult to schedule in much more time and research outside of the classroom. Therefore, alternative teaching and learning techniques should be considered.

For example, a teacher can learn about students simply by having the students describe their neighborhoods and communities for themselves. One assignment might be to have students write an essay describing an aspect of their daily life. Inform students that they interact with culture every day and ask them to write about and describe that culture. Allow them to observe and interpret everyday practices—the neighborhood church, community center, the playground, a school athletic event, their family kitchen, etc. Also, students should be encouraged to think critically about there observations. Ask them what they learned, what they liked or did not like about their observations, and how they felt during the observation. However, this simply should not be a voyeuristic activity on the part of the teacher. Culturally aware teachers and teachers who practice culturally relevant methods view themselves as part of the larger surrounding community and see themselves as giving back to this community (Ladson-Billings, 1994). Therefore, truly committed teachers of urban students should feel comfortable visiting and interacting in those locations and contexts that students have described in their writings, whether that's the local church, a community organization, or a family's dinner table.

From students' observations and writings, one learns about the contexts that students participate in, and how they give meaning to those activities. Furthermore, by asking questions about students' observations and interpretations, the teacher learns more about her students. Once I found myself teaching a group of students who were mostly White and from rural farm communities. For a social science assignment, I had them go out and observe a "slice of culture." I wanted the students to understand that every behavior had meaning and required the students to observe in any social setting that they participated in over the course of a week. Students observed factory labor, birthday parties, religious institutions, bars, bowling leagues, gay culture, and the daily customs of soybean and corn farm workers. The students took from the assignment the lesson that most Americans behave similarly but that the everyday habits that we take for granted have significance for participants. As an outsider (i.e., an African American woman from urban America), I discovered many similarities and differences between rural culture and larger American culture. I also had the benefit of learning how students spent their time outside of the classroom.

More importantly, I was able to draw from their observations examples to use in class lectures and discussions. For example, it was not uncommon for me to lecture on supply and demand using the example of barrels of wheat versus the distribution and consumption of some abstract material that did not apply to their lives. The majority of my rural students were familiar with the toil of growing wheat, selling barrels of wheat, and bidding a price to make a sustainable profit from their labor. Teachers of urban girls can put into practice similar culturally relevant assignments in their classrooms. According to Ladson-Billings (1994), culturally relevant teaching pedagogically "empowers students intellectually, socially, emotionally, and politically by using cultural referents to impart knowledge, skills, and attitudes" (p. 18). In other words, culturally relevant pedagogy builds knowledge from students' experiences. Also, culturally relevant assignments, such as the example I just provided, allow teachers to learn more about their students, teach students how to observe and reflect on their communities, let students know that the teacher cares about their customs, allow students to feel comfortable with discussing and sharing their outside world within the school walls, and allow the teacher to directly (or indirectly) interact with the families and other social groups discussed by the students. The overall goal is for teachers to begin to view themselves as participants in the cultural milieus they drive into and teach in for nine months out of the year. Teaching and learning then becomes a two-way process with both the teacher and pupil learning about the larger social and cultural context in which teaching and learning takes place.

Gender- and Cultural-specific Pedagogy

Because urban Black girls behave and are educated within gendered bodies, teachers of urban girls must encourage students to examine the social construction of gender and its root, patriarchy. Then, teachers should go a step further and provide students with a safe space to examine, critique, and deconstruct gender. Undoubtedly, most African American girls know that sexism exists without the teacher naming it. Like most White American girls, Black girls realize that boys are allowed more often to help the teacher by carrying books and other heavy items down the hall; they know that they are required to do more housework at home; they are told not to have sex while their brothers are warned to wear condoms; they are told to walk and talk like a lady even when they want to run and shout like a human. Also, like all girls they are confused by the opposing images of Snow White and Cinderella alongside Britney Spears and Christina Aguilera. In the case of urban girls, not only are they bombarded by White European images of beauty, they are also torn between the more urban fabricated sex symbols that are proliferated and consumed by mainly White Americans. Young urban African American girls' gendered identities are influenced by unending messages from the mass media, patriarchy, and urban culture. Of course, from a post-womanist perspective none of the aforesaid is dichotomous but is a simple extension of the other and works together in an intricate web of sorts. Urban girls are aware that they are treated differently in school based on their gender and societal images of them.

Why is it important for urban teachers to examine sexism in the lives of urban girls? Even more important, how can teachers build relationships with urban Black girls that serve to support their students' achievement? First of all, I believe that urban teachers should be concerned with the effects of gender discrimination on all their students. It would benefit African American boys and girls and any other students in the classroom to understand how patriarchy and its consequences are played out in their daily lives. The first step that the teacher can take is to open up dialogue in the classroom between the students and herself. She can simply ask students whether boys and girls are treated differently. More than likely, the students will put forth the argument that men and women are treated differently in our society. Based on my work with diverse groups of adolescents in different settings, I am willing to predict that the boys are even going to argue that the girls have it easier than boys. Sexism is played out differently in every situation and context, and it is oppressive to all in our society. Also, racism and sexism tend to go hand and hand. In the words of bell hooks (1990), "Any individual committed to resisting politics of domination, to eradicating sexism and racism, understands the importance of not promoting an either/or competition between the oppressive systems" (p. 64). Racism and sexism are damaging to Black boys and girls; therefore, the teacher should not try to persuade the group that one segment is more affected than another.

The purpose of having discussions about sexism is to open up dialogue between the teacher and pupil. However, it is important that the teacher further facilitates discussion on how students are treated differently in regard to gender. It is not enough to talk about whether students are discriminated against. For instance, a good assignment would be to have the students observe culture. Have them explain how girls or boys behave in social situations. The teacher might ask students who were the leaders in group activities, how did females behave in the observed situation, who were the primary decision makers, how many men and women were involved in the activity, what were individuals wearing, what were the roles of the women and men involved, who talked the most, and/or did participants greet you based on your gender status?

Another assignment might be to have students discuss in class how urban males and females are portrayed in the mainstream media. Both assignments combine the intersections of gender and students' cultural environment. Of course, it is not expected that students become cultural critics overnight, but the assignment serves the purpose of relationship-building between the teacher and students. For such a relationship to develop the teacher must also share her own experiences with sexism as an adolescent or an adult without dominating the discussion. From class dialogue on sexism, the students now know that the teacher is aware of and has acknowledged that gender discrimination is a reality that confronts them.

Furthermore, a discussion of sexism and gender roles should not be a one-day discussion or a one-time class assignment. Gender- and cultural-specific pedagogy requires that the teacher be totally committed to the eradication of sexism and racism in all of its forms. The assignments and discussions serve to inform and demonstrate to the students and others in the school building that the teacher's classroom is a safe space for such a discussion. However, the teacher should not just talk about it; she also must be "about it." She should be constantly challenging and deconstructing traditional gender roles and sexist practices. Simultaneously, she is responsible for interweaving discussions about gender and cultural inequality into lessons on a daily basis. The teacher has to be comfortable with making gender- and cultural-specific pedagogy a political project. The next step is to create or participate in gender-specific programs for girls only. Teachers can develop these programs as after-school programs or to take place during traditional school hours.

Educationally resilient African American girls admit to participating in programs that are for girls only in their own neighborhoods, facilitated by other women, and related to their career and educational goals (Evans-Winters, 2003). Based on this knowledge, once I developed and implemented a grant-funded after-school program called the "Circle of Sisterhood." The program targeted African American females in grades six through eight, and took place at a Black majority urban middle school. As a part of the curriculum, we discussed topics such as teenage sexuality, media images, hygiene and health, conflict resolution, and community responsibility. I allowed the students to develop the curriculum based on their own interests. However, participation in the group required students over an eight-week period to read books about Black women, participate in community service, and interview female role models.

Besides interviewing female role models at home, at school, or in the community (e.g., mothers, grandmothers, mentors, teachers, etc.), they had to write up the interviews in oral narrative form. Although the students asked to do so, they were not allowed to interview me, for I wanted the students to learn how to access other adult resources. Furthermore, I attempted to make sure that each girl played a significant role in the group as a leader (sometimes this required that students share roles). For instance, students served as historians, attendance takers, group leaders, griots, and presidents. Also, students were responsible for maintaining a journal of their reflections in the group and keeping their grades and behavior up to standard. If a student violated these rules, the other members had to examine her situation and determine if she should remain in the group. We never had to revoke a member's participation because all the girls wanted to keep up the reputation of our group. There was one White student in the group, but the rest of us were Black. All the teachers in the building were White; therefore, the girls wanted to show their teachers that they were worthy of and appreciated such a group. The "Circle of Sisterhood" after-school program was our safe haven.

The purpose of the "Circle of Sisterhood" program and similar ones is to provide girls a separate and safe space that makes them feel special. Such programs cultivate positive adolescent development. As a normal phase of adolescence, children begin to question their identity. Not only do they ask "Who am

I?" but they are also concerned with how others perceive them. African American adolescents as a part of their identity formation also begin to think of themselves in relation to their racial/ethnic identification (Tatum, 1997). As Black girls, African American female students may be interested in getting together with other adolescents who look like them and share similar cultural experiences in the United States. They may benefit from a space to engage in and explore their ethnic identities (Tatum, 1997). African American female students may also benefit from relationships and extracurricular programs that help them construct positive identities as urban girls.

For urban girls, as a part of their identity formation, they also have to combat negative societal images of low-income and working-class inner-city girls. As articulated by Tatum (1997), "Resisting the stereotypes and affirming other definitions of themselves is part of the task facing young Black women in both White and Black communities" (p. 57). In adolescence, Black girls, like all adolescents, experience multiple identities that affect their development and student status. Therefore, teachers of urban Black girls can help promote educational persistence by developing and implementing programs that meet urban girls' social, educational, health, and emotional needs. Two important questions that might be asked are: (1) Can White teachers implement such programs? and (2) Can male teachers implement gender- and cultural-specific programs that target Black girls? White women can definitely be a part of such a program as long as the students' topics of interest are addressed and the students are facilitators of group discussions.

Also, natural mentors (i.e., women who are a part of the Black community) should be invited in to discuss various topics with the girls. I would recommend that male teachers not participate in gender- and cultural-specific programs, because it should be a space for girls only; thus, they can feel comfortable expressing their concerns and needs based on their experiences. I am not sure that such a climate can be created by male teachers, Black or White. Nevertheless, if a male teacher is dedicated to post-womanist pedagogy and educational reform, he should advocate for such a program at his school or in his community. Maybe he can recruit an in-school female teacher, parent, college volunteer, or community member to assist in the implementation and facilitation of the program.

The larger created gender and cultural space within the school also serves the larger purpose of consciousness raising. O'Connor's (1997) study of urban school children found that resilient African American female students were students whose parents not only shared their stories of racism and sexism but also discussed with the children their own efforts to combat racism. The study concluded that resiliency may be fostered by raising the consciousness of low-income and working-class Black female students to both the effects of racism and gender inequality and the strategies to combat such inequality. From a feminist perspective, consciousness raising means raising the level of consciousness, of awareness one has about the feelings, behaviors, and experiences surrounding sex roles (Ruth, 1990). From a Black feminist perspective, consciousness-raising programs have the additional task of helping girls become more aware of how political, social, economic, and/or cultural issues play out in their everyday lives (Collins, 2000). In my view, such a task is accomplished through dialogue, and research. Consciousness raising is paramount to the positive educational development of African American girls. Pedagogically, it means building stronger relationships and promoting strong identity formation within students that can only facilitate the development of competent cultural workers. In my experience, the girls' grades and behavior improved. At the end of my program, we had a rites of passage ceremony that introduced others to these culturally and educationally dedicated young women.

Self-determination

Too often I have been observing at a school and I heard the resounding words "You ain't my mama" being hurled out of a student's mouth at a teacher. Those of us who are a little bit more familiar with the Black fictive-kin network and community social structure know that one does not necessarily have to be a child's mother in order to tell that child what to do or how to behave. Therefore, it is almost an insult to hear these words come out of a Black child's mouth. There have been plenty of times I have directed a neighbor's child or a "play" niece or nephew to do or not to do something with little retort or "back talk." Knowing that I have exercised that right inside and outside of the school building, I am always astonished that so many Black students have pretty much told a teacher that he or she does not have a right to tell them what they can or cannot do. I believe much of the tension between students and teachers is due to a cultural disconnection. Much of the strife and tension that we are witnessing in many urban classrooms is a result of teachers' and students' struggles for autonomy and respect.

It is interesting that all of the resilient girls that I have talked to about their educational experiences have complained about the level of stress that some of their teachers and other authority figures at school cause them. Young women have complained about teachers who try to control how they dress, how much they talk, when they talk, and their movement. Some students even mention that there is often ongoing harassment between themselves and particular teachers. I even thought that it was interesting that by the fifth grade most teachers had implemented stricter classroom policies that served to restrict movement in the classroom. More girls reported that by fifth grade their teachers "didn't let them do nothing." In most cases, the students were not even allowed recess time. It seems that prior to middle school, teachers encourage students to take on more active leadership roles in the classroom. For example, students are assigned the role of hall monitor, line leader, chalkboard cleaner, calendar changer, office helper, etc. However, by middle school, students begin to take on fewer leadership roles in the classroom, and they begin to feel like it is not their school. The students are forced to react more like robots after being directed too often to sit still and follow directions which causes school to become disenchanting.

As a result, for girls who report more restricted behavior and more classroom rules, school becomes boring (Evans-Winters, 2003). It appears that by the middle school years, urban teachers are trying to have more control over their students and classrooms, at a time when most students are striving for autonomy. As Tatum (1997) reminds us, in middle school adolescents are figuring out who they are as girls and African Americans. Urban girls, who are experiencing very strong race, class, and gender identification, may be in conflict with culturally different teachers who are trying to instigate power or hold on to their authoritarian power. As a result, you have both teacher and student competing for autonomy and respect.

What is interesting is that traditionally neither group has had much power. Since the beginning of the social construction of the urban education crisis (Miron, 1996), many teachers have not had much say about educational policy, in the curriculum, or the day-by-day functioning of the school. Their lack of power might only be confounded if they are women. The classroom may be the one place where they have some autonomy and power. Urban girls have little voice in a world that favors White/middle-class/boys. The continuous possibility of being matched in a classroom with a resentful teacher may leave many Black girls even more overpowered. Consequently, what are left in many urban classrooms are two disempowered groups that are always, so to speak, bumping heads.

Most teacher education programs and textbooks continue to maintain the notion that classroom management is the day-to-day control of student behavior and learning. Many teachers' approach to teaching involves control of student behavior. A lot of classroom management is exercised in how the classroom is arranged (e.g., rows of desk); how information is disseminated (e.g., teacher as main speaker); rules of student engagement (e.g., the student raises her hand until the teacher calls on her); and methods of discipline (e.g., suspension or detention). Notice that in this type of classroom protocol, the student has little power. Based on the traditional principles of classroom management, the student is a docile body that needs rules and regulations to be controlled. In the words of Foucault (1984):

The aim of disciplinary technology, whatever its institutional form — and it arose in a large number of different settings, such as workshops, schools, prisons, and hospitals — is to forge a "docile body that may be subjected, used, transformed, and improved." This is done in several related ways: through drills and training of the body, through standardization of actions over time, and through the control of space. Once established, this grid permits the sure distribution of the individuals who are to be disciplined and supervised. (p. 17)

Foucault reminds us that most teachers have been professionally trained (and socialized) to understand schools as natural settings to control and improve upon students' behavior. Their classrooms become controlled sites that are a part of the discipline process. In my discussions with students and parents, it is no wonder that they describe schools as being synonymous with prisons, boot camps, and mental wards. Teachers of urban students may be even more overzealous in their attempts to control and transform the thinking and behavior of their students, for urban students have been socially constructed as lacking self-control. In addition, I have heard preservice and master teachers claim that urban low-income Black families simply do not care about education or see it as important.

Therefore, many teachers of urban (and rural) students try to control students' behaviors and thinking in the classroom, because "those people just don't know any better." Well, if I might speak for thousands of urban students, they know better. Many times students do not readily show deference to teachers and classroom rules, because they do not want to be controlled by people who believe they lack self-control in the first place. Thus, in many urban classrooms, one may witness ongoing tension between students and teachers.

In order to decrease the tension between girls and their teachers, teachers must advocate for African American female students to exercise self-determination. Self-determination is the freedom of a people to determine the way in which they shall be governed and whether they shall be self-governed. African American female students deserve the right to determine what type of education they want to receive and how their education will be delivered. They also deserve the right to be involved in their educational experience as participants, not just as recipients. The right to self-determination may be difficult for most teachers, because it requires that they relinquish control.

Relinquishing control does not negate the teacher's obligation of authority. For instance, once a preservice teacher informed me that she feared that she would not be able to control her students' behavior. The student had been observing in a racially and economically mixed urban classroom. The student thought that the teacher she was observing lacked control of her students as measured by the students talking out of term and walking around the classroom without permission. Like the majority of White female preservice teachers, this was a young woman who excelled at her predominately White suburban school, because she "valued" education and followed the rules. Therefore, for her, it was a part of the teacher's role to control students' behavior. She also thought it natural that students would want to obey and submit to their teachers in order to receive a better education. From my point of view, this soon-to-be teacher was already associating urban students' academic failure with the lack of respect for authority figures, students' misbehavior with their failure to see the value of education, and urban students' "bad behavior" as a precursor to urban under-achievement. She came to the conclusion that for urban students to achieve their behavior had to be controlled. I responded, "It is not your job to control students' behavior. It is your job to facilitate student behavior."

As hinted at in my swift response, we need more teachers who are willing to exercise authority in the classroom as a facilitator. Authority is necessary to assist in the development of schools as democratic spheres and teachers as transformative intellectuals. The teacher exercises authority to include students in discourses of freedom and preparation for critical citizenship (Giroux, 1997). As facilitator of an emancipation agenda, the educator develops and locates resources, assists students in overcoming obstacles and celebrates accomplishments, and requires maintaining a belief in the possibility of her students and the other people involved in the learning process. The teacher-as-facilitator framework views the teacher as part of a larger group that keeps the group focused, imparts new skills, practices new skills with the students, and makes known available resources that empower.

As facilitators, teachers of urban girls can begin to promote educational resiliency in students by involving their students in the teaching and learning process. Facilitation is the lowering of resistance to make progress easier for all involved in the group. Nonetheless, in proper facilitation, being a part of the group means that the teacher is not in control but has an active equal part in the process. Along with her teacher, the student has an equal role in facilitating discussion, change, and the completion of task. In other words, students have an equal and just as important part in the day-to-day functioning of the classroom. When students are actively involved in determining classroom structure, they form high attachment to the classroom. Furthermore, they learn responsibility and the principles of self-determination. To decide for themselves how they will be governed (or if they will be governed) is most synonymous with the democratic process. Students are taught to be critical thinkers and participants in their own life outcomes; they also learn that their behavior has consequences.

Self-Reflexivity in Practice

Of course, in order to give up "control," teachers first must examine why they desire control in the first place. Many educators go into the teaching profession with preconceived notions of who is a good student, who deserves to be educated, and who is capable of learning. Individuals in our society are bombarded with images of urban youth who are culturally deficient. Sometimes these messages even enter the halls of higher education. Once at a small Midwestern college, I was walking down the hallway on my way to teach an introduction to American education class. Posted directly outside my classroom on a bulletin board was a newspaper headline that read, "Inner-City Children Are Victims of Brain Damage." In my mind, without even reading the body of the article, I concluded that the headline was perpetuating racism and class elitism. Needless to say, I snatched the article off the bulletin board and threw it into the recycle bin. I learned later that a White female psychology professor posted the article. I was appalled that directly outside of an education class students were being sent subliminal messages about the cognitive abilities of urban students.

I was even more appalled when a White female colleague (friend) insinuated that I was overreacting and explained that the article was posted for psychology students to understand more about the impact of the environment on young children's brain development. Maybe that was the point of the article, but in bold black print was the message that Black inner-city children simply lack the capacity to learn because of conditions in their environment. The message caught readers' attention and reinforced their assumptions about low-income Blacks living in urban areas. That particular message was being sent out to mainly White middle-class psychology, education, sociology, political science, and child development majors, who probably did not even bother to read the small-print body of the article. As this example demonstrates, many urban teachers prior to even meeting their students, enter the classroom with the assumption that their students will have behavior problems and lack cognitive abilities to learn and/or behave.

All educators of urban girls have the obligation to examine their assumptions about the abilities or the lack thereof of African American female students. To speak more bluntly, teachers must reflect on the racist beliefs that they hold and how their racism is played out in the classroom. More specific to urban girls, teachers should also examine how their racist beliefs are tied to other forms of patriarchy like racism and sexism. Too many girls have informed me that they feel their teachers treat them differently from their White peers. In addition, too many report that their schools have strict policies that function to control how they dress and behave. Because of individual and institutional racism, sexism, and classism, Black girls' bodies are restricted against their will.

Many teachers do not recognize or ignore how racism is played out in their own classrooms and lives outside of the school building. Some teachers even assert that that students use accusations of racism as an excuse not to conform to classroom or school rules. The teachers further claim that "If I were racist, I definitely would not be teaching down there with those kids." Usually this self-observation is followed by a hearty laugh. Obviously, people do not understand how racism is revealed in everyday discourse. Nonetheless, the result of deflecting students' and parents' cries of racism is that the teacher's racism goes unexamined.

Most teachers, like most Americans, do not want to admit that they are racist or that they benefit from racism. Racism is the belief or doctrine that phenotypical traits and/or genetic differences determine cultural or individual achievement and/or that one's own race is inherently superior to another's. It also includes the acceptance of the way goods and services are distributed in accordance with these beliefs. I know that this is too simplistic of a conceptualization of racism, but it is a working definition of racism that most individuals can understand and later critique with personal and intellectual growth. It is also the definition that most Americans start from without being able to articulate it.

First, I believe that most teachers conclude that they are not racist because they actually come in contact with African Americans. Somehow we have constructed this view of a racist as a person who chooses not to even come in contact with people of color. Second, a racist has been limited to someone who wants to do physical harm to non-White people or one who denigrates "colored" people. The problem is that most of us in education fail to make the connection that our beliefs that a student's physical traits can actually determine how one will behave, one's ability for academic success, or one's ability for social mobility are all racist beliefs. These are beliefs from which most teachers and school personnel approach decisions about classroom structure, pedagogy, and interactions with students and parents on a daily basis. Yet we all want to think that because we drive down to their neighborhoods five days out of the week for nine months out of the year, then we must be working on their behalf and in their best interest. As Carby (1999) explains:

> Like missionaries these teachers have not examined their own racism in their preoccupation with their own spiritual regeneration through "doing good" to black youth. Neither have they examined their own positions as agents of the state in a hierarchy of relationships in which they are in a position of control and ultimate authority in the classroom. It is in the lack of this form of analysis that "anti-racist" teaching has become a mere substitute for political action. (p. 206)

From this standpoint, if a teacher fails to scrutinize his or her own racist beliefs, he or she is no longer working on behalf of the students. Such teachers will remain contributors, sustainers, and facilitators of oppression and domination. Last, a critical pedagogy requires that teachers of urban girls further explore and reflect on how racism unevenly distributes goods, resources, services, and power in society. It is impossible for teachers of urban girls to build relationships with their students without examining teachers' (and students') intimate relationship with racism. Also, it is negligent for teachers of urban girls to hold low expectations for and prejudice against Black students as previous research studies has suggested (Foster, 1997). Racism and its consequences are only perpetuated when students are allowed to fall behind their White and middle-class peer groups. It does not benefit the students, teachers, or the Black community when curriculum and content are watered down, because teachers have low expectations of and are prejudiced about their students' perceived abilities.

Questions that teachers might explore are: How does racism affect who I am as a person? How has racism affected the decisions that I have made in my life and career? How does racism determine where I live, whom I sleep with, and whom I spend my leisure time with? How does racism impact my students' lives and educational experiences? How do my own racist beliefs play out throughout the school day? How do my racist beliefs affect how I communicate with students and their parents? How do my racist beliefs affect how I perceive students' behavior? Do I view behavior as Black behavior or simply student behavior? How does my own Whiteness (or Blackness) determine power relations in the classroom? As a victim and benefactor of racism, how can I help to eradicate and/or alleviate the negative effects of racism and patriarchy in my own life and those of my students?

By continuing to reflect on one's participation in racism, one becomes a more self-reflective and authentic intellectual. However, with self-reflexivity the educator is not only reflective or thoughtful of racism but becomes responsive to racism. Self-reflexivity calls for a move to action. As transformative intellectuals, they feel obligated to speak out and against notions of race and racism. They are also obligated to mobilize others to combat systematic oppression against Black girls, their families, and the larger Black community.

Cultural Aesthetics

When I was a graduate student, a principal who was familiar with my research and interest in urban students invited me to become a permanent substitute at his middle school. One day as teachers were preparing the students for state testing, I was assisting in a seventh grade science class. The teacher was absent and the instructions that were left for me asked me to have students write down and define any word on the practice examination that they did not know the meaning. Of all the assignments and lessons I have planned, I would definitely vote that one as the most boring, and nonrelevant to the students. One male student refused to participate in the assignment. After much discussion and inquiry about why he did not want to complete the assignment, he informed me that he knew the words; therefore, he did not need to complete the assignment. He told me that he was too smart for that class. He further explained to me that he was a rapper and that he needed to practice some rap lyrics that he had been working on for an upcoming performance.

In response to the student's indifference to the science lesson and my so-called authority, I decided to challenge his rap skills and his academic abilities. I told him that if he finished the assignment early, then I would let him practice his lyrics with the remaining class time. However, I also raised the challenge by telling the student to prove to me that he is a rapper with skills. I challenged him to include vocabulary words of his choosing from the practice tests and include them into a song. Every time that I tell this story, I am still amazed that that young man took several basic and advanced words from the test and wrote and rapped a fluent song that completely baffled me and the students in the class. In short, this example shows that some students are talented, but their talents go unnoticed because their way of learning and displaying their knowledge does not conform to societal standards. Even more, it shows how some students may be identified as behavioral problems because teachers fail to closely probe what might motivate that student to learn and actively participate in the school environment.

Admittedly, I am a consumer and advocate of hip hop and rap music. I also choose to look at the talent and knowledge that is evident in those who participate in this artform. Furthermore, because I nearly worshipped the earlier radical artists like Chuck D, KRS 1, Queen Latifah, and Public Enemy, I continue to hold on to the transformative qualities of hip hop/rap from which the current genres of this music have been born and evolved from aesthetically. Cornel West (1999) contends that rap music is different from previous forms of Black music.

> Black rap music is primarily the musical expression of the paradoxical cry of desperation and celebration of the black underclass and poor working class, a cry that openly acknowledges and confronts the wave of personal cold-heartedness, criminal cruelty and existential hopelessness in the black ghettos of Afro-America. In stark contrast to bebop and techno-funk, black rap music is principally a class-specific form of the Afro-American spiritual-blues impulse that mutes, and often eliminates, the utopian dimension of this impulse. (p. 482)

Hip hop/rap music defines, informs, shapes, reflects, and simultaneously speaks to and speaks against urban Black culture. Critical urban teachers of

Black girls are aware of both the contradictions and bona fide expressions of this unique artform. Teachers must also be aware of how hip hop/rap complicates and complements Black girls' existence. Of course, I am not putting forth the argument that all urban teachers should go out and learn rap or attempt to use it in their classrooms, but I am advocating a critical pedagogy that brings aesthetics back into teaching and learning. According to hooks (1990), "aesthetics then is more than a philosophy or theory of art and beauty; it is a way of inhabiting space, a particular location, a way of looking and becoming" (p. 104). Hip hop/rap should be brought into the classroom along with jazz, blues, classical, opera music, and other forms of art. By bringing hip hop/rap into the classroom, teachers are bringing students' culture and voices (mind, body, and spirits) into the classroom. It can also serve as a very important and significant reference point that is open to both interpretation and critique. Socially and politically, a pedagogy that embraces aesthetics also embraces the physical and mental presence of urban Black youth.

The Beauty of Dress

Urban hip hop culture also reminds us that aesthetics also plays a part in determining who youth respect and take seriously. In Black culture, dress or how one presents him- or herself is important. Many Black church leaders, community activists, and political figures, and even hip hop/rap musicians are revered, because they are judged to be "fresh" and "clean" to the observer's eye. As a part of Black culture, children do associate people who are to be taken seriously with those who are well dressed. Although rap musicians may be dressed differently from the church minister, dress plays a significant role in their stage presence. If teachers want to be taken more seriously, they should also take their students seriously. Once, in confidence, a middle school principal mentioned that the teachers at his school did not even respect the students enough to bother dressing professionally. He asked, "How could the students take the teachers seriously if the teachers did not take their jobs seriously?" The principal informed me that he purposely wore a suit every day to work as an example to the teachers and students of the importance of "looking good," and he thanked me for making the same effort.

Every day that I prepared to observe or teach at the school, I made the effort to dress in a professional manner. I knew how important (stage) presence was to students and how useful it was to me for conveying a message. Dress captures urban youth's attention while conveying the message that the topic is of importance to the speaker. Teachers who practice culturally relevant pedagogy are concerned with their dress as a sign of professionalism (Ladson-Billings, 1994). Critical urban educators must understand that dress is very important for at least three reasons: (1) it informs students about how serious a teacher is about her profession; (2) it tells them that the teacher views herself and her students as important persons; and (3) it tells them that to succeed in larger society the way that you are dressed can ultimately determine your success. Again, how one is dressed is concurrently linked to long-term and short-term goals. Therefore, we do not have to separate aesthetics or beauty from intellectual growth. African Americans concern with what is beautiful and visually appealing can be assimilated with their educational experiences. Also, it is important for urban educators to demonstrate (rather than criticize) for our young sistahs the messages that attire sends to others about our commitment to ourselves and our community.

Furthermore, urban hip hop/rap music reminds us of the significance of language as a form of artistic expression, political voice, and culture (re)production. Through hip hop/rap not only do we find that language makes us feel good but it also tells stories. It is an alternative voice for urban youth. As an alternative voice, critical urban educators know that the language used in urban music is not youth's primary form of communication. Most urban youth through everyday communication with adults, like ministers, parents, Black leaders, and even Black teachers, learn how to slip in and out of formal Black English. In other words, most Black children know when it is important and appropriate to use either Black slang or formal English. Ask any Black child and they will tell you that they can tell whether their mother is talking to a White person or a Black person by voice change and the words used. Since slavery, spoken and unspoken language has been used as a social and political tool among Black people.

Critical urban educators believe that all Black children are capable of learning the dominant discourse while retaining their own linguistically diverse language form. If teachers try to criticize or take away from students' mother tongue in the classroom, they threaten to take those students' sense of identity and uniqueness. Also, because we know that adolescent students are in search of ethnic and gender identity, they are going to gravitate toward what they believe makes them fit in with their peers. Urban Black English is hip and political right now, and most youth are going to be interested in participating in this emotionally stimulating form of communication. However, by not teaching the dominant discourse, teachers may be limiting students' possibilities of social and economic mobility. Teachers of urban girls understand that language is important in challenging and confronting oppression.

As for the urban Black girl, in the words of Dowdy (2002), "She must operate from behind the mask of the 'white' language" (p. 11). Formal English is simply another tool that equips Black girls for educational resiliency and mobility. Of equal importance, a critical pedagogy would also have students participate in a deconstruction of language discourse. Students should learn why educational institutions and urban communities are battling each other in this cultural war of words. Whose language is under attack and why? Whose interest does it serve that the dominant group's language is spoken and proliferated in our school systems? Why is it important for Black students to know both their home language and the language of the European elite? How is language and linguistic censorship a part of hegemony and oppression? How can we use hip hop/rap as a separate and exclusive form of communication that is both private and public simultaneously? For most Black urban youth, it would be in and of itself empowering to participate in one's home language and the dominant's group language form.

Humor

One last point that I want to make, as it relates to cultural aesthetics, is the importance of humor. If educators believe that beauty and emotions are significant and connected to intellectual development, they have to understand to have humor is to be human. Notice that both words have in common the root word *hum*, which means "to make sound." To be human is to have a sense of humor. However, sometimes teachers become stoic and robotic in their daily activities and interactions with students, and they expect the same mode of behavior from students. If the student gravitates from a serious state, the student is reprimanded or punished. Urban students, like other students, appreciate a teacher who has a sense of humor.

Too often teachers take their students' words or actions too seriously. No, African Americans are not always interested in laughter and entertainment, especially for the amusement of others, but most of us do view humor as an essential part of life. Humor, satire, and laughter have been nearly critical to our survival in a hostile world. Humor is also strongly tied to our language and music. Even my son has been praised for his language development by his White female teacher, who noticed that he has mastered sarcasm at the age of four. Often one will hear my son lightheartedly reciting, "I'm just playin'. I'm just playin'."

Like my four-year-old son, it is not unusual in schools to hear students say to each other and teachers "I'm just playin'," or "I'm just kiddin'." I know that there are probably readers saying, "Well, school is not a place to play." Schools may not be a place to play, but if you do not connect with your students, it also won't be a place to learn. Pedagogy is a creative artform, and we need strategies that will help teachers connect with their students, emotionally and intellectually. Furthermore, some students have a gift of making others laugh. These students have been traditionally labeled the class clowns. Now, because of stricter school rules, which are marked by the "no-tolerance" rules that are sprawling up across the country, the class clown is threatened by school dropout or pushout factors.

What teachers and other school personnel may be overlooking is that the class clown not only may have advanced language skills, but he/she may also have advanced interpersonal skills. How can urban educators capitalize on humor? The simple answer is, have a sense of humor, use it in class, and allow others to possess it. By participating in and allowing humor, teachers might decrease student-to-student and teacher-to-student tension and animosity in classrooms. Humor is culturally appealing to many urban students because it is stimulating and at the same time anecdotal. Critical urban educators understand its cultural relevancy and its significance in pedagogy.

A Negotiated Artwork

As we hear in the voices of the resilient students, African American female students' identities are creative, negotiated, and constructed projects. Through everyday cultural practices, Black girls' student identities are constructed vis-à-vis their race, class, and gender roles. In everyday cultural practices, like "doing hair" and getting her "head done," Black girls are sent messages of how to be a good girl, the linguistics of adult Black English, and issues of trust and responsibility. Many of these gender- and cultural-specific practices are passed down to girls by adult women. In an ideal world these cultural cues would be validated and supported by social institutions like the schools. Must young women learn that their school environment is not always in congruence with the norms of their homes? Thus, some negotiation is required on the part of the student, family, community, and school.

When we were little girls, our brothers, cousins, and neighbor boys looked upon us with both envy and sympathy, as the daughters in the village had our heads worked into a tapestry of art. The village that I speak of and remember so vividly was not located in some remote part of Africa; instead it was a small neighborhood of familiar faces. It was a community made up of distant kin, "play" cousins, and other mothers. Most of the time it was our own mothers, aunts, older cousins, and godmothers who were in charge of maintaining the females in the village *heads*. Other times, it was the neighborhood braider, who was known for being able to "do some hair." Constantly we were warned "Don't let anybody in yo' head." To let someone in your head was a matter of intimacy, trust, and skill.

Getting your head done was a daunting task for the girls, for we were required to sit for long hours, at times endure pain, and be able to position our heads at the perfect angle for the stylist. Our heads were the artists' palettes, and we knew that our sacrifice would bring us both special recognition and praise. The artwork was constructed at the kitchen table, in family living rooms, or more often, especially during the summer months, on front porches. How well the daughter's *head* was *done* was a reflection on all involved in the process. The mother, daughter, and artists' hands were all recipients of the compliments and attention the young woman received. It attested to the young woman's patience and obedience, the artist's creativity, and the mother's level of care for her daughter's maintenance and self-esteem. At school age, our female caregivers are forced to pass on a similar kind of trust and creative endeavor to teachers and school personnel. They are required to allow those outside of the village to "get into their daughter's heads." It is hoped that teachers approach such a task with care, creativity and diligence, with the goal of co-constructing a piece of artwork that is both transformative and critically engaged with the struggle of her community and overall humanity.

References

American Association of University Women. (1992). *Shortchanging girls, short-changing America*. Washington, D.C.: American Association of University Women.

Anderson, J. (1988). *The education of Blacks in the south: 1860–1935*. Chapel Hill: University of North Carolina Press.

Anthony, S.B. (1990). Speech before the legislature, 1860. In S. Ruth (Ed.), *Issues in feminism: An introduction to women's studies* (pp. 465–470). Mountain View, California: Mayfield.

Anyon, J. (1997). *Ghetto schooling: A political economy of urban educational reform*. New York: Teachers College Press.

Ashford, J.B., LeCroy, C.W., and Lortie, K.L. (1997). *Human behavior in the social environment: A multidimensional perspective*. Pacific Grove, California: Brooks/Cole.

Bagley, C.A., and Carroll, J. (1996). Healing forces in African American families. In H.I. McCubbin (Ed.), *Resilience in African American families* (pp. 117-142). Thousand Oaks, California: Sage.

Baker, J. (2004). Triangulism. In L. Delpit and J.K. Dowdy (Eds.), *The skin that we speak* (pp. 49–66). New York: The New Press.

Ball, S.J. (1990). Self-doubt and soft data: Social and technical trajectories in ethnographic fieldwork. *Qualitative Studies in Education, 3 (2):* 157–171.

Blakey, M.L. (1997). (2nd ed.). Man and nature, white and other. In F. Harrison (Ed.), *Decolonizing anthropology: Moving further toward an anthropology of liberation* (pp. 16–24). Washington, D.C.: American Anthropological Association.

Borman, K. M., Mueninghoff, E., and Piazza., S., (1988). Urban Appalachian girls and young women: Bowing to no one. In L. Weis (Ed.), *Class, race, and gender in American education* (pp. 230–248). Albany, New York: State University of New York Press.

Britzman, D.P. (2000). "The question of belief": Writing poststructural ethnography. In E. St. Pierre and W. Pillow (Eds.), *Working the ruins: Feminist poststructural theory and methods in education* (pp. 27–40). New York: Routledge.

Canino, I.A., and Spurlock, J. (1994). *Culturally diverse children and adolescents: Assessment, diagnosis, and treatment*. New York: Guilford Press.

Caraway, N. (1991). Segregated sisterhood: Racism and the politics of American feminism. Knoxville: University of Tennessee Press.

Carby, H.V. (1999). *Cultures in Babylon: Black Britain and African America*. New York: Verso.

Cashmore, E. (1996). (4th ed.). *Dictionary of race and ethnic relations*. New York: Routledge.

Cauce, A.M., Hiraga Y., Graves D., Gonzales N., Ryan-Finn K., and Grove K.. (1996). African American mothers and their adolescent daughters: Closeness, conflict, and control. In B.J.R. Leadbeater and N. Way (Eds.), *Urban girls: Resisting stereotypes, creating identities* (pp. 100–116). New York: New York University Press.

Clark, M.L., and Scott-Jones, D. (1986). The school experiences of black girls: The interaction of gender, race, and economic status. *Phi Delta*, 67: 520–526.

Collins, P.H. (1998). *Fighting words: Black women and the search for justice.* Minneapolis: University of Minnesota Press.

Collins, P.H. (2000). (2nd ed.). *Black feminist thought: Knowledge, consciousness, and the politics of empowerment.* New York: Routledge.

Conver, B. (1957, March 11). Negros reach to professions. *Peoria Journal Star*, pp. A1, A3.

Davis, A.B., and Rhodes, J.E. (1996). Supportive ties between nonparent adults and urban adolescents girls. In B.J.R. Leadbeater and N. Way (Eds.) *Urban girls: Resisting stereotyping, creating identities* (pp. 213–225). New York: New York University Press.

Davis, A., Gardner, B., and Gardner, M.R. (1941). *Deep South.* Chicago: University of Chicago Press.

Davis, A.Y. (1983). *Women, race, and class.* New York: Random House.

Dehyle, D. (1995). Navajo youth and Anglo racism: Cultural integrity and resistance. *Havard Educational Review, 65 (3):* 403–444.

Delgado Bernal, D. (1998). Using a Chicana feminist epistemology in educational research. *Harvard Educational Review, 68 (4):* 555–579.

Delpit, L. (1995). *Other people's children: Cultural conflict in the classroom.* New York: The New Press.

Denzin, N.K., and Lincoln, Y.S. (Eds.).(2000).(2nd ed.). ·*The handbook of qualitative research.* Thousand Oaks, California: Sage.

District 150. (1999, November). *Peoria public schools: School report card 1998–1999.*

Dove, N. (1998). *Afrikan mothers: Bearers of culture, makers of change.* Albany: State University of New York Press.

Dowdy, J.K. (2002). Ovuh dyuh. In L. Delpit and J.K. Dowdy (Eds.), *The skin that we speak: Thoughts on language and culture in the classroom* (pp. 3-14). New York: The New Press.

Duren, F. (1992, February 19). Black Peorians play in tricentennial history. *Observer*, p. B–10.

Early history of the Negro in Peoria: Negro education. (1998, January). *The Traveler*, p. 7.

Edwards, T. (1996, October 30). 99.75 percent of White and getting whiter. *Peoria Journal Star.*

Emerson, R.M., Fretz, R.I., and Shaw, L.L. (1995). *Writing ethnographic fieldnotes.* Chicago: University of Chicago Press.

Erkut, S., Fields, J.P., Sing, R., and Marx, F. (1996). Diversity in girls experiences: Feeling good about who you are. In B.J.R. Leadbeater and N. Way (Eds.), *Urban girls: Resisting stereotypes, creating identities* (pp. 53–64). New York: New York University Press.

Evans-Winters, V. (2003). *Reconstructing resilience: Including African American female students in educational resiliency research.* Unpublished dissertation. Urbana: University of Illinois.

Feagin, J. (2000). *Racist America: Roots, current realities, and future reparations.* New York: Routledge.

Fine, M. (1991). *Framing dropouts: Notes on the politics of an urban public high school.* Albany: State University of New York Press.

Fine, M., McCormick, J., and Pastor, J. (1996). Makin' homes: An urban girl thing. In B.J.R. Leadbeater and N. Way (Eds.), *Urban girls: Resisting stereotyping, creating identities* (pp. 15–34). New York: New York University Press.

Foley, D.E. (1990). *Learning capitalist culture: Deep in the heart of Tejas.* Philadelphia: University of Pennsylvania Press.

Fordham, S. (1988). Racelessness as a factor in students' school success: Pragmatic strategy or pyrrhic victory? *Harvard Educational Review, 58 (1):* 54–84.

Fordham, S. (1996). *Blacked out: Dilemmas of race, identity, and success at Capital High.* Chicago: University of Chicago Press.

Foster, M. (1997). *Black teachers on teaching.* New York: The New Press.

Foster, M. (1999). Race, class, and gender in education research: Surveying the political terrains. *Educational Policy, 13 (1):* 77–85.

Foucault, M. (1984). The subject and power. In P. Rabinow (Ed.). *The Foucault Reader* (pp. 208-226). New York: Random House.

Garibaldi, A.M., Reed, W.L., and Willie, C.V. (Eds.). (1991). *The education of African Americans.* Boston, Massachusetts: William Trotter Institute.

Garrett, R.B. (1973). *The Negro in Peoria.* Peoria, Illinois: Peoria Public Library.

Geertz, C. (1973). *The interpretation of cultures: Selected essays.* New York: Basic Books.

Gibbs, J.T. (1996). Health-compromising behaviors in urban early adolescent females: Ethnic and socioeconomic variations. In B.J.R. Leadbeater and N. Way (Eds.), *Urban girls: Resisting stereotyping, creating identities* (pp. 309–327). New York: New York University Press.

Giroux, H.A. (1992). *Border crossing: Cultural workers and the politics of education.* New York: Routledge.

Giroux, H.A. (1997). *Pedagogy and the politics of hope: Theory, culture, and schooling.* Boulder, Colorado: Westview.

Goldberg, D.T. (1993). *Racist culture: Philosophy and the politics of meaning.* Cambridge, Massachusetts: Blackwell.

Grant, C.A., and Sleeter, C.E. (2003). *Making choices for multicultural education: Five approaches to race, class, and gender.* New York: John Wiley & Sons.

Grusky, D.B. (2001). (2nd ed.). *Social stratification: Class, race, & gender in sociological perspective*. Boulder, Colorado: Westview.

Gulbrium, J.F., and Holstein, A. (1997). *The new language of qualitative method*. New York: Oxford University Press.

Guy-Sheftall, B. (Ed.). (1995). *Words of fire: An anthology of African-American feminist thought*. New York: The New Press.

Haertel, G.D., Walberg, H.J., and Wang, M.C. (1994). Educational resilience in inner cities. In E.W. Gordon and M.C. Wang (Eds.), *Educational resilience in inner-city America* (pp. 45–72). Mahwah, New Jersey: Lawrence Erlbaum Associates.

Hall, R., Russell, K., & Wilson, M. (1992). *The color complex*. New York: Doubleday.

Harding, S. (Ed.) (1987). *Feminism and methodology*. Bloomington: Indiana University Press.

Henderson, N., and Millstein, M.M. (1996). *Resiliency in schools: Making it happen for students and educators*. Thousand Oaks, California: Corwin Press.

Henry, A. (1998). Invisible and womanish: Black girls negotiating their lives in an African-centered school in the USA. *Race, Ethnicity, and Education, 1(2)*: 151–170.

Hine, D.C. (1989). *Black women in White: Racial conflict and cooperation in the nursing profession, 1890–1950*. Bloomington: Indiana University Press.

Hine, D.C. (1991). Black migration to the urban Midwest: The gender dimension. In J.W. Trotter (Ed.), *The great migration in historical perspectives*. Bloomington: Indiana University Press.

hooks, b. (1990). Homeplace: A site of resistance. bell hooks, *Yearning: Race, gender, and cultural politics*. Cambridge, Massachusetts: South End Press.

Hurston, Z.N. (1937). *Their eyes were watching God*. New York: HarperCollins.

Ianni, F. (1996). *Meeting youth needs with community programs*. New York: ERIC Clearinghouse on Urban Education.

Johnson-Bailey, J. (1999). The ties that bind and the shackles that separate: Race, gender, class, and color in a research process. *Qualitative Studies in Education, 12 (6):* 659–670.

Kelley, R.D.G., and Lewis, E. (Eds.). (2000). *To make our world anew: A history of African Americans*. New York: Oxford University Press.

Kincheloe, J.L. (2004). Why a book on urban education? In S.R. Steinberg and J.L. Kincheloe (Eds.), *19 Urban questions: Teaching in the city* (pp. 1-27). New York: Peter Lang.

King, D. (1995). Multiple jeopardy, multiple consciousness: The context of Black feminist ideology. In B. Guy-Sheftall (Ed.), *Words of fire: An anthology of African-American feminist thought* (pp. 294-318) New York: The New Press.

Ladner, J.A. (1987). Introduction to tomorrow's tomorrow: The Black woman. In S. Harding (Ed.), *Feminism and methodology* (pp. 74-83). Bloomington: Indiana University Press.

Ladson-Billings, G. (1994). *The dreamkeepers: Successful teachers of African American children.* San Francisco, California: Jossey-Bass.

Ladson-Billings, G. (2000). Racialized discourses. In N. Denzin and Y. Lincoln (Eds.), *Handbook of qualitative research* (pp. 257–278). Thousand Oaks, California: Sage.

Leadbeater, B.J.R., and Way, N. (Eds.). (1996). *Urban girls: Resisting stereotyping, creating identities.* New York: New York University Press.

Lee, C.D. (1992). Profile of an independent black institution: African-centered education at work. *Journal of Negro Education, 61 (2):* 160–177.

Lee, C.D. (2003). Why we need to re-think race and ethnicity in educational research. *Educational Researcher, 32(5):* 3–5.

Lindstrom, D. (1977). *School desegregation in Peoria Illinois: A staff report of the U.S. Commission of civil rights.* Washington, D.C.: The Commission.

MacLeod, J. (1987). *Ain't no making it: Aspirations and attainment in a low-income neighborhood.* Boulder, Colorado: Westview.

Madriz, E. (2000). (2nd ed.). Focus groups in feminist research. In N. Denzin and Y. Lincoln (Eds.), *Handbook of qualitative research* (pp. 835–848). Thousands Oaks, California: Sage.

Marshall, G. (1998). *A dictionary of sociology.* New York: Oxford University Press.

Martinez, R., and Dukes, R.L. (1991). Ethnic and gender differences in self-esteem. *Youth and Society, 22 (3):* 313–338.

Masten, A.S. (1994). Resilience in individual development: Successful adaptation despite risk and adversity. In M.C. Wang and E.W. Gordon (Eds.), *Educational resilience in inner-city America: Challenges and prospectus* (pp. 3-25). Mahwah, New Jersey: Lawrence Erlbaum Associates.

McAdoo, H.P. (1998). African American families: Strengths and realities. In H.I. McCubbin, (Ed.), *Resilience in African American families* (pp. 17-30). Thousand Oaks, California: Sage.

McCarthy, C. (1988). Rethinking liberal and radical perspectives on racial inequality in schooling: Making the case for a nonsynchrony. *Harvard Educational Review, 58:* 265–269.

McCubbin, H.I. (1998). Resiliency in African American families: Military families in foreign environments. In H.I. McCubbin (Ed.) *Resilience in African American families* (pp. 67-98). Thousand Oaks, California: Sage.

McCubbin, H.I., Thompson, A.I., Futrell, J., & L.D. McCubbin. (1996). *Promoting resiliency in families and children at-risk: Interdisciplinary perspectives.* Thousand Oaks, California: Sage.

Mickelson, R.A. (1990). The attitude achievement paradox among black adolescents. *Sociology of Education, 63:* 44–61.

Ministers lament small number of Negro high school graduates. (1962, January 4). *Peoria Journal Star.*

Miron, L.F. (1996). *The social construction of urban schooling: Situating the crisis.* Cresskill, New Jersey: Hampton.

Morris, A.D. (1984). *The origins of the civil rights movement: Black communities organizing for change.* New York: The Free Press.

Mullings, L. (1997). *On our own terms: Race, class, and gender in the lives of African American women.* New York: Routledge.

Murry, V.M. (1998). Variation in adolescent pregnancy status: A national tri-ethnic study. In H.I. McCubbin (Ed.) *Resilience in African American families* (pp. 67-98). Thousand Oaks, California: Sage.

Nolde, G.C. (2000). *All in a day's work: Seventy-five years of Caterpillar.* Chicago: Triumph Books.

Obbo, C. (1997). What do women know? ... As I was saying. In M. Vaz (Ed.), *Oral narrative research with black women* (pp. 41–63). Thousand Oaks, California: Sage.

O'Connor, C. (1997). Dispositions toward (collective) struggle and educational resilience in the inner-city: A case analysis of six African American high school students. *American Educational Research Journal, 34 (4):* 593–629.

Ogbu, J.U. (1978). *Minority education and caste.* New York: Academic Press.

Ogbu, J.U. (1987). Variability in minority school performance: A problem in search of an explanation. *Anthropology and Education Quarterly, 18 (4):* 312–334.

Ogbu, J.U. (1991). Immigrant and involuntary minorities in comparative perspective. In J.U. Ogbu and M.A. Gibson (Eds.), *Minority status and schooling: A comparative study of immigrant and involuntary minorities* (pp. 3-33). New York: The College Board.

Ogbu, J.U., and Simmons, H.D. (1998). Voluntary and involuntary minorities: A cultural ecological theory of school performance with some implications for education. *Anthropological and Education Quarterly, 29 (2):* 155–188.

Oliver, M.L., and Shapiro, T.M. (1997). Black wealth/White wealth: A new perspective on racial inequality. New York: Routledge.

Omolade, B. (1994). *The rising song of African American women.* New York: Routledge.

Orenstein, P. (1994). *School girls: Young women, self-esteem, and the confidence gap.* New York: American Association of University Women.

Pattillo-McCoy, M. (1999). *Black picket fences.* Chicago: University of Chicago Press.

Payne, C.M. (1994). *Getting what we ask for: The ambiguity of success and failure in urban education.* Westport, Connecticut: Greenwood Press.

Payne, C.M. (1995). *I've got the light of freedom: The organizing tradition and the Mississippi freedom struggle.* Berkeley and Los Angeles: University of California Press.

Peng, S.S. (1984). Understanding resilient students: The use of national longitudinal databases. In M.C. Wang and E.W. Gordon (Eds.), *Educational resilience in inner-city America: Challenges and prospects* (pp. 73–84). Mahwah, New Jersey: Lawrence Erlbaum Associates.

Peoria School District 150. (1998). *Illinois school report card.*

Pillow, W. (2000). Exposed methodology: The body as a deconstructive practice. In E. St. Pierre and W.S. Pillow (Eds.), *Working the ruins: Feminist poststructural theory and methods in education* (pp. 199-220). New York: Routledge.

Pipher, M. (1994). *Reviving Ophelia: Saving the selves of adolescent girls.* New York: Ballantine.

Rigsby, L.C. (1994). The Americanization of resilience: Deconstructing research practice. In M.C. Wang and E.W. Gordon (Eds.), *Educational resilience in inner-city America: Challenges and prospects* (pp. 85–96). Mahwah, New Jersey: Lawrence Erlbaum Associates.

Roberts, D. (1997). *Killing the black body: Race, reproduction, and the meaning of liberty.* New York: Random House.

Robinson, T.L., and Ward, J.V. (1991). Cultivating resistance among African American adolescents: A model for empowerment. *Women & Therapy, 11*: 3–4.

Ruth, S. (1990). *Issues in feminism: An introduction to women studies.* Mountain View, California: Mayfield Publishing.

Schwandt, T.A. (2001). (2nd ed.). *Dictionary of qualitative inquiry.* Thousand Oaks, California: Sage.

Siddle Walker, V. (2000). Valued segregated schools for African American children in the south, 1935–1969: A review of common themes and characteristics. *Review of Educational Research, 70 (3)*: 253–285.

Smith, E.J. (1982). The Black female adolescent: A review of the educational, career, and psychological literature. *Psychology of Women Quarterly, 6 (3): 261–288.

Smith, P.J. (1999). Our children's burden: The headed hydra of the educational disenfranchisement of black children. *Howard Law Journal, 42 (2)*: 133–239.

Stack, C. (1974). *Call to home.* New York: Basic Books.

Stanfield II, J.H. (1998). Ethnic modeling in qualitative research. In N. Denzin and Y. Lincoln (Eds.), *The landscape of qualitative research: Theories and issues* (pp. 333–358). Thousand Oaks, California: Sage.

St. Pierre, E.A. (2000). Poststructural feminism in education: An overview. *International Journal of Qualitative Studies, 13 (5)*: 477–515.

Sullivan, A.M. (1996). From mentor to muse: Recasting the role of women in relationship with urban adolescent girls. In B.J.R. Leadbeater and N. Way (Eds.), *Urban girls: Resisting stereotypes, creating identities* (pp. 226–254). New York: New York University Press.

Tatum, B. (1997). *Why are all the black kids sitting together in the cafeteria?: And other conversations about race.* New York: Basic Books.

Taylor, R. (1994) Risk and resilience: Contextual influences on the development of African American adolescents. In M.C. Wang and E.W. Gordon (Eds.), *Educational resilience in inner-city America: Challenges and prospects* (pp. 119–130). Mahwah, New Jersey: Lawrence Erlbaum Associates.

Thirty-six Negros arrested for CILCO sit-in: Thirteen are jailed. (1963, July). *Peoria Journal Star.*

Tierney, W.G. (2000). (2nd ed.). Undaunted courage: Life history and the postmodern challenge. In N. Denzin and Y. Lincoln (Eds.), *Handbook of qualitative research* (pp. 537–554). Thousand Oaks, California: Sage.

Tillman, L. (2002). Culturally sensitive research approaches: An African-American perspective. *Educational Researcher, 31 (9):* 3–12.

Trotter, J.W. (1985). Black Milwaukee: The making of a Black proletariat: 1915–1945. Urbana: University of Illinois Press.

Trotter, J.W. (1988). *River Jordan: African American urban life in the Ohio valley.* Lexington: University Press of Kentucky Press.

Trotter, J.W. (1991). *The great migration in historical perspective: New dimensions of race, class, and gender.* Bloomington: University of Indiana Press.

Truth, S. (1990). Ain't I a woman? In S. Ruth (Ed.), *Issues in feminism: An introduction to women studies* (pp. 463–464). Mountain View, California: Mayfield Publishing.

United States Census Bureau. (1940). *Inter-university consortium for political and social research. Study 0003: Historical demographic, economic, social data: U.S. 1790–1970.* Ann Arbor, Michigan: Inter-University for Political and Social Research.

United States Census Bureau. (1996). *State and county quick facts: Peoria County.* http://quickfacts.census.gov/qfd/states/17/17143.html

United States Census Bureau. (2004). *State and county quick facts: Peoria County.* http://quickfacts.census.gov/qfd/states/17/17143.html

United States Commission on Civil Rights. (1977). *School desegregation in Peoria, Illinois* (DHHS Publication no. 726–943/376). Washington, D.C.: U.S. Government Printing Office.

United States Department of Commerce, Bureau of the Census, Current Population Survey (CPS), October 1998.

United States Department of Education, National Center for Educational Statistics, Common Core of Data (CCD), Public Elementary/Secondary School Universe Survey and Local Education Agency Survey, 1997–98.

Valenzuela, A. (1999). *Subtractive schooling: U.S. Mexican youth and the politics of caring.* Albany: State University of New York Press.

Van Maanen, J.V. (1988). Tales of the field: On writing ethnography. Chicago: University of Chicago Press.

Vaz, K.M. (1997). *Oral narrative with black women.* Thousand Oaks, California: Sage.

Vidich, A.J., and Lyman, S.M. (2000). (2nd ed.). Qualitative methods: Their history in sociology and anthropology. In N. Denzin, and Y. Lincoln (Eds.), *Handbook of qualitative research methods* (pp. 37-84). Thousand Oaks, California: Sage.

Villenas, S. (2000). The ethnography called my back: Writings of the exotic gaze, "othering" Latina, and recuperating Xicanisma. In E. St. Pierre and

W. Pillow (Eds.), *Working the ruins: Feminist poststructural theory and methods in education* (pp. 74–95). New York: Routledge.

Wang, M.C., and Gordon, E.W. (Eds.). (1994). *Educational resilience in inner city America.* Mahwah, New Jersey: Lawrence Erlbaum Associates.

Ward, J.V. (1996). Raising resisters: The role of truth telling in the psychological development of African American girls. In B.J.R. Leadbeater and N. Way (Eds.), *Urban girls: Resisting stereotypes, creating identities* (pp.85–99). New York: New York University Press.

Way, N. (1996). Between experiences of betrayal and desire: Close friendships among urban adolescents. In B.J.R. Leadbeater and N. Way (Eds.), *Urban girls: Resisting stereotypes, creating identities* (pp. 173–192). New York: New York University Press.

Welsing, F.C. (1991). *The Isis papers: The keys to the colors.* Chicago: Third World Press.

West, C. (1999). *The Cornel West reader.* New York: Basic Civitas Books.

Wilson, W.J. (1996) *When work disappears: The world of the new urban poor.* New York: Random House.

Winfield, L.F. (1994). *NCREL monograph: Developing resilience in urban youth.* Naperville, Illinois: NCREL Urban Education Program.

Wolcott, H. (2001). *Writing up qualitative research.* Thousand Oaks, California: Sage.

Wollenstonecraft, M. (1990). A vindication of the rights of woman. In S. Ruth (Ed.), *Issues in feminism: An introduction to women's studies* (pp. 444–449). Mountain View, California: Mayfield Publishing.

Studies in the Postmodern Theory of Education

General Editors
Joe L. Kincheloe & Shirley R. Steinberg

Counterpoints publishes the most compelling and imaginative books being written in education today. Grounded on the theoretical advances in criticalism, feminism, and postmodernism in the last two decades of the twentieth century, Counterpoints engages the meaning of these innovations in various forms of educational expression. Committed to the proposition that theoretical literature should be accessible to a variety of audiences, the series insists that its authors avoid esoteric and jargonistic languages that transform educational scholarship into an elite discourse for the initiated. Scholarly work matters only to the degree it affects consciousness and practice at multiple sites. Counterpoints' editorial policy is based on these principles and the ability of scholars to break new ground, to open new conversations, to go where educators have never gone before.

For additional information about this series or for the submission of manuscripts, please contact:

Joe L. Kincheloe & Shirley R. Steinberg
c/o Peter Lang Publishing, Inc.
275 Seventh Avenue, 28th floor
New York, New York 10001

To order other books in this series, please contact our Customer Service Department:

(800) 770-LANG (within the U.S.)
(212) 647-7706 (outside the U.S.)
(212) 647-7707 FAX

Or browse online by series:

www.peterlangusa.com